COLLABORATIVE FORM

COLLABORATIVE FORM
Studies in the Relations of the Arts

THOMAS JENSEN HINES

THE KENT STATE UNIVERSITY PRESS
Kent, Ohio, and London, England

© 1991 by The Kent State University Press
All rights reserved
Library of Congress Catalog Card Number 90-46804
ISBN 0-87338-417-2
Manufactured in the United States of America

Library of Congress Cataloging-in-Publication Data

Hines, Thomas Jensen, 1940–
    Collaborative form : studies in the relations of the arts / Thomas
Jensen Hines.
        p.   cm.
    Includes bibliographical references and index.
    ISBN 0–87338–417–2 (alk. paper)∞
    1. Arts. 2. Ut pictura poesis (Aesthetics) 3. Group work in art.
I. Title.
NX170.H56   1991
700—dc20   90-46804

British Library Cataloging-in-Publication are available.

To Susan, Joshua, and Susanna

Contents

Acknowledgments

I am grateful to the libraries of Kent State University, the Cleveland Museum of Art, the University of Washington and the Bibliothèque Nationale, Paris, for help in retrieving the works of René Char, Oskar Kokoschka, Wassily Kandinsky, and Arnold Schoenberg that would otherwise have been difficult to find. I am especially indebted to M. François Chapon, curator of the Bibliothèque Littéraire Jacques Doucet for access to the collaborations of René Char with numerous painters of the twentieth century and to the curators of the Städtische Galerie im Lenbachhaus, Munich, for the early editions of Kandinsky's writings.

I would also like to thank M. Chapon for permission to reprint revised versions of essays originally published in the *Bulletin du Bibliophile:* "L'Ouvrage de tous les temps admiré: *Lettera amorosa* de René Char et Georges Braque" (73–1) and "*A la santé du serpent:* René Char et Joan Miró" (81–1). I would like to thank Rudolf Kuenzli for allowing me to reprint a revised version of my article "Collaboration of Forms in a One-Man Show: The Performance of *Mörder Hoffnung der Frauen*" which first appeared in *Dada/Surrealism* 4 (1974).

For permission to reproduce the lithographs of Georges Braque, I would like to thank M. Claude Laurens, executor of the Braque estate and the Artists Rights Society of New York, exclusive agent of ADAGP for the United States. For the right to reproduce pages of Joan Miró's graphic work from *A la santé du serpent,* I wish to thank the publisher, Guy Lévi-Manos of *GLM* and Rosa Maria Malet, director of the Fundació Joan Miró in Barcelona, as well as the Artists Rights Society of New York, exclusive agent for ADAGP for the United States.

Permissions to reproduce portions of Arnold Schoenberg's score for *Herzgewächse*, Op. 20 (copyright 1920 by Universal Editions, Vienna; copyright renewed), have been granted by Belmont Music Publishers for the United States and Canada and by European American Music Distributors for the territory of the world excluding the United States and Canada.

I would like to thank the estate of Oskar Kokoschka and its representatives, the Artists Rights Society of New York, exclusive agent for the ADAGP for the United States, for permission to reprint the graphic works of Oskar Kokoschka related to the performance and subsequent publication in *Der Sturm* (1910) of *Mörder, Hoffnung der Frauen*.

I am grateful to Alwin Nikolais of the Nikolais and Louis Dance Company for permitting me to work in the Chimera Foundation Archives and to observe the creation and recreation of several of his choreographies with his dancers. Mr. Nikolais gave me permission to republish photographs from several of his dances and I want to thank him for that as well as for sitting through several interviews.

Finally I want to thank those who have given me the time to complete the research and writing of this book. First, I am grateful to the National Endowment for the Humanities for giving me an opportunity to go to France and Germany to study painting, graphic works, and sculpture. Next, I want to thank the Research Council of Kent State University for awards of quarters and semesters free to pursue specific parts of the research for this book. Then, I would like to thank the American Council of Learned Societies, the Fulbright Program, and the Deans of Research and Sponsored Programs at Kent State University for travel funds without which I could not have completed this book.

In conclusion, I want to add a note of gratitude to those students, colleagues, friends, and family members who patiently attended to the raveling and unraveling of collaborative form in those years when they might have had something better to do and something less elusive to imagine.

COLLABORATIVE FORM

COLLABORATIVE forms are the direct result of combining two or more different arts to make composite art works. The following study is an attempt to define and explicate this kind of art. While I refer to the combinations and syntheses of the arts that I have chosen to examine as collaborative forms, they have been given other names as well.

In the history of composite art works, beginning with Greek tragedy, no single term has quite sufficed to characterize the variety of intentions and results associated with the synthesis of the arts. Jack M. Stein rightly points out that "since the renaissance, the idea of synthesis has been associated most persistently with the stage, principally opera, which indeed originated in an attempt to revive the form of Greek tragedy."[1] However, with the advent of Romanticism in Germany and England, the ambition of the artists grew and the goal of synthesis of the arts came to include all the arts. William Blake's integration of poetry, painting, and music is as central to the ideal of synthesis in the Romantic sense of the term as the songs and settings of Schumann, Schubert, and Wolf. In Germany, two generations of Romantic writers and artists including Goethe, Schiller, Tieck, Wackenroder, Novalis, Brentano, Hoffmann, and Runge constructed theories and, occasionally, works of collaborative form. The terms they used to describe the synthetic work varied from artist to artist and from text to text. The major philosophical spokesman for the Romantic vision, Friedrich W. J. Schelling, lifted composite art to its highest position in theory when he called for the combination of all the arts into a single new form. Schelling envisioned this ideal synthesis as the most powerful purveyor of the "vision and expression of the indwelling spirit of nature."[2]

1

Das Gesamtkunstwerk, that infamous term associated with Richard Wagner, suggests the same Romantic ideal of all-encompassing synthesis. In Wagner's early prose, he theorized that the synthesis of the arts would take place when music and poetry were combined in his music dramas.[3] In spite of his occasional statements to the effect that the music drama was the universal art form, Wagner's clearest remarks on synthesis concern only two arts, poetry and music. His use of the different arts changed significantly between his theoretical explanations in *Oper und Drama* (1851) and his actual practice in *Der Ring,* beginning with *Das Rheingold* (1854) and *Die Walküre* (1856).[4] In his earlier writings, music, poetry, and drama were all placed on an equal plane and the syntheses of the three arts in opera were understood to come from an interdependence of equals. Later, Wagner believed that the music of the operas of *Der Ring* so surpassed the other arts that the balance he had predicted was inaccurate. Consequently, he revised his theory of synthesis in favor of music. By Wagner's own confession, music became primary and the *Gesamtkunstwerk* began to have a peculiar connotation.[5]

In spite of the fact that Wagnerian collaborations illustrated only one kind of combination, subsequent admirers of the composer tended to speak of his operas as the ideal forms of syntheses in the arts. This misunderstanding led to several mistaken conclusions concerning the history of syntheses of the arts. First, many subsequent discussions of composite form began and ended with Wagner, thus precluding examination of syntheses created by Schubert, Schumann, Hugo Wolf, Richard Strauss, Gustav Mahler, and many others. Second, discussions that were based on Wagner almost inevitably concluded that music is the primary art form and that the highest form of synthesis must follow the Wagnerian model. These have created formidable limitations on discussions of collaborative form. And while some of Wagner's operas are interesting examples of the *Gesamtkunstwerk,* they nonetheless form a limited set of works which all combine the same arts. They are products of the same mind and the same method of combination.

Subsequent devotees to the "total work of art" sought to add further dimensions to Wagner's model. They collaborated to produce a less homogeneous texture (as in the case of Richard Strauss and Hugo von Hoffmansthal's *Elektra* [1909]). They also incorporated other arts to fill out the nascent form. "New arts" like decorative sets and props in avant-garde styles as in *Parade* (1917), photographs and filmstrips projected on the stage as in Piscator's epic theater of the

1920s, and even the choreography of modern dance movements on the stage of an operatic production as in Kandinsky's *Der gelbe Klang* (1909), were brought together in experimental creation. Each addition marked another kind of *Gesamtkunstwerk* even though the Wagnerian idea had nothing to do with increasing the total number of arts that were brought together. Wagner's original assumption was simply that two arts were better than one.[6] To achieve the effects of interaction that he desired, Wagner composed his "poem" (the libretto) and his music (the vocal and orchestral score) so that ideas, emotions, and rhythms would be built upon the synthesis of the parts. In the history of collaborative form Wagner is certainly the most prolific creator of his century. He popularized an idea that has only rarely been studied outside his principal realm: opera. Because of his public success Wagner received credit for originating the idea of the *Gesamtkunstwerk* even though the idea had been the public dream of the earlier generations of Romantic poets and composers. Furthermore, it was only after Wagner that the dominant artists of the avant-garde in the late nineteenth and early twentieth centuries began to speak and write as if the synthesis of the arts were the absolute goal of the arts. And such was the power of the Wagnerian model that the ideal of the *Gesamtkunstwerk* seemed viable even though few subsequent artists actually attempted to combine any arts in collaborative works.

In the twentieth century, other terms have been invented to name collaborative art and, though none of these names would replace the *Gesamtkunstwerk*, all were invented so that their referents might be distinguished from Wagner's model. Wassily Kandinsky, for example, calls such composite forms *Monumentalkunst*, a word he transliterates to German from Russian and French. Although he is openly critical of Wagner, Kandinsky envisions combinative effects that are very similar to those announced by Wagner for the *Gesamtkunstwerk*.[7] Similar terms like *total art, total theater, multi-media,* and *mixed-media* have since emerged to describe various combinations of arts. However, since each of these terms has been used to name a certain historical manifestation of the idea of collaboration, all have limited application across the range of possible combinations of the arts. Recently, the term *performance art* has come to describe a rather wide range of activities performed by artists who often combine several arts in their work. Yet, even the concept of performance art is limited to a set of quasi-theatrical assumptions and would not include collaborative works like opera, lieder, or illuminated books.

Collaborative forms may be "collaborative" in two senses. First, such works may be the product of several artists. This is the usual meaning of the term and, in ordinary usage, collaborations refer directly to work artists do together to produce a joint creation. While I do not wish to remove the artists from their works, there is, nonetheless, another sense of the term *collaboration*. Whenever two or more arts are brought together in a single work, the combined effect can be said to be a collaboration of the contributing arts. When we confront a composite work, we experience most immediately the effects of the "collaboration of the arts" rather than the acts of collaboration of the artists, whether historical or performative. For this reason, I shall use the work *collaboration* to describe the relations of the arts as well as the cooperation of the artists (where the latter applies). I should remark here that it is not always easy to distinguish one from the other. Nevertheless, I intend to analyze combinations of the arts created by one artist in quite the same way as those combinations achieved by more than one artist. I want to be clear at the outset about how I have enlarged the meaning of this key word because I wish to emphasize the relations of the arts rather than the relationships of the artists.

Each of the following seven chapters examines one work of art that is collaborative, often in both senses of the term. I have used two complementary methods in my analysis of these works: (a) a summary, historical account of the background of each participating artist, and (b) an interpretation of the work that concentrates on the effects of the interactions of the arts. I adopt the first approach to inform the general reader of the formal conventions of the relevant arts. In doing so, I have had to discuss aspects of each artist's development as well as his relationships with the artistic currents (painterly, musical, literary, etc.) of his time. Because each chapter examines a different set of arts and artists, both methods of analysis (historical and interpretive) are repeated for each different work. It will appear that I have had to start all over again in each chapter and, to a certain degree, this is true. Each collaborative work exemplifies a specific kind of problem—a different set of arts, a different mode of presentation, a different level of complexity—and such variation requires that thorough exposition precede innovative elaboration. Each chapter is so constructed that it could stand alone as a complete (though abbreviated) study of a unique work of collaborative art.

Further, the structure of this book enables each chapter to serve as one of a limited number of similar (but not identical) examples of the nature of collaborative works. As the discussion moves from example to example, it prepares the way for a set of rules for these collaborative forms. The methods of analysis and the order of the chapters are designed to clarify and explain the rules of collaborative form which constitute the conclusion to this study. My selection of the works to be examined is not random, even though it will occur very quickly to most readers that the works are not studied in an identifiable historical order. Instead, I have chosen certain kinds of collaborations to represent a minimal range of possibilities. Thus, instead of analyzing seven operas or seven illustrated books, or seven musical settings of poems (any set of which might constitute one kind of collaborative form), I have chosen to analyze seven works which combine seven different sets of arts.

There are two distinct measures for organizing sets of composite works: by artists and by arts. In either case, there are relative degrees of complexity. The traditional view holds that the complexity of the relationships of the arts depends upon the number of artists involved. By these rules, a work completed by one artist was "simple," by two "less simple," and a work involving a number of artists "complex." As long as everyone was interested in the artists and not the art work, this view was useful. This measure made poetry "simple" and theatrical productions "complex" even if the poetry was illuminated and the theatrical piece was a one-man show. It is obvious, however, that counting the number of artists who took part in a work's creation does not provide a useful way of categorizing art.

The plainer and more functional formula proposed here will describe one measure of the degree of relation of the arts and also reflect the format of this book. This study moves from four simple collaborations to three complex collaborations. I assume that the base measure in any discussion of the arts is a single art. The traditional historical and critical divisions of the "arts" are founded upon the idea of a clear delineation of the separate arts. And, it is usually against the norm of a single art that any collaborative form is measured. In fact, the overwhelming prevalence of the single art as the basis for historical and critical studies is so pronounced that those who try to broaden that base are immediately suspect. But why draw attention to the "unity and coherence" of each art if it is obvious? Only to demonstrate that what I am undertaking here goes against the natural, self-protective tendencies of the respective critical traditions of each of the arts involved. Even studies of "traditional" collaborative forms such as opera, theater, dance, and film often downplay their interdisciplinary bases. The typical modern approach to collaborations emphasizes the art of one's specialty to the detriment of the "other arts." Hence, operas are analyzed in terms of music, plays as literary texts, and films as the art of their strongest part (as novel, as play, as camera work, as editing, etc.).

Collaborative form redefines the concept of form against the intrusions of "primary form." Where one form is made primary in a combination of the arts, there can be no collaborative form. Combinations that emphasize one art at the expense of the contributing arts tend to enhance the primary form rather than create a new form from the resulting interactions. Since the beginnings of Romanticism, most of the rules of combination invented by composers, directors, and choreographers are rules for the use and enhancement—in short, the accompaniment—of a primary form. In this way, we can understand the approaches of composers like Schubert, Schumann, Wagner, Strauss, and Schoenberg in much the same way that we understand the practices of film directors like G. W. Pabst, Fritz Lang, Jean Renoir, John Ford, and Stanley Kubrick. The controlling artist combines the arts so that his art has full advantage. This will be the major issue in most combinations of the arts and, as we shall see, rather few works will remain in the field of collaboration once the rule prohibiting "primary form" is enforced.

For collaborative works, the minimum standard relation is between two arts. Whether these two arts are combined by one or several artists, this level of relation is the norm against which both single arts and multiple combinations are compared. In effect, this is the simplest level of collaboration and this level is represented in the following study by Georges Braque and René Char's *Lettera amorosa* (1963), Joan Miró and René Char's *A la santé du serpent* (1954), and Maurice Maeterlinck and Arnold Schoenberg's *Herzgewächse* (1909). A fourth example is included, the collaborative editing of Wassily Kandinsky and Franz Marc in *Der Blaue Reiter* (1912), but this case is less pure since there are more than two arts involved in the work.

I have designated another level, the complex relation, to describe those cases where more than two arts are combined in one work of art. Whether one artist (as in Oskar Kokoschka's *Mörder, Hoffnung der Frauen* [1909]) or several (as in the team of Cocteau, Satie, Picasso, and Massine, who created and produced *Parade* [1917]) combine three or more arts, the key to complexity is the number of arts involved. The chart of relation shown below illustrates the clear sequence developed in this book:

The Three Levels of Relation in the Arts

1. None   The basis for most study of the arts precludes relation. We study one art at a time even where several arts might constitute a movement, school, or period.

2. Simple   Two arts are combined. This is the simplest level of relation.

3. Complex   More than two arts are combined. Wherever more than two arts are combined, the difficulties increase exponentially.

The organization of this book follows the order of complexity inherent in this chart. Starting with the standard level of collaboration (Simple), I examine four discrete examples of this level of relation. The last three chapters are devoted to "complex" works. In each of these last chapters, the works examined are versions of the ideal "complex" art work, the *Gesamtkunstwerk*, though all three creators might deny any such pretension. In Kokoschka's *Mörder, Hoffnung der Frauen* (1909), Kandinsky's *Der gelbe Klang* (1909), and Nikolais' *Triad* (1975), the difficult ideal of the *Gesamtkunstwerk* is pursued in three completely different ways.

The reader should be forewarned that this division in my examples between simple and complex is adopted for formal rather than historical reasons. There is certainly a need for a history of collaborative forms, but I have not attempted to fill that need here.

I have chosen a certain set of works and a certain order of presentation for formal, not historical or cultural or linguistic reasons. I move from the simple to the complex, from the single to the multiple and so the order of the chapters stands, not as a unified argument but as a set of examples, arranged in an order that speaks of the form itself, a form that I am trying to make intelligible. In my study of collaborations, I find something that other critics have not remarked upon. I take my first task to be that of making clear what I am calling collaborative form (particularly since I am the first to name it as such). There can be no history of collaborative form until someone demonstrates its existence and proposes, by way of definition, some rules governing its functions. Once that is done, someone else should be able to work out the historical development of the form and organize a field of study along more traditional lines (origin, transmission, influence, and its relation to cultural and historical settings). I hope that this book will make that task possible.

The larger claims that I make for the nature of collaborative forms do not depend on any one set of composite works any more than the rules that I derive depend on a historical period, national origin, or a set of arts. For those artists who wish to combine the various arts, the first task has always been the same: to breach the walls that stand between them. In the examples that I have chosen, there seem to be two strategies for solving this problem. The first is the most obvious and the most difficult: to combine the most forceful effects of each art with parallel effects of the others. In this case, the artist uses those very aspects of each art that are the essential features of that art (or, at least, its distinct advantages). For such "strong" approaches, there are two abiding difficulties. First, as practiced by Wagner, Scriabin, and Kokoschka, the strong approach requires a mastery of each of the arts the creator uses. This, by itself, is no small feat. As a master painter once pointed out, *le peintre s'écrit à peine.*[8]

The second difficulty is not as obvious, though it is just as challenging. Whoever would combine the arts must first overcome the inertia that is discovered when one attempts to compel any art into combination. The very forces that characterize an art form (definition, conventions, habit, and historical precedent) create a significant resistance to any interaction with other arts. The forces that traditionally hold the arts apart are so strong that even Wagner could not always put them together. His own productions were often projected toward an audience little prepared to perceive his goal. Even today *Die Walküre* ride (excerpted) up the Rhein without words and the instrumental excerpts of the "Forest Murmurs" are performed as if the leitmotif did not concern the absent Siegfried and the unheard opera of his fate. Even if Wagner's performances had achieved the level of interaction that he claimed, it is doubtful that such effects could have been recognized by more than a few spectators. For not only must the collaborative artist discover the means to combine the arts, he must also prepare the way for the reception of his work, tasks that are rarely completed.

The second strategy for combining the arts does not attack the weight of difference directly. Instead of creating an open juxtaposition of the formal strengths of the several arts, the artist abstracts individual elements from their respective aesthetic contexts. He may then freely recombine these elements within a structure that is not conventional for any of the abstracted elements. For example, in *Der gelbe Klang* (1909), Wassily Kandinsky composes a series of scenes upon a stage. Each scene is called a picture (*Bild*) and is made up of elements of music (notes played by an orchestra, vocal parts, and short sections of combined choral and orchestral music), poetry (fragmented lines and words, incomplete vocal sounds), drama (each picture is performed on a stage), painting (colored sets, colored props, and colored light projected on the stage), and dance (choreographed movements of five giants, of flying objects, of individual dancers, and finally of a large group of dancers). Kandinsky abstracts these elements from their conventional surroundings, recombines them in a larger context, then composes a set of serial and simultaneous interactions on his stage. Since none of these elements is directly linked to its conventional source, none contains formal reference to its mother art. In this way, the combination of the elements creates effects that are purified of the residual cultural weight that would otherwise function to keep the elements apart for the perceiver. However, abstract combinations like *Der gelbe Klang* can become trapped in the very strategy of their presentation. For, with the elimination of traditional sets of expectations, abstract collaborative works frequently offer no familiar ground for the audience. And where the work is not prepared for an audience, an audience must be prepared for the work. Abstract collaborations are rarely produced because of the additional demands upon both artist and audience.

In both strategies, the viewer of the collaboration is asked for a different kind of attention than required by conventional art works. For, even though the aims of the collaborative work are no different from those of any art work, the audience must suspend its usual expectations so that it can perceive the new form. When several arts interact in a single work, viewers must expand their perspective to include all of the collaborating arts. Such a change of viewpoint draws attention to the interactions that make up the whole. This alteration of expectations is rarely built into the collaborative work. The more conventional the collaboration, the more aware the audience of the demands of such works. Thus, for example, spectators for the opera are more acutely aware of the complexities of that form than are spectators of a collaborative stage event for which there are few conventions.

Each of the artists of collaborative form suffered the disappointment of discovering that the actual effect of composite work is not quantitatively different from the actual effect of any single art work. This rule (which I will refer to in the conclusion of this study as the rule of equality of forms, one of the rules of collaborative form) is not in accord with the expectations declared by nearly all the artistic and philosophical spokesmen for the *Gesamtkunstwerk*. The celebrity accorded any artist is thus unlikely to come from experiments, however successful, in collaborative forms. The most obvious reasons for this fact are implied in the series of difficulties just discussed. However, the historical disadvantages of composite art do not end there. The ideal of the *Gesamtkunstwerk* seemed always to promise more than it was likely to deliver. Not only were the difficulties inherent in combining art forms underestimated, but the subsequent comprehension of such works nearly always contradicted the artists' confident prophecies. After all, if it has taken nearly two hundred years to discover the full importance of William Blake's collaborative forms, can any lesser poet, painter, or composer expect better?

Each of the arts involved in this study has its own history, its own criticism, and its own set of limits as a formal activity. Certainly the critical tradition of each art contains the arcane lore, the unique assumptions, and the different scholarly methodologies that any specialist might expect. However, it would be foolish to reject them out of hand. The advances in the knowledge of each art are still communicated in the criticism of that art. Good criticism is as necessary to the art as to its audience. In the study of the relations of the arts, the critical assumptions of each of the arts must become part of our working knowledge of the art. There can be no substitute for the history, conventions, and critical approaches of each of the arts involved in a collaborative work. Such a restatement of the ground rules of scholarship would be out of place were it not for the fact that some recent writing on the relations of the arts has displayed a striking refusal to account for those matters of scholarship that are assumed by specialists in the field.

In fact, it is my view that the critic of collaborative form always multiplies his tasks, for he must take on the traditions of every art that he would discuss. And surely in doing so, he faces a two-headed demon at every turn, a demon that despises analogy. He must satisfy the specialists in each art he touches upon while, at the same time, remaining clear to the general reader (i.e., the general, educated reader who would be interested in the related arts). There is no fury like that of an art historian watching a literary critic discuss art history unless it be that of a musicologist listening to an art historian analyze a piece of music. And there should be no relief from these scholarly demands merely because one crosses and recrosses traditional disciplinary boundaries. On the other hand, criticism of collaborative works cannot be expected to conform to the limits of any particular art (or the critical theories thereof). The scholar of a certain art can be counted on to defend the integrity (read identity) of his specialty and, in so doing, defend the barriers that separate it from the other arts. Works of art that combine several arts implicitly threaten the identity of each art. Hence, my task, if I am to be effective, will be twofold: to survive the threshold of hard attention from the specialists while avoiding the kind of specialized critical language that would baffle the general reader. I have tried to interest both audiences. I have, wherever possible, deleted critical jargon that would only be grasped by specialists. I am aware that in some cases this has meant opting for clarity rather than precision and I have accepted that risk as a necessary part of any original explanation of an art form without a critical tradition.

Collaborative works always stand at the fringe of the accepted *oeuvre* of any artist. As a result, the form that I am setting out to define will seem, at first glance, obscure. Part of the explanation for this fact is that collaborative forms do not fit the usual formats for reproduction and assessment in the arts. The most celebrated twentieth-century collaborations are reproduced only with difficulty and even then are hardly available to everyone. Thus, attempts to recreate the first performance of Stravinsky's *Sacre du Printemps* (1913) using the original choreography and score; to reproduce Picasso's collaborations with Paul Eluard; or to reproduce the first performance of *Parade* (1917) complete with Satie's score, Picasso's costumes and sets, Cocteau's scenario, and Massine's choreography remain historically interesting and yet inaccessible to the majority of those who would be most interested in seeing the works reproduced. Collaborations between painters and poets are immediately negotiable artifacts in the world of art and disappear in limited editions into the collections of those who can afford them. The collected works of poets nearly always appear without illustrations, music, or choreography that originally may have made up the whole context of the work. In books and articles on these same artists, collaborative works are usually ignored.

Combinations of the arts will not be found in anthologies and catalogues. Yet, if the example of William Blake has any lesson for critics and readers, it is that ignorance of collaborative forms (even if backed by a hundred years of expert deletions by editors and commentators) only serves to misinform scholars, students, and general readers. The "rediscovery" of Blake's drawings, etchings, and illuminations has forced a reassessment of the poet's major works. The collaborative forms of the artists I have chosen to discuss here express (like the collaborative forms of William Blake) a central aspect of each artist's vision. If I can demonstrate how such combinations might be best treated, we need no longer assign combinations of the arts to the fringes of knowledge of the arts.

In the past decade, a resurgence of critical interest in comparing the arts has opened up new areas of study. In 1952, the Modern Language Association organized an annual bibliography of literature and the other arts and since then has offered sections at its meetings on this general topic. A few scholars have produced excellent studies of the relations of poetry and painting, poetry and music, the novel and film, and other dual relationships, all within traditional, literary periods. However, the tendency to examine only two arts within a restricted historical period has limited the direction and scope of study. More often, critics pursue influences and analogies rather than actual works that combine the arts. Many of the comparisons of the arts are made from the standpoint of one art as the primary form. Following Suzanne K. Langer's insistence on the necessity of a dominant form, these studies have emphasized the primacy of music over poetry in settings of poems, the superiority of music over drama in opera (following Wagner's lead), and the prevailing strength of cinema over its screenplays and sources (whether novels or plays). In spite of these shortcomings, the attention presently directed toward the relations of the arts is a positive, though ambivalent, sign of renewal in the study of the arts.

I have accepted the absence of a unified theory of the relations of the arts as one of the enduring problems to be confronted in each analysis of a collaborative work. For a study such as this, the lack of general theory is a positive advantage. The writer is then free to observe the general rules of collaboration from the examples at hand rather than having to answer a proscriptive model at every step. The

question of a general theory can be overemphasized. Having no theoretical starting place should make collaborative forms no more in-
timidating than any one of the several arts. After all, there is no
compelling single theory of opera, painting, dance, or film. The absence of such theoretical constructs may encourage a fresh approach
or an original methodology.

It is in this context that I propose to examine a set of collaborative
works to see if I can lay out the ground rules of this form. I would
like to induce, from these separate studies, a set of rules that binds
all collaborations. Hence, the goal of this study is to understand
what happens when several arts are combined in a single work. Part
of this goal will be completed in each chapter where a different kind
of collaboration is explained. The second part will be achieved in the
conclusion, where I will culminate these studies by discussing the
rules of collaborative form.

ONE

THE WORK ADMIRED
IN EVERY AGE
Lettera amorosa

IN the twentieth century, the arts have been brought together in a wide variety of ways. The major movements in literature and painting (the plastic arts) have contributed new ideas and new approaches for crossing the traditional lines of the separate disciplines but all these movements have sought in common what Wassily Kandinsky called "a synthesis of art forms." Whether we speak of Impressionism in painting, music, and poetry; cubism in painting and poetry; futurism in poetry, graphics, music, film, painting, and total performance; or Expressionism as it touched nearly every art form in Germany during the period 1905–22, we find a common fascination with bringing the arts together in a larger, unnamed form. Not that the idea was new in the twentieth century. Richard Wagner's *Gesamtkunstwerk* preceded both in theory and performance the attempts of the modern artists to fuse the different forms. But the modern experimental movements in the arts have been curiously unanimous in their separate espousals of such a total work which would, in theory, use the unique advantages of the respective forms together to achieve a totality which transcended the sum of its parts. Hence, from such simple experiments as Apollinaire's "Les Fenêtres" to such complex works as Kandinsky's *Der gelbe Klang*, the modern artist has felt an apparent urge to cross the formal boundaries of the disciplines in his creations.

The range of possible effects of such syntheses is only limited by the number of ways in which the different arts can be brought together. Thus, whether one simply adds the various possible combinations of art forms that could function together or contemplates the kinds of creativeness involved and their potentials in combination, he can soon imagine a maze of possibility. However, a surer way to begin a discussion of the phenomena is to talk specifically of certain models of collaboration between the arts before attempting to formulate a theory of collaboration.

The simplest model of collaboration is provided by those artists who have mastered more than one art and who then bring these arts together in their work. This model is provided in the works of Kandinsky, Paul Klee, Arnold Schoenberg, Paul Valéry, Hans Arp, and Oskar Kokoschka, to name a few. There are obvious advantages for the critic in beginning with a "one-artist collaboration." First, since only one artist is involved, the critic can assume a certain unity and wholeness in the collaborative work. Such variables as the artist's style, his development, and his idiosyncrasies tend to carry over from one art to the next, thus making discussion and understanding considerably easier. Second, for the art historian (as well as for the literary critic), such knowledge of the entire *oeuvre* as is necessary is a priori limited (even though this *oeuvre* may be in a variety of art forms and immensely complex, as is the case with Kandinsky, Schoenberg, and Valéry).

The classic model in poetry and painting of a "one-artist show" is the work of William Blake, an English engraver, poet, painter, and craftsman of the early Romantic period. It was not until the middle of the twentieth century, however, that the collaborative nature of Blake's work began to attract the serious attention of his readers and critics. Once discovered, the illuminations and graphic works became indispensable parts of Blake's work, parts that can no longer be ignored in favor of the poetry edited in "collective" editions. The interactions in Blake's manuscripts and first editions between the texts and the illuminations create a constant flux, back and forth, between the two arts wherein each form both completes and complements the other. Such constant and profound interaction enriches the reading of the work in such a way that the resultant aesthetic experience transcends the isolated experience of either distinct art form in the total work. In *The Four Zoas,* for example, there are many sections of the manuscript wherein one cannot easily make reasonable distinctions between the effects of the two arts since they are so nearly inseparable from the whole. Critical attempts to come to grips with this problem have not been wholly successful but have nonetheless attested that Blake's illuminated works cannot be broken into separate aesthetic forms without changing the nature of the work drastically. Hence, the peculiar nature of Blake's collaborations demonstrates how effective such a fusion can be. Even though problems remain in finding adequate critical approaches to such a work, these problems are simplified somewhat by the fact that a single artist is the center of study. What one assumes about Blake the poet, his craft, his imagination, his poetic world, his images, and his symbols can frequently be carried over into the illuminations themselves. The major difference is that of the form used.

The second model, that of a collaboration between two artists, is more difficult to discuss in spite of the fact that it is the most common mode of interaction between the arts. For this reason, I have chosen to pursue the nature and qualities of a collaboration of this mode to some length to show how such works achieve their ends and what kinds of critical perceptions of the total experience of the collaboration are possible. The collaboration, in this case, is between two arts: poetry and lithography. Two artists bring their respective arts together to create a new work, composed of interaction and, at best, transcending the effects available in either art form separately.

Lettera amorosa is the kind of *oeuvre* that literally merits the description *beau livre*. Produced together by René Char and Georges Braque, the book was published in 1963 by Edwin Engelberts of Geneva, Switzerland, in a limited edition of 230 *exemplaires*. It was printed in Paris at the Imprimérie Union in folio size (In-4°) and bound in folds which permit full-page sections to be removed for viewing. Nearly every one of its fifty-five pages contains a color lithograph by Braque and one or several fragments of a poem by Char.

Char recounts that he wrote the first version of the poem of the same title in 1952 and subsequently published it in a separate edition in Paris (NRF Gallimard, 1953). He later altered the poem several times; first for republication in a selection of his poems, translated and edited by Jackson Mathews in *Hypnos Waking* (New York: Random House, 1956); and later, in another variant published in *La Parole en archipel,* a collective edition published in Paris in 1962 (NRF Gallimard). Between these editions, he worked on a third, collaborative version with Georges Braque after the painter himself singled out *Lettera amorosa* as the one poem of Char's that he particularly wanted to rework with the poet.[1] However, it was not until 1958 that Braque and Char agreed on a publisher and on the general concepts that were to guide the new work.[2] It should also be emphasized that, at this stage of the work, neither Char nor Braque intended their combined effort as a simple joining of a set of lithographs to a set of preexistent lines of poetry. Rather, there was to have been a great deal of flexibility on the part of both artists as they gradually resolved and united their respective ideas into a single work which is neither an "Art Book" nor a "Poem" per se but rather *L'Ouvrage,* a curious combination that defies traditional definitions in the critical language of either art form. In this case, the *beau livre* is to be more than a container for the play of forces that each art form introduces and leaves for the other to fulfill. In this case, *L'Ouvrage* is itself a work of art as few books in their entirety are: *"L'Ouvrage de tous les temps admiré."*[3]

Char and Braque commenced this work with a full appreciation of their shared experience and a rare communality of spirit. This undercurrent of understanding is nowhere more apparent than in the mutual respect for one another's art, a respect that is reflected in the work. Char alters lines, changes typography, and adds fragments to complete the movements begun in Braque's figures. Braque, at the same time, reinvents the imagery of the poem and unifies the major motifs within the images of the natural world of the Sorgue River and the Vaucluse. Most importantly, the painter honors the poet's controlling image—the multivalent symbol for woman, love, deity, cosmos—the *Iris d'Eros, iris de Lettera amorosa* ("Sur le franc-bord," *Lettera amorosa,* 55) by invoking floral images of similar shape and color in the movement of lithographs from the cluster cosmos of the first stone (10) to the flowing petals of the last stones (46, 48, 49, 51).

In appearance, the book is extraordinarily simple: a series of fragments of poetry intertwined (like the *liseron* with its roots and branches) with a series of color lithographs. However, the structure of *Lettera amorosa* is neither linear nor serial (though such structures might be inferred from a first glance at the work). Braque's lithographs are not necessarily created to illustrate their respective pages of poetry. Nor is there a consistent one-to-one relationship between poem and lithography in the order of revelation of themes and motifs. Rather, like two complementary structures moving simultaneously toward each other, the fragments and the lithographs take formally different paths to arrive at the point of completion. In other words, to use a figure to describe the work's structure, the poetry and the lithography form two sides of a circle that opens and closes within the work itself. The viewer's experience of the work is never easily divisible since once he has seen the circle unfold and complete itself, he can rarely discern which part is made up of poetry and which of painting. This aspect is, in fact, one of the best descriptions of a successful collaboration between two art forms.

The central idea of the text is to present an exchange between two persons: one speaking, one listening (though absent). The form of Char's poem, that of a letter, is not gratuitous. The original version of the poem, which was more specifically a personal letter between two people, has here been altered so that the exchange is not so simply between the lover and his absent loved one, but also explicitly between a more universal mind and its images and, at the same time, on another level, a *conversation souveraine* between poet and painter.[4] The text was changed then to make more general the particular, more erotic the sexual, and more universal the moments of shared, private experience. In effect, Char opens the poem outward by each of his deletions and projects the poem toward universality by each addition.

The form of the letter gives two specific kinds of expectations to the reader, each of which is vital to the function of the *ouvrage*. First, the letter invites intimacy not only with the addressee (the *tu* to whom segments are addressed) but with the larger audience as well. Such an intimacy of tone breaks down the characteristic expectations of the reader concerning "Poetry." In fact, the tone (as part of the form) reverses the formal expectations connected with poetry, thus freeing the reader to accept the interaction between the poem and the lithography. Second, the assumption of a shared experience, which is basic to the process of letter-writing, is extended to the work itself, wherein the larger context of the collaborative *ouvrage* is implied as a sequel to the particular unspoken whole relationship implied between lover and loved one. The fragments of poetry— which often seem distinct and not specifically related to the development of themes or ideas—operate nonetheless within an unseen horizon which is assumed to be the field of shared experience between the speaker and his loved one. As the poem opens, this private horizon of mutual experience and common assumption expands to include the broader world of relations accessible to all readers. Such an opening of the field of concern of the poem is advantageous since it creates the possibility of the *ouvrage* through the intertwining collaborative relationship between text and lithographs. *Lettera amorosa* is thus from the lover to his beloved, then from the mind to its forms, and finally from the poet to art itself as each of these relationships is explored *de la base au sommet*.

The entire process of opening begins with the first lines of the text which are in juxtaposition with the lithograph *Profil:*

> Temps en sous-oeuvre, années d'affliction. . . . Droit Naturel!
> Ils donneront malgré eux une nouvelle fois l'existence
> à l'Ouvrage de tous les temps admiré. (9)[5]

With neither special emphasis (except that it occurs at the beginning) nor explication, the concept of the *Ouvrage* ("the Work") is announced even before the specific lover's vow ("Je te chéris") that is traditional in a dedication.[6] The *lettera* begins after a long period wherein time is measured (qualified) by personal suffering. The idea of beginning *again* implies a sense of a cyclic rhythm in which the season of suffering must be followed by rebirth and renewal. The closed past has been broken and the cycle of creativity is renewed *(une nouvelle fois).* Once more, *L'Ouvrage* will be given existence as if the idea had always been latent, needing only the opening of the *nouvelle fois* to take its shape. The announcement is juxtaposed between the first model, Monteverdi's avowal from *Lettera amorosa* quoted as epigraph, and the poet's repetition of this form.[7] The changes in diction, tone, and elevation between Monteverdi and the speaker are introduced through the notion of the *ouvrage:* a form which takes a different shape with each succeeding age.

Char's introductory epigram, remarks, and announcements are juxtaposed with the lithograph *Profil* (see figure 1) which makes dominant the silhouette of the absent loved one, the woman to whom the entire love letter is ostensibly addressed. In the first lithograph, Braque establishes not only the central figure toward whom the *Lettera amorosa* might be said to move on a literal level, but also other major forms, structures, and color motifs of the work. Moreover, he sets up these parts of the whole with miraculous simplicity. The largest image portrayed is the central figure of the woman's head in black surrounded by the signs of the cosmos. More precisely, her profile is ringed by space and set off by star clusters, two irregular large star shapes, and two spirals. Each of these forms a direct relation to part of the text of the poem adjacent to the lithograph.

Furthermore, each of these forms is suggestive of larger meanings that are not at all explicit to the reader at this point in the work. The woman is dominant over all cosmic forces, for her gray shadow takes precedence over the other figures wherever there is an overlap. The

Fig. 1. Georges Braque, "Profil" from *Lettera amorosa* (Copyright 1990 ARS N.Y./ ADAGP)

central position of her head in the frame establishes her as both the central object of desire at this moment and as that being *("Absent partout où on fête un absent")*, defined as absence itself, which over-powers even those extreme and constant figures of cosmic stability (the stars, the moon, the galactic form of the spirals, and the voids of space) which are invoked explicitly (as on page 16) and by juxta-position (as on pages 28 and 29). Her absence becomes, like Heidegger's *Das Nicht*, a negative ground that reveals itself *als nicht*, a force that is most fully realized by its not-being-there. The implied absence of the loved one in the poem is immediately juxtaposed to the power of absence in the lithography, a juxtaposition that leads the viewer to behold the contraries of finite absence and cosmic presence.

In this case the two arts seem to function together most effectively where they are able to complete both sides of the opening circle. In this way, the reader is presented a double perspective and hence, a simultaneous sense of the opposites at work. Whether the difference in perspective is spatial (as seems the case in this example), temporal (as suggested in subsequent fragments), or simply a matter of pro-portion, the inherently different advantages of the separate art forms are used to modulate the reader's experience in ways that are not available to either of the forms singly. Hence, even where the woman is understood to be *"absent partout,"* and, in spite of the fact she is as clearly the cause of the writer's malaise as of his joy of ex-pectation, she is a distinctly mental presence. She is, in other words, poised outside of time and space by Braque's opening stone and thus *de la pensée, pas de la terre.*

The poet writes in a period of waiting. He creates an indefinite time lapse in the middle of which he begins to speak. The text opens after *"années d'affliction,"* between beginning and ending, between separation and reunion. He ends the letter at a point different only in duration. He remains in the middle. The expected reunion never is announced in the text and the poem does not end. It simply stops after a passage of recognition. The only sense of an ending and of subsequent fulfillment in union is provided by the lithographs.

In the first "Profil" of the *bien-aimée*, Braque suggests the future *"rapport à présent invisible"*[8] by creating symbolic forms that surround the woman's head in pairs. Thus, where the male appears in the poem as a voice in solitude and the female appears alone in the first lithograph, the union of the couple, like the closing of the circle, is only completed when the two are together, in the same temporal and spatial plane. The form of the love letter inherently disallows such an event, for the distances implied cannot be closed. Man and woman, absence and presence, poetry and painting are brought together at the end, not in the text, but in the final lithograph.

Braque's use of pairs in the first lithograph suggests, at the beginning of the *ouvrage,* the visual mating of the pairs which is represented in the final lithograph of the work. The composition of the figures on the first page implies the finality of a cosmic pairing in the universe and a lasting union as if the spirals closed upon themselves to achieve the perfected form. But while the presence of the symbolic pairs in the lithographs prepares for *commune présence* as completion, the couple represented in the final stones, both in floral and in human form, are more than symbols of concluding union in the real world of the speaker and his loved one. Since there is no reconciliation in the literal world of the poem, such a meeting takes place only in the mind of the reader, who watches the fictive signs of the visual imagination moving toward a state of union. Such an imagination achieves momentary summits in the work, but all such "instants" collapse:

> Ce n'est pas simple de rester hissé
> sur la vague du courage quand on suit
> du regard quelque oiseau volant au déclin
> du jour.[9]

The bird's flight is both a rise (a model for the speaker's balance) and a fall *(au déclin du jour).* Like Wallace Stevens's "casual flocks of pigeons" which "in the isolation of the sky, at evening . . . make ambiguous undulations as they sink/Downward to darkness on extended wing," Char's random bird contains an inexplicable beauty and a contradictory motion.[10] Braque's *L'Aile et les oiseaux* brings forth a vision which unnerves the man who tries to travel on his own wave. The apparent ideal in this passage would be a lasting balance *"sur la vague du courage."* But such extended durations are simply fictions which tell more of the speaker's desires and deprivations than of his actual time. In *Lettera amorosa,* the meaningful balances occur only between couples wherein equal but opposite forces are fused.

> Celui qui veille au sommet du plaisir est
> l'égal du soleil comme de la nuit. Celui qui
> veille n'a pas des ailes, il ne poursuit
> pas. (40)[11]

A more Romantic poet would have called here for a man who can hold summits, stay at the crest of the breaking wave, or, more graphically, stop the undulation of time. Such a man would, then, by extension, need nothing, neither the imagination's wings nor the mind's rapacious pursuit. But, as aphorisms sometimes imply more than they denote at first reading (or, perhaps imply the opposite of what they seem to say, given the fuller context of the poem), we must look more closely at this fragment of Char's to see the full implications. He who desires a still summit, a static wave, a lasting sexual climax, or *l'instant* sustained wishes for the timeless, spaceless unity of Being wherein all the fragmented perceptions close together in a whole. Such a man (*"celui qui,"* that is, a generalized someone without name or qualities) would have attained finality, unchangingness, hence stasis. He would no longer be human. As Char writes, he is identified with the cosmos (*"L'égal du soleil comme de la nuit"*) as an unchanging constant through which human time would course as the earth spins through sunlight and darkness. But, the wish for permanence is a two-edged knife. Permanence would eliminate cares, but in so doing it would eliminate the very center of what is fleetingly human: imagination's flight and the emotion's ecstasies. The dual edge of Char's lines serves as an adequate reminder of his understatement and of the careful irony of his diction, both of which prepare and conceal the ambiguity inherent in his style. One wishes for eternity, the still center, and the perfect union, but such wishes are and must remain fictive. For at their core is a refusal to accept what is human as what is. For the poet of summits and depths, not to have wings, not to pursue would be the imagined hell of absolute solitude, all relations having ceased.

Char's ambiguity and occasional hermeticism are matched by Braque's reticence and elegant simplicity. In the first stone, the face of the woman in profile is primitive, masklike, and undifferentiated. Her silhouette is representative of the style that Braque uses in the entire suite of lithographs. At this point in Braque's career, he had begun to simplify natural forms into instants of form and color. Braque's devotion to such animal forms as fish and birds as well as his interest in such plant images as flowers, fruits, and leaves, began in the extended still-life studies he completed during and after the Second World War. Since his first version of Char's *Le Soleil des eaux* in 1949, he had shown a particular fascination with the flora and fauna of the poet's Vaucluse. The best example of Braque's later style, which we also find interspersed in *Lettera amorosa*, is the extended study of birds in flight. With each bird or set of birds, whether in oil, *eau-forte*, lithograph, or pen and ink, Braque captures an instant of flight, suggesting not only the literal photographic form of the bird but the quality of flight as well. In *Derniers Messages,* these studies attain their most abstract (nonrepresentational, distorted) form as the motion of wing and head, tail and neck assume the archetypal, often primitive, shape of prehistoric flight, captured in the color and texture of the imagination. The natural forms presented in *Lettera amorosa* are developments of the same subjects to which Braque had attended for over twenty years (if not a lifetime). They each represent Braque's own manner of reticence, which declares as little as possible as explicit commentary and yet suggests through color intensity and hue as well as through movement of line and figure a particular instant captured as part of that eternal recurrence of forms in flight. Thus, not only are birds drawn in suspended motion, but flowers, trees, leaves, roots, and the river are all caught in acts of motion. Flying, flowing, blowing, exploding, sailing, floating, imploding: these are the motions suggested on each page. Braque's simplicity of presentational form is seldom more appropriate than in union with Char's compressed and fragmented statements. The subsequent lithographs in this work show a similar primitivistic figuration wherein the artist uses color and simplified form to achieve results that are both symbolic of and partially illustrative of the world of the poem. More fully explained, these lithographs perform multiple functions in the context of the work. There are a number of lithographs that seem to be illustrations of the text. For example, the gray and yellow *rapace* on page 44 (see figure 2) serves adequately as an illustration for the bottom fragment on page 50:

> Ma convoitise comique, mon voeu glacé: saisir
> ta tête comme un rapace à flanc d'abîme. Je
> t'avais, maintes fois, tenue sous la pluie
> des falaises, comme un faucon encapuchonné.[12]

The *rapace,* formed of intertwining yellow and gray rings, hangs in the air like a kestrel, before striking its prey. In Char's fragment, a similar ravenous quality is described and the hawk, as metaphorical figure, serves well to illustrate the poet's *"convoitise comique."* However, we must add several observations that take away from the purely illustrative value of Braque's lithograph. First, it precedes its matching fragment by six pages, thus diluting somewhat its possible

Fig. 2. Georges Braque, lithograph "Le Rapace" from *Lettera amorosa*, 44 (Copyright 1990 ARS N.Y./ADAGP)

effect as illustration and explanation. Second, it serves also as an illustration for the "oiseau volant au déclin du jour" which I have already discussed. Furthermore, its structure suggests both in texture and in detail an incipient fragmentation. The form of the bird is composed of small, partial circles, linked together like a chain-mail coat. However, none of the links seems quite secure and the overall impression is that the raptor itself is on the verge of falling into pieces in flight. Such potential disintegration qualifies rather severely the pose of the *rapace,* which is the pose of a bird of prey about to strike with the wings outstretched and the tail tucked beneath and bent for braking.

In similar ways, the lithographs of the *Trèfle* (page 18; see figure 3) *La Nuit* (page 16), and *L'Iris* (25, 32, 41, 46, and 49) appear at first to be possible illustrations of an adjacent text. However, like the example of the *rapace,* each of these lithographs does far more than render a concrete, visual representation of an image in the poem. When seen in the context of the work as a whole, each of these lithographs serves just as importantly to give direction, to act as simultaneous rejoinder, to pose a contrary, or to present a complementary flight of image, idea, or form to the poetic text. In *Lettera amorosa,* where neither the text nor the series of lithographs can be said to make up the whole of the *ouvrage,* both forms must be seen as they function in relation to each other and to the whole. Their respective movements, meanings, and significances must be constantly qualified by the context that the other simultaneously creates.

The words and images used to evoke the opposition and, at the same time, the potential union of two forces provide a powerful series of motifs that play back and forth through every level of the *ouvrage.* From the most obvious couple (the man and the woman) to the least obvious, though everpresent pair (the poet and the painter), the opposition of the parts in pairs is repeated in numerous variations. The rhythm of couples, pairs, and contraries is suggested, even in the context of Char's passages of devastating isolation, by Braque's complementary forms. The example discussed in the first illustration introduced the motif of the pair even though the explicit couples in the lithograph were relegated to the background. However, the periods of cyclical evolution that follow create a complex rhythm between text and plastic form wherein the variations on the theme of the couple are played over the full spectrum of possible images.

Thus, where the letter actually begins (page 13) and the fragments and paragraphs of poetry approach the mundane level of letter-writing at its most recognizable, the apparent couple implied

Fig. 3. Georges Braque, lithograph "Le Trèfle" from *Lettera amorosa*, 18 (Copyright 1990 ARS N.Y./ADAGP)

in the letter is neither supported nor illustrated by the accompanying lithograph. Instead, the ordinary echoes the ordinary. A still-life composition of lemons in a bowl serves as ironic response to the specifics of the letter-writer's news of health and weather.

But after the text has moved from ordinary day to a less ordinary night, the opposing *lunes et nuit* are evoked as sinister masks upon the waking of his love:

Lunes et nuit, vous êtes un loup de velours noir, village, sur la veillée de mon amour.[13]

These images and fragments of nocturnal activity move in turn to dream and finally to the ripeness of insomnia in which *"L'Amour hélant, L'Amoureuse viendra . . ."* impregnating the night with *"Gloria de l'été, ô fruits!"* The positive quality of the poet's sleeplessness (which takes the form of a nocturnal vision of fulfillment) is offset by the dark irregular circle (much like black clouds or smoke) that surrounds the trèfle (see figure 3) and makes ominous the

> miniature semblable à l'iris, l'orchidée,
> Cadeau le plus ancien des prairies au plaisir
> Que la cascade instille,
> Que la bouche délivre.[14]

The clover, a natural product of the complete cycle from the source to the sea and a small facsimile of the symbolic iris (first mentioned here), is explicitly hymned and implicitly threatened. Its place and meaning rest between two poles, unresolved.

The explicit couples of the lithographs (see especially pages 22, 25, 31, 32, 41, 42, 49, and 53) function as variations upon the major theme, and each time a pair is evoked, whether as a momentary union in the air (as in *oiseaux couple* [22], or the *oiseaux fulgurant* [31], or simply as the double image [*Doppelgänger*, as in *Les Volubilis, La Nuit,* or *Migration*]), each variation reinforces the reader's sense of both potential and actual union. The opposites are brought together, the poles are bent toward the center, and those pairs that were separate are fused. As a motif, as a theme, as an interaction between two separate arts, *the relation between unlike things* (whether opposites in a literal sense or merely differing parts of the whole) becomes the center of the work itself.

The couples presented in the final lithographs, both in floral and in human form, cannot be the direct illustrations of the fusion or union in the text (see figure 4). The text itself contains no fusion at the end, no union of lovers and, finally, no ostensible closure as would normally be expected of a long poem.

Instead, the text stops at a seemingly arbitrary point in time, space, and emotion. The stop is marked only by a lyric recognition of the power of the iris and an incantation to the flower (which reminds the reader of the epic invocation of the Muse). However,

Fig. 4. Georges Braque, "Le Couple" from *Lettera amorosa*, 53 (Copyright 1990 ARS N.Y./ADAGP)

nothing has forewarned of so abrupt an end. Were this the whole work, one's expectations might well be deceived. But it is exactly at this point that the text stops, even though the work is obviously unfinished. The ending, like the beginning, works on a principle of complementary interaction. It is most clearly in search of an ending that we are led to look once more at the final lithograph, in which the format, color, tone, and figuration used in the first lithograph are repeated. Repeated, that is, with one variation: the man who is the speaker of the poem has virtually entered the world of the woman. The two facing silhouettes affirm the union at the end that was left unstated in the text. In this way, the ending toward which the work has moved from the beginning is fulfilled and the two arts, like the two lovers, are brought together in visual action as well as in formal fusion.

I have chosen to study the combination of poetry and lithography in *Lettera amorosa* as my first example of the new form because it involves two artists and two arts. I will now progress from the "simple" case of collaboration to several combinations that are more complex in the sense that either more arts or more artists are called into play. I should also remind the reader that the order of my examples is formal rather than historical so the subsequent leap backward in time will not be perplexing. Before moving to my next example, however, I would like to emphasize several points that I demonstrate in my study of *Lettera amorosa:* First, that collaborative form is a definable art form in and of itself; second, that the form discovered is the result of the interactions of the two arts that are combined; and third, that the form is unique and not traceable to either of its constitutive arts. These three points must be shown before they can be asserted as the basis for defining the new form. It should also be evident at this point that collaborative forms can be analyzed, that is, discussed and debated. Once we have established the existence of such forms that result from combinations of the arts and, by discussion, have shown that these forms are available to audiences which otherwise might not have perceived them, we will have taken a considerable step toward removing the veils of mystification and vagueness that have haunted combinations of the arts since the *Gesamtkunstwerk* was invoked as a symbolist ideal. It is also the case that once we have shown how one example of collaboration works, we can begin to explore works that are more difficult than the "simple" case.

TWO

THE WARMTH OF THE FACE OF THE NEWBORN
A la santé du serpent

THE unique exposition, *René Char: Les Manuscrits enluminés par les peintres du XXe siècle,*[1] serves as a timely reminder that, in France, the distance separating poetry and painting is never as great as it seems. While the exhibition was small, it nonetheless documented a series of special collaborative activities between the poet and his friends, the painters, that otherwise might have been difficult to discover. For René Char, whose handwritten poems are the constant of the exhibition, each combination of manuscript and *enluminure* corroborates what his readers have already come to know of his enduring and intense relationships with an imposing array of the major painters of this century. Char quite literally began his career by combining poetry and painting. His first book of poems, *Les Cloches sur le coeur* (1928), was accompanied by an illustration and his first collective edition, *Le Marteau sans maître* (1934) contained a *pointe-sèche* by Wassily Kandinsky.[2] Since then, he has consistently made a place in his writings for painters whose illustrations have been, at times, an integral part of his work. He has also devoted considerable critical attention to the plastic arts in essays, prefaces, and introductions to catalogues of expositions.

In fact, Char would seem to fit into a distinguished series of French painters and poets whose relationships have served as models of the ways in which artists from different arts work together, a series that begins with Charles Baudelaire and includes, among others, Rilke and Rodin, Apollinaire and the Cubist painters, Eluard and Picasso, and Reverdy and Braque. However, with Char, there is one conspicuous difference. His "rapports" are not with one, but with twenty painters. Furthermore, each of his relationships is expressed differently. While his work with his friends, the painters, represents an enormously varied example of the ways in which poetry and painting can be combined, the successful combination of poet and painter does not occur as easily or as naturally as some critics have been led to say. While it is certainly not news that modern painting has lost its illustrative function, the phenomenon has further ramifications when one considers the possibilities of combining painting and poetry in books. For where the dominant direction of painters has been away from the figure, the landscape, and representational forms, the tendency of this kind of painting has been to illustrate nothing but itself. But that is only half the problem. René Char's poetry presents a reduced format for the painters. As his work approaches the maxim, the aphorism, and the fragment, the amount left unsaid becomes a measure of the power of the poem. Even if the painters were to look for an imagistic base as they sought affinities with the poet's works, they would discover a paucity of pure description that matches the absence of representation in their own works. One result of these differences has been that the traditional meaning of the term *illustration* cannot be applied. The painters who have worked with Char have felt little compulsion to explain, either figuratively or pictorially, the lines of poetry on the page. No two painters adopt quite the same strategy. However, an overview of the works Char has completed with his chosen painters does permit a sense of the range of possibilities for combining the two art forms.

Pablo Picasso's contributions to several of René Char's works define one extreme of "indirect illustration." One cannot but admire the drawings and lithographs even though they have little apparent relation to the texts which they accompany. They are Picassos first and then, as if coincidentally, part of a literary work. However, there are notable exceptions. For example, in *Dépendance de l'adieu*[3] the juxtaposition of Picasso's minotaur to the text poses the strength of the drawing against the strength of the poem. Here, the fierce independence of the two forces creates a context that enhances both text and illustration. This is not so clearly the case in the illustration accompanying the definitive version of *Le Marteau sans maître* published in 1945 or in the gravures that appear in *L'Escalier de Flore* and *Pourquoi la journée vole.*[4]

A number of painters have illustrated the poems more directly. For example, where Char's works are combined with those of Jean Hélion, Jean Hugo, Pierre André Benoit, Victor Brauner, Luis Fernandez, Greta Knutson, or Denise Esteban,[5] one finds the painters selecting pictorial forms from their own work and applying these to the poems. In each case, the color, line, shape, and figuration expand the imaginative range of the book, adding elements that become vital contributions. With these painters, the traditional sense of the term "illustration" is appropriate in describing their work for they portray the text. They give emphasis to images, colors, and lines that are already present in the poem.

Georges Braque, Henri Matisse, Hans Arp, Alberto Giacometti, and Joan Miró constitute a third group of painters who work through the poems with sets of complementary forms that verge on abstraction. In each case, these forms are discovered by the painter independently and then adapted to the needs of the collaborative work. These forms vary from Braque's almost representational leaves, flowers, birds, and figures in *Le Soleil des eaux, La Bibliothèque est en feu,* and *Lettera amorosa* and Giacometti's attenuated figures in *Poèmes des deux années* and *Retour Amont,* to the suggestive forms and signs of Arp in *Guirlande terrestre* and Miró in *A la santé du serpent, De moment en moment,* and *Nous avons.*[6] While none of these painters illustrates the text directly, each invents a complementary structure of graphic forms that, in turn, becomes not just a part, but a necessary part of the collaborative work.

On the poet's side, Char's fascination with the unions and divergences of poetry and painting has been the constant feature in the combinative works he has taken part in. His appreciation of each painter is explained most succinctly by his own constant quest for the essential. In his writings on his favorite painters, he declares that the essential is expressed most directly in the painter's extremes. While this is certainly a converse rule of recognition, it does account for Char's propensity to discover painters whose work subsequently turns out to be vital for him.

Of all the painters with whom Char has worked, none has had a larger place than Joan Miró. The poet and the painter have completed thirteen books together. As Jacques Dupin recounts:

> Le poète et le peintre se sont connus, se sont croisés, à l'époque du surréalisme, rencontres chaleureuses et brèves dont ils se souviendront l'un et l'autre. Mais le ciel était à l'orage, et chacun d'eux si absorbé par la nécessité de fortifier son langage pour résister à la monstrueuse montée des périls, qu'il leur fallut attendre l'après-guerre et un espace plus serein pour que leur amitié donne ses premiers fruits.[7]

They became reacquainted through Guy Lévis-Mano, who brought the two artists together for the publication of Char's *Fête des arbres et du chasseur* in November 1948. The color lithograph that Miró created for Char's small volume is the first example of the collaboration of the two men. At the same time that Miró was preparing this lithograph, he also worked on a series of Char's manuscripts that were to be presented to Yvonne Zervos. In his work on the thirteen manuscript poems, Miró not only sealed a lasting relationship with the poet, but he also presented proof of the unusual effects possible in such works. The painter's inventive and remarkable solutions to the problems of language and space in Char's manuscripts were so masterful that they became the model for the whole series of "illuminations" displayed in the 1980 exhibition. Describing this particular set of *manuscrits enluminés*, Antoine Coron writes:

> Miró qui prouva souvent et avec quel éclat un sens du livre quasi infaillible et une si remarquable intelligence du graphisme accordé au poème, traita, comme Wifredo Lam quatre ans plus tard, chaque double page comme un tout, alternant surfaces brillamment colorées et espaces plus sombres, jouant de tout le clavier des possibilités qui lui étaient offertes. L'encre de Chine, la gouache, l'aquarelle, les crayons de couleur, le fusain, la cire, mêlés ou utilisés séparément, déterminent ainsi des zones, rythment le recueil, en un accompagnement graphique qui s'accorde aux poèmes de manière si juste dans l'économie des moyens et le paradoxe des signes . . . qu'on est confondu de tant de liberté et de fantaisie dans la réplique, la ponctuation graphique.[8]

For René Char this lithograph marked, as well, the beginning of an impressive series of collaborations in the books he has completed with Joan Miró. This subsequent series, though, is somewhat different in theory and in practice from the illuminated manuscript, and while it may appear that very much the same kind of collaboration occurs, these differences are often controlling. First, in *enluminure,* neither poet nor painter need concern himself about the processes of reproduction. For the poet, this is simple enough. He writes out each poem in his own hand, skipping the setting into type, the galley and page proofs, and all the other potentially intrusive processes of publication. (Very few of the poems in manuscript form that Char has given to the painters are *inédits,* hence he is usually reproducing his own published work when he writes out the poem.) The poems, then, do not usually change from their original form except in the subtler sense in which they are changed by the poet's calligraphy.

For the painter, on the other hand, the essential freedom given in the process of illumination is the freedom from the limits imposed

34

by reproduction. In this sense, an illumination is not altogether different from drawings, watercolors, and paintings. The pages illuminated are individual, unique, and, like a painting or a watercolor, not to be copied or reproduced. Faced with a poem on an otherwise empty page, Miró uses the full array of his tools, a choice of weapons not otherwise available for gravures, eaux-fortes, and lithographs unless he wishes to return to each copy to add an effect, to overlay another medium, or to enhance the color values. The tools that Coron lists (charcoal, crayon, chalk, lead, ink, wax, and oil) are important because they are the very techniques that cannot be reproduced except by photograph. These methods make clear how the illuminated manuscript is a special form and must be distinguished from the artist's works reproduced in books.

Yet, there is one important effect in Miró's illuminations that does carry over into the illustrated books. In the illuminations that Miró accomplished for René Char, there appears on each page the rough-hewn quality of improvisation. This appearance is deceptive, though, and may very well be the mark of the ease with which a master senses the tone and rhythm, the content and form of the poem he wishes to complete. For with Miró, as with Braque, Picasso, Matisse, and Arp, the elegant simplicity with which he completes a page conceals, in the seemingly casual configurations, a unique signature that is recognizably his own. This improvisational quality is less evident in the forms, signs, and hieroglyphs created for the illustration of texts. Miró's finished signs appear not to have been improvised (even though they passed through stages of refinement). They seem to come from a long-lost text containing the original calligraphy of the gods. They are almost legible, yet they preserve a strangeness that bars linguistic interpretation. Miró himself does not explain how or where he obtained his graphic vocabulary: "Les choses viennent lentement. Mon vocabulaire des formes, par exemple, je ne l'ai pas découvert d'un coup. Il s'est formé presque malgré moi."[9] Yet these same forms are, as he confirms, "des signes póetiques et graphiques purs." He connects their origin to the beginning of his series of *Constellations* when he writes, "[J'ai voulu] considérer cette série de toiles comme des signes schématiques poignants, de pure poésie, cri de l'esprit comme les futures eaux-fortes."[10] As he discovered the bases of these forms, he identified them as *signes* and, thus, gave the term a special sense in his work: "ces signes schématiques ont un énorme pouvoir suggestif, autrement ils seraient une chose abstraite et par conséquent une chose morte."[11] From the point of discovery (which Miró modestly calls their "appearance"), the artist works through variations toward a model. For Miró, perfecting each sign entails a process of rereading his own ambiguous texts. But he does not clarify the referent of his sign. He simply finds its simplest representation, which is always a reduction into pure graphic terms. The lifelong habits of a great painter are evident in his improvisations as well as in his final forms and, in Miró's *signes*, one sees improvisation and final form coalesce.

In the books completed by the poet and the painter, several categories can be distinguished. First, in five books, Miró contributes single graphic works which serve as frontispieces for the volume of poetry.[12] In every case, the relation of the graphic work to the text is indirect. A lithograph or gravure is inserted to enhance the book in a general way as well as to increase its value for collectors. The method most often used in this kind of illustration is simple juxtaposition. While the painter's page may establish a tone, a mood, or an expectation, it is not a necessary part of the book (a fact further demonstrated whenever the illustration is limited to the *exemplaires en tête de série* [13]).

However, it is never safe to ignore works in this format since occasionally a poet and painter will work together closely (along lines that are not immediately apparent) to create a specific effect from a single page. One such exception to any general rule about single illustrations occurs early in Miró's work with Char. In *L'Alouette*, Miró accompanies a short poem of the same title with a drawing that encircles the sense of the poem. In this case, the painter has worked closely with the poet and his graphic work is the equal, in its separate domain, of the beauty and suggestiveness of Char's four lines.

The second category of combination of the arts can be located at the other end of the spectrum of illustrated books. Where single illustrations tend to be irrelevant to the understanding of the literary texts, a large suite of illustrations often turns out to be its own justification. Here, the term *illustration* is again questionable, since frequently the series of graphic works so collected can remain completely independent of the texts printed on the opposite page or on intervening pages. Hence when a book of poems is republished in a large format by an art gallery or editor of art books, one is justified in suspecting that the interaction of poetry and painting may not be the central concern. And, while most such books juxtapose painter and poet to no visible effect, some serve nonetheless to open frontiers between the arts that otherwise could not have been foretold. One such book is the reissue of René Char's first collective edition, *Le Marteau sans maître* by Le Vent d'Arles in 1976. Joan Miró contributed twenty-three eaux-fortes in color on an oversize format (44 x 33.5 cm). On first appearance, this book would seem to fall into the category of oversize art books described above. However, in this case, the book represents something more than a convenient wrapper for Miró's graphic work. The painter chose the texts because of an enduring interest in Char's poems dating from their first meetings at the edges of *Surréalisme*. Like a conductor returning to the original music of his youth, Miró goes back to the poems of *Le Marteau sans maître* to renew his source of inspiration. Miró's eaux-fortes reencounter the poems on new ground. For the reader, this book provides a unique chance to read the early poems anew, through the signs and colors of Miró. *Le Marteau sans maître* is nevertheless an exception to the rule. Frequently the juxtaposition of a number of poems (which are works of art) with a large suite of graphic works (which are works of art) makes a lovely book that is not a work of art. The principle at work is that of the showcase rather than that of the *oeuvre combinée,* and such a distinction need imply no negative connotation. Such works give a painter's work access to a larger public than the analogous exposition and, as books, are both more interesting and more enduring than a catalogue.

One other category exists in the books published by René Char and Joan Miró. Of the five texts in this group, each contains graphic works that are necessary to the effect of the book. Thus, in *A la santé du serpent* (GLM, 1954), *De moment en moment* (PAB, 1957), *Nous avons* (PAB, 1958), *Nous avons* (Louis Broder, 1959) and in an illuminated manuscript that was subsequently published as a broadside, *Six patiences pour Joan Miró,*[14] both poet and painter present separate parts to function in combination. The end, in each of these cases, is a collaborative form, a work that is the sum of its interactions. The first book in this series is both the most unusual and the most successful collaboration. In *A la santé du serpent,* Miró chose to work with a set of aphorisms that René Char had first published in 1946 in the review *Fontaine* and then republished in the first edition of *Le Poème pulvérisé* with a gravure by Henri Matisse as frontispiece.[15] Thus, the poem Miró chose had been previously published and previously illustrated. In fact, before Miró began work on the set of fragments, René Char had sent manuscript versions to Wifredo Lam who, in turn, in 1952, illuminated (in ink, aquarelle, and gouache) all forty-four pages of the handwritten aphorisms.

Miró and Char were once again brought together by Guy Lévis-Mano, who proposed a simple union of painter and poet on a scale that would permit a larger run of books than the usual *beau-livre*. As Wifredo Lam, Georges Braque, and Luis Fernandez had already demonstrated,[16] the aphoristic form of Char's poems allowed each artist an unusual flexibility. The variable space between Char's fragments opened the possibility of a much closer spatial relationship of graphic work and text. Miró had discovered the advantages inherent in these spaces in the manuscripts he illuminated in 1948. In *A la santé du serpent,* Miró invents another use of the spaces given over by the poet's text: the serial order. He creates, through repetition and variation, a structural harmony using his signs as motifs. Miró's strategy implies two distinct prior acquisitions: first, forms that can be reduced to less than a quarter of a page and then expanded to nearly a full page and, second, a vocabulary of forms that will permit him to make identities recognizable (thus permitting repetition). His *signes* fulfill both prerequisites. One step from the logical identities inherent in any system of signs (such as languages, number systems, etc.), Miró's *signe* can refer to a more generalized system without requiring identification with that system. *Signes* suggest a plurality of referents but they function best in a context where partial reference is given, either by a text or by preceding *signes.* Their allusive function serves to complicate rather than simplify their interpretation. They are obviously drawn (thus begin at the level of picture), yet they present themselves, on the page, at a point very near abstraction (a point where no representational sense or symbolic meaning is evident). Between these two poles, they resist the reductions of either extreme. Miró humanizes the *signes* by giving each an emotive tone (from joy to melancholy) whether through the figures (the referents) suggested by the *signe* or by the addition of patches of color.

In *A la santé du serpent,* Miró points his signs in a specific direction (parallel to the direction of the poems) and orders them, much as a composer orders musical motifs. The repetition and variation of a limited set of *signes* creates a complementary relationship between text and *signes,* and they proceed on a double track. Like a second serpent, Miró's work is coiled alongside the whole of Char's text, extended in front and behind it as well. The set of *signes* commits itself to a parallel meaning that is neither a visual commentary on the poems nor an interpretative reading. Instead, the full set of *signes* serves as the painter's declaration of union with the poet in

Fig. 5. Page 7 of *A la santé du serpent* (Copyright 1990 ARS N.Y./ADAGP)

the making of something larger: "Miró qui n'énonce pas, Miró qui indique, Miró qui imagine les noces."[17]

Miró creates this series of *signes* especially for the text of *A la santé du serpent*. The very absences that mark Char's text dictate to the painter that there are ellipses to imagine, bridges to construct, and an underlying unity to derive. The fits and starts of awakening, the summits and valleys of an inconstant meditation, these are also the motions of the *signes*. Miró finds the gaps between the poems an adequate space for apposite creation. In this sense, if one can accept the analogy, Miró, too, works aphoristically. In the series of *signes* that accompanies the text, there are twenty-seven different motifs and all of these are repeated at least once. The single exception is the *signe* that appears on the first page and is neither introduced nor repeated. Miró begins his part of the book with a three-page prelude (6, 7, 10) that announces all the forms except one. This *ouverture* is placed before the title page and in front of the color lithograph on page 12. Miró's object in these introductory pages is not merely decorative. First, the format of his introduction places the *signes* on each page so that they simulate a linguistic text (such as the text he is purportedly illustrating). The compact unity of each of his *signes* further imitates and also prepares for the compressed format of Char's "parole en archipel." Second, Miró serves his own graphic purposes. Each of the *signes* presented is repeated in the text (reproduced above a certain fragment or aphorism of Char) and several are subsequently repeated as many as five times in the book.

The order of presentation in the introductory pages of the book emphasizes the graphic affinities of the *signes* and plays upon their abstract and suggestive relationships with one another. Miró thus presents a parallel language that will function hereafter in relation (both spatial and thematic) with the poem. Like musical motifs, the *signes* introduce the themes of the whole work. Unlike music, however, the three pages of introduction are very nearly complete, as if a composer played all the themes in full in the prelude and withheld only the variations.

The format for the re-presentation of each *signe* is straightforward and apparently direct: on every page except the first, there are two *signes* and two aphorisms. In each case, the *signes* seem to precede the aphorisms in such a way that they suggest immediate relationships (figures 7 and 8).[18] However, the illustrative function of the *signes* is neither direct nor representational and the reader of the book will not be able to discern a collaborative effect in any one set

Je chante la chaleur à visage de nouveau - né, la chaleur désespérée.

Fig. 6. Page 15 of *A la santé du serpent* (Copyright 1990 ARS N.Y./ADAGP)

Combien durera ce manque de l'homme mourant au centre de la création parce que la création l'a congédié?

Chaque maison était une saison. La ville ainsi se répétait. Tous les habitants ensemble ne connaissaient que l'hiver, malgré leur chair réchauffée, malgré le jour qui ne s'en allait pas.

Figs. 7 and 8. Illustrations from pages 18 and 19, *A la santé du serpent* (Copyright 1990 ARS N.Y./ADAGP)

Produis ce que la connaissance veut garder secret, la connaissance aux cent passages.

Ce qui vient au monde pour ne rien troubler ne mérite ni égards ni patience.

of texts and *signes*. The sense made by the *signes* occurs on two other levels: that of the whole combination (the book) and that of a step-by-step parallel wherein the poet's words are read first and then are modified by the presence of Miró's *signes*.[19]

Each of the aphorisms defines itself in a fully human context, bred of the consciousness of the difficulty of being human. The poet's style had changed as radically as Miró's during the period of the Second World War. The difference between the difficult syntax, exotic diction, and purposeful obscurity of his surrealist period and the terse, clear, epigrammatic form of the poems collected in *Fureur et mystère* (1948) and, especially, in *Le Poème pulvérisé* (1947) is nowhere more clearly shown than in this set of poems. Each line of *A la santé du serpent* appears to be pounded out by *Le Marteau du maître*. While this effect is consistent, the particulars of each aphorism (the tone, clarity, and texture) all change from fragment to fragment. There is, nonetheless, an undeniable identity in each fragment. Like Miró's *signes*, these fragments come from the same hand and are marked with an invariable, underlying signature.

The beginning of the poem announces the origin of the text, the theme of the work, and the ambiguous presence of that "chaleur à visage de nouveau-né" (the warmth of the face of the newborn) which is both subject and cause of the poet's song (see figure 6).

The first song is introduced by a new sign, not included in the prelude of *signes*. Its unique appearance links it symbolically to the song of the warmth of the face of the newborn. The illustration separates the parts of the potential *signe* as if we are about to see a new *signe* born. Displayed separately, each part of this potential *signe* is simplified as if Miró wished, for the first time, to break down the sophisticated *écriture* invented in the prelude. Four elements are encircled in the space of the illustration. First, the dark spot introduces the barest minimum of the concept of line: the point. It stands highest in the drawing and, thus isolated, stands for Miró's *"nouveau-né"* of painterly space. Second, the largest form approaches several letters and is an integral part of several of Miró's *signes*. It suggests two *t*'s as well as a deformed *H*. It dominates the enclosed space by the length of its lines and their darkness. Suggesting calligraphy, it remains ambiguous until linked with other parts. The third form is the heavy crescent shape that traditionally represents the moon in Miró's paintings. Here, though, Miró lays it on its back and, in so doing, suggests a primitive curve. The weight of this form is typical of certain biomorphic shapes that appear in Miró's drawings and, like

Arp's concretions, suggests a condensation of life forms (fruit, a seal, a worm). Finally, the two black points linked by a heavy line (the barbell) is double-ended, open, and slightly biomorphic. It is a rudimentary illustration of line (linking two points) and can suggest an imminent split, as in cell division. Disconnected, each form attracts the viewer's attention separately. They are related to one another, however, by the fact of their apparent containment.

The encirclement is accomplished by a chain of small dots that sets off and highlights the set of forms. The contained space is merely suggested by the repetition of the points. The viewer completes the circle. In a complementary way, Char's introductory fragment represents a similar, simplified beginning. The lines are reminiscent of the Homeric invocation of the Muse except that Char refuses to give the Muse a name. He announces the theme that he will sing and the mode of his song: the song of immediacy will be sung in the warmth of the face of the newborn. The specific referents may not be as singular as one might first suppose. The "chaleur" can be both that of new life and that of new song (as the extended conceit of Mallarmé's "Don du poème" suggests)—hence, a warmth desperate to be alive and desperate to be sung.

The poet begins with the first-person pronoun, making us the recipient of his words. His pronouns imply an intimacy. He addresses himself as he addresses others. Yet, where the first-person pronoun appeals to the normal separation of speaker and audience, the second-person familiar creates an opposite effect: "Tu es dans ton essence constamment poète, constamment au zénith de ton amour, constamment avide de vérité et de justice. C'est sans doute un mal nécessaire que tu ne puisses l'être assidûment dans ta conscience."[20] At least two people are addressed: first, the poet addresses himself, partly by way of self-definition and partly by way of self-justification. Second, the statement is directed to all those who identify with the description of the state of the poet. To these, the last sentence may serve as consolation as well as justification. The simple and effective repetition of the adverb that defines each of the poet's tasks suggests far more than mere solidarity with poetry. Included in the three-part rhetoric of definition is also an intense expression of the inescapable pressure that poets are sometimes the last to become aware of. The price of poetic power is that absence from one's conscience (or is it absence from consciousness?) that leads to terrible acts. The speaker recognizes this price and seems almost casual in his acceptance of it. "C'est sans doute un mal nécessaire . . . ," he writes, and leaves this clause in a position that raises doubts almost as surely as it attempts to excuse these same doubts as necessary evils. Only the precision of the poet's diction prevents an abandonment of conscience in the cause of poetry. The word *assidûment* turns the equation around so that the reader can qualify the poet's assertions. Why, after all, should a poet be assiduously in his conscience? Char implies, in raising the question, that the stakes are higher in poetry and that the ordinary moral lapses are multiplied precisely in proportion to the increase in consciousness gained by the poet.

The itinerant moralist in Char (and, here, I mean moralist in that French sense that includes Pascal, Nietzsche, and Camus) surfaces often enough to forewarn the reader of the depths of his sayings. Certainly it is in the tradition of the moralist to recognize the delicate balance between the truth of observation and the clear statement thereof. Char joins that high tradition wherever he strikes a unity between the contraries of visionary experience and poetic expression. He resists the double temptation in that he neither mystifies nor explains. In the only fragment added after the original publication of the poem, he proposes a cryptic rule: "Il n'est pas digne du poète de mystifier l'agneau, d'investir sa laine."[21] For if the poet leaves his illuminations too close to their source, the resulting poems may have the effect of making more mysterious the mystery, thus adding haloes instead of light. At the same time, the terms of the speaker's prohibition imply a unilateral dignity for poets.

There are other forms for the moralist's observations. Occasionally the poet applies a sudden circularity to wrap up a fragment. It is also the advantage of the aphorism that it need not present an equation that is balanced: "Les larmes méprisent leur confident."[22] This line could have been part of several aphorisms that precede it. It is not. It stands alone, a terse definition of tears. In the world of emotion, there is no equivalent for tears, for they are the natural language of feelings. Tears break down the discourse in which "confidants" are made. They also draw attention to open emotion which in turn attracts new "confidants." But, who is the "confidant" of tears? Is it not those who cry as well as those who attend to crying? The double sense is both contradictory and, at the same time, perfectly representative of the compression of Char's writing. His terseness leads one, on first reading, to a level of meaning that is apparently simple and clear. This illusion of simplicity lasts as long as one is willing to ignore the precision of his diction and phrasing. His aphorisms do not accept paraphrase. Nothing is quite as satisfying to the poet as that fragment that balances two contradictory meanings without giving way before one or the other. The closer the poet's phrase comes to achieving that precarious balance, the more aptly he defines by example rather than by statement. In the present case the simplicity of the phrase works against itself. Like one of Molière's gay ironies, it springs lightly into its own trap.

If Char's poems were composed completely of these kinds of fragments, that fact would describe a certain talent as well as a certain limitation. However, the fragments are not as specialized as critics like to make them and do not lend themselves to tidy summary. Furthermore, an aphorism that may seem, on one level, to deliver a moral directive may function as well on other levels. For example, the poet avoids direct statement when he declares, "Si nous habitons un éclair, il est le coeur de l'éternel."[23] The conditional nature of his sentence demands that the first clause be the case before the second comes into play. While this may seem like elementary grammar, close attention to the syntax of Char's sentences often eliminates unnecessary confusion. We must be able to imagine the first condition in order to be able to imagine the second. The two statements have to do with different kinds of time. Literally, to live in a lightning flash is a state that cannot be ascribed to a temporal condition. In it we leap immediately outside time. Hence, the conditional "if" clause presupposes an immediate, elliptical acceptance of a metaphorical state, the state of illuminated existence. In that state, the contrast of the instantaneous and the eternal is rendered into an identity. Outside that state, the aphorism introduces an impossible condition as the prerequisite for comprehending the unknown. This is the same poet who would write "l'éclair me dure."[24] Audacious statement? Certainly the immediate and abrupt assumption of the mystic's metaphor creates an enormous ellipsis. Yet, the power of this fragment depends upon the shock of the ellipsis. The literal sense of the statement describes the relation of unlike things: a lightning flash and a man. To allude to the arc of electricity that unites two opposing fields of force assumes only the world of natural experience. Yet, we too must imagine the brevity of lightning, for we are unable to see it as it occurs. The image of the flash is retained in the eye of the beholder, causing him to perceive a duration that is much longer than the millisecond of its existence. From that duration of perception, which for consciousness is the minimum, the poet creates the full metaphor of ellipsis. And, while it is literally the case that the flash of lightning lasts, for him as for the rest of us who watch it, the sense of the poet's fragment only begins here. The statement is audacious, not because of the precision of the image, but because of the ambiguity of the phrase. He does not write "l'éclair m'a duré" or "l'éclair me durera." The present tense confirms (paradoxically, almost oxymoronically) a continuing state. The pronoun (the only one possible) contains several shades of meaning. Does the lightning last him? Or does it last for him, with him, in him, to him? Each of these alternate phrasings is possible as translation, but not as paraphrase. Char's phrase contains them all.

In stating the relation of poet and illumination, Char chooses the same image that Heraclitus chose to link the natural world with the mystical: "La foudre pilote l'univers."[25] Yet where the presocratic thinker evokes a causal relation as part of a fragmentary cosmology (alluding and not alluding to Zeus), the poet reverses this direction. He takes the lightning inside him and describes the subsequent implosion with a brevity that matches its meaning. The fragment is suffused with hubris, full of wonder (to be the one for whom the lightning lasts), and linked to the terrible (an illumination without reprieve). Spiritually, the poet has become a vessel for the *éclair*, the extreme state of which is personified by the holy and the insane. But Char corrects the extremes of the imagination and seeks his balance in the statement of his condition, thus conducting the voltages of the *éclair* into the amperes of poetry.

Returning to the fragment, "Si nous habitons un éclair, il est le coeur de l'éternel," the lightning flash is the heart of the eternal *only if* we inhabit it. The controlling verb, *habiter*, is so common that we almost accept it in this context. Yet the paradox is obvious and purposeful. The poet forces a break with ordinary comprehension, then insists upon his conditions. The *éclair* needs us to fulfill its identity; we are the only ones who can so identify it with the eternal. Is this a statement about the mystery, *la morale*, or the poetry? The beauty of Char's language consists of the way in which he implies bridges between these unbridgeable regions. Inside the fragment, the circle of meanings is drawn tight against a metaphor, leaving out distinct referents. The aphorism then serves as the example of its own statement. It balances danger with delight, playing the threat of blatant misreading against the pleasure of imaginative discovery. The poet who dares to assure us that "l'éclair me dure" has already assumed the risks of his poetry. He knows that in a central poetry much is at stake and that the lightning may not last forever.

The set of ellipses that I have thus far attempted to describe creates the rhythm that Miró accentuates in the *signes* that he applies to the texts. And, where one could profitably extend the discussion to each fragment of the poem, I prefer instead to imitate both artists by selecting examples that demonstrate the effect of the whole. For Miró, the book itself is such a whole. He applies his *signes* where he senses their appropriateness. He then organizes the whole through a structure of repetitions and variations that control, more than the individual relationships of the *signes* to the fragments, the parallel meaning of the book as a collaborative form. One way of demonstrating this structure and its effects is to select those *signes* for discussion which, by their repetition and exact placement, are emphasized by the painter.

Reading from left to right, the first *signe* occurs initially in the upper left side of the first suite of the *ouverture* (6–7) and recurs four times.[26] It is vaguely calligraphic (see figure 9) and is placed in a dominant position because it recalls the title of the work and, in one sense, the parallel structure as well. On the third page of the poetic text (7), this *signe* appears above the following fragment: "Dans la boucle de l'hirondelle un orage s'informe, un jardin se construit."[27] The *signe* suggests (as calligraphy) an abbreviation of the title which, in its link to the third form (the *A* that is stopped at the lower right by the rounded point), is joined to the Alpha of the beginning. The double *S* signals the double track (the two serpents) of the *signes* and the poem. Char's aphorism appears below the *signe* and follows the models previously discussed. It poses one possible image as a prior condition for subsequent images. The two latter images are placed inside the circle that is framed momentarily in the sky by the trace of the swallow's flight. From one image to the next are projected distant cause-and-effect relations. The discordant resonances are resolved in the imagination's leap to future possibilities. Metaphorically, this leap revalues the loop *(la boucle)* of the swallow, for it is the primary image of the moment in which all is present. The three-part process of ellipsis forces a return to the origin without saying, without having to say, anything about the wonder of the *hirondelle*. In the two distant sequels, the poet captures the exhilaration of the flight of the bird. Miró's *signe* subtly reinforces the movement of the poem with the double *boucle* inside the loops. Like the aphorism, it leaps, but does not explain. Between the two, the balance is like that between the loop of the swallow's flight and the images it contains.

*Dans la boucle de l'hirondelle
un orage s'informe, un jardin
se construit.*

*Il y aura toujours une goutte
d'eau pour durer plus que le
soleil sans que l'ascendant du
soleil soit ébranlé.*

Fig. 9. Page 17 of *A la santé du serpent* (Copyright 1990 ARS N.Y./ADAGP)

A similar process occurs on the next page of the text where Miró repeats *signe* 23 above another fragment by Char (see figure 7). This aphorism applies most directly to poetry, which, for Char, is not a product of *"la connaissance."* But the tone is made lighter by the appositional phrase poking fun at the pretensions of knowledge. Like a secret agent working within an institution to give away its secrets, the last phrase carries out the directive of the fragment, uncovering one of the secrets that *la connaissance* would prefer to keep hidden. Miró's figures match the tone of Char's words. He produces a lyric *signe,* a dancing, heavy-footed *A,* that swings its double bar out to the two archetypal stars. Both phrase and *signe* ironically devalue as they place their weight on the page.

Immediately below this set is an opposite, balancing set of *signes* and aphorism (see figure 7).

Like Homer's secondary figures in the *Odyssey,* the Phaiakians, those who go out of their way to avoid contention are destined for oblivion. Their identity is concealed in the vaguest of pronouns. However, the speaker affirms an invincible line of defense, since he who disturbs nothing will scarcely come into the range of active *égards* or *patience.* At the first signal of conflict, he disappears. Miró weights the *signe* with four darknesses: a darkened sun and moon surround a darkened double figure. The *A,* so lyrical in the *signe* directly above on this page, is here tied to a motley, floating figure (a variation upon the *A*). Each dark area adds weight and a somber tone. Miró contrasts this *signe* with the normal figures of sun and moon and *A* as well as with the specific aphorism and *signe* directly above it on the same page. Another reading of this set of figures is suggested by Miró's anecdote of the escaping clown. In this version, the motley hat tries to escape the grip of the squeezing *A,* but is held. The gravity of the darkened sun and moon is balanced to add weight upon the escaping figure. In either case, whether one prefers an almost intelligible *signe* or an overly simple anecdote, the central, lyric figure is surrounded by (if not held by) three darker figures.

On the facing page, two pairs of *signes* and aphorisms complete this series and culminate the major themes. Miró places emphasis on these sets through his repetitions of the *signes.* Both *signes* (*signe* 26 and *signe* 27; see figure 8) appear four times in the same form and *signe* 27 appears another time in an inversion (19).

According to the myths of origin, man has not been at the center of creation since the first man. The myth of the garden of Eden precludes man's presence at the center as part of the explanation of human mortality. Adam could not die in Eden; he had to leave to die. *L'homme mourant* is, by definition, outside, and his position vis-à-vis the center serves, in the myth, to explain his suffering. But, was it creation that sent man out from the center? Or, is the poet altering the myth? So long as man defines himself as mortal, the poet can have it both ways, at least so long as the reader insists upon the old myths as the key to the poem. It is difficult to speak of new myths without breaking through the structure of reality, and yet the poet's question suggests another possibility. Where creation takes place in the present tense instead of in the verb tense of the eternal, there *L'homme mourant* finds himself, once again, at the center. This possibility breaks apart the old tautology and makes the original question in the fragment intelligible. In this case, the question might be restated as follows: How long will it take for mortal men to make themselves the center of creation, the center they have for so long denied themselves in the hope that something better was there? Miró does not repeat the question. He creates a parallel in the figure that precedes the text. The outline of a human figure (rudimentary but recognizable) stands slightly off-center, holding a weapon in one hand (in a menacing gesture), and reaching through the earth with the other. In the distance, on the other side, is the star. The figure brandishes and searches. Can this be man's eternal position? He is part of the poet's question. Yet, neither figure nor fragment is rhetorical. The answer is not given. It must be searched out.

The figure at the bottom of the page (see figure 8) is *signe* 27 of the prelude, drawn upside down. The inversion is not accidental. Char's fragment describes a perpetual stagnation wherein winter is continual. This climate of the mind is without seasons (even though the houses of the village suggest a variety of seasons). The image of warmed flesh on an invariable winter's day inverts the cliché, creating a terse portrait of minor hell. Miró's characters, turned upside down, echo the stasis as if they too were still-born, an impression that is confirmed by comparing this set to the original set on pages 10, 29, or 33. Yet, the supposedly uniform hell of the village's consciousness does not describe the village itself. These are the vagaries of repetition: the houses of the village are as different as the seasons of the year. Like the year, the village repeated itself. But the definition of a place is not its houses. The village mind stays forever where it is, locked in the winter of its inability to imagine change. Hell, in this case, is a failure of the imagination.

On the last page of the text, Miró repeats this *signe* with one significant variation. After righting the figures of the sign, he then subtracts one of the three components (see figure 10). The spiral lines move out to the right, in the same direction, and suggest a parallel, fluid movement of eddies, the very hesitations of water that poetry avoids. The missing part is the *pont* of the stepping *A*. Since it is the part that poetry passes without holding itself up to see its reflection, it is omitted. Once again, Char's metaphor describes his own practice. The poetry that, like *"les eaux claires"* to which it is metaphorically connected, goes by its own bridges, is a poetry whose movement does not reflect upon itself. Were the missing *pont* present in the *signe*, it would alter the configuration of unilateral, parallel movement (replicated but not identical). To achieve the effect he desires, Miró changes his forms by deletion, the only case of subtraction in the book.

Char's second phrase (a fragment, held in apposition) clarifies the original sentence by restatement. The level of the metaphor in the first sentence very nearly escapes the intelligence. The waters are clear and their insistence is hard to see. Poetry is an activity, not a record. Poetry is not its poems (those already written) nor its poets: hence, *la vie future*. But why only for *l'homme requalifié*? Is he the only man in whom poetry, that future life, lives? If he were merely *"qualifié,"* one might assume that he was capable of holding *(à l'intérieur)* the future life at issue. However, the term that Char coins in this fragment is precise. *L'homme requalifié* is that man who must lose his future life in order to regain it through poetry. *La poésie*, thus defined, expands to an extreme value. Each word in the fragment "requalifies" the definition, charging the metaphor of the first sentence with the precise terms of the appositional phrase. Like many of the other examples of diction discussed above, the compacted wisdom of Char's neologism forces the reader to retrace the implied steps in his imagination. At the risk of being obscure, the poet seeks clarity. Miró's parallel variations suggest the path necessary to the full reading of the work.

All but one of the *signes* that I have illustrated recurs on a single page after the poem has ended. Miró accepts the task of concluding the book, continuing his progression after Char's last lines: "Une rose pour qu'il pleuve. Au terme d'innombrables années, c'est ton souhait."[28] The years that have passed for poet and painter are those of illness, exile, war, and resistance. The rose calls forth an abundance

53

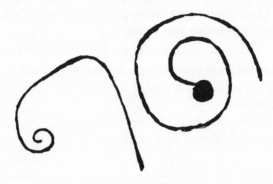

La poésie est de toutes les eaux claires celle qui s'attarde le moins aux reflets de ses ponts. Poésie, la vie future à l'intérieur de l'homme requalifié.

Une rose pour qu'il pleuve. Au terme d'innombrables années, c'est ton souhait.

Fig. 10. Page 28 of *A la santé du serpent* (Copyright 1990 ARS N.Y./ADAGP)

of associations for both poet and painter, but its singleness stands out as a sign of a hard-earned simplicity. This wish is attributed to all readers but only Miró continues his work as if to fulfill it. His page follows with an abundance of *signes*, repeated from the prelude and the text, which restate themes and mark resonances (29).

These themes are then narrowed down to four in the final, two-page reproduction of *signes* 23, 24, 27, and 26 (pages 32 and 33). Each of these *signes* is enlarged to fill a half page in this concluding statement. The movement in the suite of engravings from calligraphic forms presented in groups (before the text begins), to symbolic forms presented individually with certain fragments of the text, and finally to restatement of the central motifs after the text has ended defines the appearance of Miró's *signes*, but not their structure. The structure is that of the parallel form, first suggested as parallel calligraphy, then as double serpent, and finally as a parallel modification of the text and of the book. In this way, what begins as a formally organized suite of signs (invented from the same letters he appears to illustrate), develops into a statement and restatement of major motifs that the painter has chosen to emphasize in the poem. These motifs function to complement Char's fragments, but not merely those fragments that are linked spatially with the dominant motifs. Just as Char forges his fragments and aphorisms into a poem (insisting on invisible bridges), so Miró reunites the same series of fragments with his series of *signes*. The distinct levels of reading, like the distinct parts of the book, are different. The identity of Char's work is never brought into question by Miró's *signes*. Each functions first on its own level. But, and this is the advantage of a parallel structure, Miró's work, because it is threaded into the weave of Char's poem after the poem was created, adds highlights, rhythms, and emphases that provoke a new unity. Taking his cue from the spaces Char leaves on each page as well as from the pulverized textual fragments, Miró finds himself free to construct a second level, parallel to the first, and replete with the unifying devices of formal and serial repetition that Char denies himself. Where there are crossovers between the *signes* of the painter and the fragments of the poet on a given page (and I have discussed some of these), direct interchanges take place between the two arts. But the parallel effect is achieved when the whole poem must be reread in light of the response that Miró brings to every page. Every rereading becomes an assurance that Miró's art changes and redirects the poem that existed before this book.

In each transaction between poet and painter, there are tangible risks for both: first, the risk that time and energy will be lost (the minimal risk), and second, the risk that *l'ouvrage combiné* will not complete itself (the actual risk). There is probably no greater *hommage* to both artists, though, than that paid, each to the other, in a work such as *A la santé du serpent*. Only where the risks of collaboration are taken freely do artists combine their work and thereby achieve the new form. For collaborative form exists only in its examples.

THREE

ON THE SPIRITUAL IN ART
Der Blaue Reiter

I N the period of German Expressionism, the most important theorist of the relation of the arts was Wassily Kandinsky and the
movement that made the most significant advance toward a synthesis
of the arts was his invention, "Der Blaue Reiter." With the help of
Franz Marc, Kandinsky initiated the exhibitions and promoted the
theories of collaboration upon which Der Blaue Reiter was based.
He also produced the crucial and timely breakthrough to abstract
(nonrepresentational) art associated with the movement. Though he
worked closely with Marc to edit the famous almanac or yearbook,
also called *Der Blaue Reiter,*[1] and organize the two exhibitions sponsored by the "Redaktion der Blaue Reiter," he alone was responsible
for the seminal ideas of the movement and for its contribution to
German Expressionism.

Kandinsky seemed to his contemporaries to have burst upon the
art scene in Munich fully armed in 1909 when he suddenly began to
promote new associations in the arts. He took the lead in the formation of the *Neue Künstlervereinigung München* (NKVM) in response to
the outworn conventions of the Munich Secession. However, as Will
Grohmann first demonstrated, Kandinsky's rise to the head of the
Munich avant-garde was scarcely meteoric.[2] He had struggled
through a difficult apprenticeship between the time he gave up a
lucrative future in law in Moscow in 1896 (at the age of thirty)
and 1909, when he formed the association of artists called *Neue
Künstlervereinigung München* (NKVM).

He had come first to Munich to enroll at the Academy of Fine
Arts, taught private classes, then spent a year near Paris, in Sevres,
France, during which time he painted his way through the prevalent
styles of the period. He had begun by painting a mixture of *Jugendstil*

and a kind of Russian Romantic style (1901–4). From there he painted through his major models, experimenting with brush stroke, texture, and subject in imitation of Van Gogh and Munch. By 1907, he had progressed to studies of the effects of light in works that resemble Monet and Cézanne. In 1909 he began to experiment more freely with color. The Fauvist models of Matisse and Derain were the last he followed before assuming painterly modes that became characteristically his. In 1910, after nearly a year of experimentation and improvisation, he painted his first abstract watercolor.[3] But, even after that accomplishment, he continued to paint landscapes, religious scenes, and other figurative works.[4] Kandinsky seemed to delight in lingering in the twilight area between pure abstraction and representational painting. He invented a nonobjective method of titling the works, distinguishing between impressions (which could have titles), improvisations (which were numbered), and compositions (which were preceded by a series of studies and which, as major works, were labeled with roman numerals).[5] Other works were titled as before, according to their subject matter. In theory at least, a title like *Composition V* suggests considerably less to a viewer than *Landschaft mit Kirch,* even though viewers have made out landscapes with churches in both paintings.

Kandinsky was characteristically modest about his achievements and about his historical role in painting. One of the reasons for this reticence was revealed in a theory that might have been called the "Great Theory of Formal Equality." Even as the first painter to create both a theory of abstraction and a set of canvases that were also abstract, he recognized that abstract painting was an inner-necessity rather than a historical necessity. He suggests in *Über das Geistige in der Kunst* and then declares in *Über die Formfrage* that abstraction is inherently neither more valuable nor more effective than realism.[6] Abstraction had merely been a necessary step in his quest for the pure effects of colors and lines. The elimination of the representation of objects (i.e., of the illusions of reality) removed misleading variables for the viewer. Pure abstraction makes possible pure effects of color and line. This allows the painter to experiment with the motions and emotions of the colors without the encroaching recognitions forced by the semblances of reality.

At the same time, Kandinsky shows, in spite of his theoretical disclaimers of the priority of abstract art, an acute awareness of the historical importance of the steps he took toward an "inevitable" pure abstraction. In the midst of the development of abstraction, at the exact stage when the transition was being made, he wrote *Über das Geistige in der Kunst* to explain and defend abstract painting. In his book, Kandinsky effectively turns over the traditional questions in painting by establishing a level of meaning that transcends them. In a later introduction, Kandinsky describes the new dialectic:

> Das Kunstwerk besteht aus zwei Elementen: aus dem innern und aus dem äussern.
> Das innere Element, einzeln genommen, ist die Emotion der Seele des Künstlers. Diese Emotion hat die Fähigkeit, eine im Grunde entsprechende Emotion in der Seele des Beschauers hervorzurufen.
> Solange die Seele mit dem Körper verbunden ist, kann sie in der Regel Vibrationen nur durch die Vermittlung des Gefühls empfangen. Das Gefühl ist also eine Brücke vom Unmateriellen zum Materiellen (Künstler) und vom Materiellen zum Unmateriellen (Beschauer).
> Emotion—Gefühl—Werk—Gefühl—Emotion.[7]

The whole tradition in art history spoke only of the outer elements: form, style, and technique. Kandinsky's introductory definition sets those issues aside and moves to a discussion of the inner. As he writes, "the emotion of the soul of the artist" contains a unique power, "the capacity to evoke a similar emotion [in the soul of] the observer."[8] Recognition of the primacy of the inner led Kandinsky to an original scheme and to an unusual analysis of color and line. Certainly, even where the inner qualities and inner necessities are prior, the external elements remain, but merely as embodiment or carrier of inner elements. From this realignment of values in art, Kandinsky deduces a corollary that is formulated succinctly in *Über die Formfrage:* All questions and arguments concerning form are nonquestions. "Hier sehen wir, dass es also in Prinzip gar keine Bedeutung hat, *ob eine reale oder abstrakte Form vom Künstler gebraucht wird. Da beide Formen innerlich gleich sind.* . . . Abstrakt gesagt: *es gibt keine Frage der Form im Prinzip.*"[9] Kandinsky's equation attempts to separate form and value in the history of art. At the same time, the principle of formal equality deflates the myth of progress and evolution in the arts, a myth that promoted a narrative history of the arts under the label of historicism.

In *Der Blaue Reiter,* the editor's insistence on the equality of forms was a natural extension of Kandinsky's theory. Hence, as a vehicle for exhibiting and publishing such immensely diverse manners and styles of art, *Der Blaue Reiter* becomes an experiment that tests

Kandinsky's ideas. He drew his examples in the arts from ancient and medieval works as well as from contemporary artists. He expanded the ordinary limits of art history by showing primitive artifacts, the products of contemporary artisans (Bavarian glass works), and archeological pieces in contexts that placed them on equal ground with El Greco and Picasso. As he was later to write about this period (and specifically about Der Blaue Reiter):

> J'avais alors l'idée d'un livre 'synthétique' qui devait effacer les superstitions, faire 'tomber les mûrs' entre les arts divisés l'un de l'autre, entre l'art officiel et l'art non admis, et enfin prouver que la question de l'art n'est pas celle de la forme, mais du contenu artistique. La séparation des arts, leur existence isolée dans de petites 'cabines' avec des mûrs hauts, dûrs et opaques était à mes yeux une des conséquences fâcheuses et dangereuses de la méthode 'analytique' qui supprimaît la méthode 'synthétique' dans la science et commençait de la faire dans l'art aussi. Les résultats suivaient: la dureté, le point de vue et le sentiment étroit, la perte de la liberté du sentiment, peut être sa mort définitive.[10]

The synthesis of which Kandinsky speaks here is the book, *Der Blaue Reiter,* and while the nature of this synthesis has only partially been understood, whatever shortcomings in comprehension have occurred can scarcely be blamed on the book's author. Though his ambitions for one volume might very well seem overstated, his book does try to tear down the walls that divide the arts and then "prove" that the essential question in art is not form but "artistic content." His attack on the status quo comes from an unexpected and somewhat metaphysical direction:

> Mon idée était alors de montrer par exemple que la différence entre l'art officiel et l'art 'ethnographique' n'avait aucune raison d'être; que la pernicieuse habitude de ne pas voir sous les formes différentes extérieures la racine intérieur organique de l'art en général pourrait finir par la perte totale de l'action réciproque entre l'art et la vie de la société humaine. De même la différence entre l'art de l'enfant, du 'dilettante' et l'art 'académique'—les differences graduelles de la forme 'achevée' et 'non-achevée' couvrait la force de l'expression et la racine commune.[11]

Kandinsky conceived of the period of Der Blaue Reiter as a time of spiritual crisis and, consequently, a time of crisis for the arts. His theory of the spiritual in the arts was not merely a back-door defense for abstract painting. It was a synthetic structure for all the arts, demonstrating the basis of their "inner identity" and showing how the arts may be brought together. As theory, it was purposefully transcendental in its premises and blatantly attractive in its ideals. It was a difficult theory to disagree with since wherever one attacked it, he attacked the concept of the artist's soul and its relation to the spiritual. Since the fundamental statement of Kandinsky's theory constituted a rejection of value judgments (at least according to current standards), *Über das Geistige in der Kunst* actually performed in practice the tasks that he lists in his a posteriori summary.

At the same time, in his description of the goals of *Der Blaue Reiter,* there are several central ideas that distinguish the yearbook in the context of German Expressionism. First, Kandinsky openly explains his desire to replace the traditional ways of valuing art works with an inner (spiritual) value system. Second, he invokes the irrational, romantic fight against the inroads of analytic modes of thought which he associated with science and to which he attributed the destructive, nihilistic tendencies of the "modern." And third, he states his own belief in the "inner-equality" of all of the arts in such a way that it leads to a synthetic theory. He then creates a model of "synthesis" as a natural demonstration of the inner-relations of the arts. To this extent, *Der Blaue Reiter* was planned to serve as an example of synthesis and collaboration of the arts.

Thus when, a year after he wrote *Über das Geistige in der Kunst,* Wassily Kandinsky wrote to Franz Marc that he had conceived of a plan for "eine art Almanach," it should not be surprising that he seems, from the start, to know what he is about.[12]

The two painters quickly reached an agreement to carry out Kandinsky's idea and set to work outlining the contents of *Der Blaue Reiter Almanach.* By September 1911, the first table of contents was sent to the prospective publisher, Reinhard Piper, owner of Piper Verlag. In the initial proposal, Marc sent a carefully structured, coherently organized plan for a journal and specified clearly how the coeditors envisioned their book. In this document, there were to be four general divisions with six articles on painting, eight on music, three stage works, and finally, a section containing three chronicles of the year's work in art. These sections of writing were to be followed by a number of reproductions from five different areas of art, a method of organization frequently used in catalogues for exhibitions.[13]

While this formulation serves as a sample, it neither resembles the final product nor gives any indication of how either the artists or the arts were to be "synthesized" within the framework of the book. One could argue that Kandinsky and Marc wished to present a relatively traditional front to Piper to convince him of both their seriousness and their ability to put together such a book. On the other hand, it could be argued that this early proposal was evidence that the form and theories of Kandinsky were only gradually worked out as the two artists compiled the book. It may well have been that problems with contributors and pressures of publication forced the two editors to abandon their orthodox format and improvise. In so doing, the organization and the shape of the book began to change to reflect not only the material they actually had in hand, but also Kandinsky's theory of the synthesis of the arts. It is clear, comparing the several early prospectuses to the complete almanac, that the editors changed the serial ordering of documents as well as the placement and rhythm of the reproductions so that all these elements would more closely reflect Kandinsky's ideas about the relations of the works included. For, as Kandinsky writes in the Introduction to the first *Blaue Reiter* exhibition, "In this small exposition, we are not trying to propagate *one* precise and specific form, but we do hope to illustrate, by the variety of forms represented how the artists' inner-wish may be variously embodied."[14] This statement of intention is subsequently expanded to a full-page announcement of the forthcoming almanac:

> Next spring [1912] there will appear . . . *Der Blaue Reiter Almanach*. A great revolution, the displacement of the center of gravity in art, literature, and music. Diversity of forms; the constructive, compositional character of these forms; an intensive turn to inner nature, and linked with it, a refusal to embellish outer nature. These are, in general terms, symptoms of a new spiritual renaissance. To show the features and manifestations of this change, to emphasize its inner connection with the past, to reveal the expression of inner aspirations in every form suggestive of inwardness—this is the goal that the Blaue Reiter is striving to attain.[15]

Few readers of these words could understand their implication for Kandinsky. He had, in his writing, developed some idiosyncratic usages by which he intended to express something more than he says literally. Hence, when Kandinsky writes that *Der Blaue Reiter* "hopes to illustrate, by the variety of forms represented, how the artist's inner-wish may be variously embodied," only the readers of *Über das Geistige in der Kunst* are likely to understand that a synthesis based on the spiritual identity of the arts is intended. Likewise, the "displacement of the center of gravity in art, literature, and music" must have seemed a rather wild metaphor with neither explanation nor evidence. Yet, Kandinsky had already written how this displacement was to take place and also how it constituted "a new spiritual renaissance."

Between the first written document outlining the contents of the book and the final text, several variants appear. From the estate of August Macke, one table of contents (in Macke's hand) shows a slightly different format with a reduction in the number of articles and an elimination of the Chronicles that had originally been the center of the yearbook idea.[16] The listing of contents places the articles in the same order: painting, music, one article on literature, Kandinsky's *Der gelbe Klang* with a foreword and an essay entitled "Konstruktion in der Malerei" followed by a list of reproductions which lists a number of the kinds of art (Benin, Egyptian, Siamese, Niger, Bavarian glass, Votive art, and Russian folk art as well as work from such moderns as Burliuk, Delauney, Le Fauconnier, Gauguin, Girieud, Cézanne, Kandinsky, Kokoschka, Marc, Matisse, Münter, Jawlensky, Picasso, Werefkin *"und so weiter!!"*). The list, in this case, is ordered so that the nonmodern arts and the modernists are grouped separately, and there is a strong expectation that they will be shown in roughly that way, i.e., at the end of the book and in something of a nonmodern vs. modern format. I emphasize this because Kandinsky and Marc did not do what might have been expected, given Marc's prospectus and Macke's later version.

The second version was produced by Kandinsky in October of 1911 for a press release advertising the appearance of *Der Blaue Reiter* in early 1912. Kandinsky lists Allard, Marc, Macke, Burljik, Thomas von Hartmann (subsequently known as Thomas de Hartmann), Arnold Schoenberg, *"Die Stilfrage,"* and himself as author of the Bühnenkomposition, *Der gelbe Klang*, and "Über Construktion in der Malerei." In addition Kandinsky notes that there will be around one hundred reproductions from various sources.[17]

Several issues are confirmed in these two versions of the contents. It appears that in October the actual composition of the book was firm and the way the materials would be put together would be fairly orthodox. However, the editors were neither scholars nor "editors" in the conventional sense, and to expect the almanac to turn out like the preliminary drawings would be like expecting their finished paintings to resemble their studies and sketches. The two artists were, up until the final copy was sent to Piper Verlag, still exploring the possibilities inherent in the medium they had more or less reinvented for themselves. Some of this free-form invention caused their publisher considerable anxiety and one of his letters to the artists, after the appearance of the book, reflects a rather testy understanding of what had occurred:

> Bei der Herstellung des Buches haben Sie mit Herrn Kandinsky aber völlig unabhängig von uns verfahren, bei der Annahme der Aufsätze und bei der Bemessung der Anzahl, sowie der Grösse der Klischees uns niemals um Rat gefragt, sondern einfach Druckauftrag resp. Klischierauftrag gegeben. Auch den Ladenpreis von M. 10.–haben Sie festgesetzt ohne Rücksicht auf die Herstellungskosten. Sie gingen ja von der an sich ganz richtigen Voraussetzung aus, dass eine Propagandaschrift nicht allzu teuer sein darf... Sie dürfen sich nun nicht wundern, wenn die Kosten des Buches zu den Eingängen trotz des ziemlich lebhaften Absatzes in einem Missverhältnis stehen... Sie haben aber auf die Kalkulation keinerlei Rücksicht genommen und *wir hatten unsererseits auf Ihre redaktionellen Massnahmen keinen Einfluss.*[18]

While Piper's complaints were justified, his tone would have been more angry had he not insisted that the two editors pay for the price of production before printing began. Piper's complaint was not merely that the book was too expensive and underpriced, but rather that the estimates of the cost of production were based on the early projections of Marc and Kandinsky and these had turned out to be altogether too modest. For example, there were 148 reproductions instead of the 50 or so works suggested by Marc's original proposal. There were 16 articles in place of the 8 listed by Kandinsky or the 12 listed by Marc (in the variant tables of contents of October 1911). Furthermore, instead of consulting with the publisher about what should be accepted and how much, Kandinsky and Marc had proceeded as if Piper Verlag were merely an employee responsible for printing and binding the book.

At the same time, one must keep in mind that the goals of variety, inner-necessity, and synthesis were still ideals to be explored rather than preestablished axioms. The fact that Kandinsky wrote the requisite essays on the questions of form and the *Bühnenkomposition* while the almanac was in its period of composition emphasizes the catalytic role of the book for Kandinsky's own theories. For while the essential ideas were suggested in *Über das Geistige in der Kunst*, the practical applications beyond the field of painting did not occur until *Der Blaue Reiter* began to take shape under his hand. The changes observed in the creation of the almanac as an actual book all indicate that Kandinsky was working out explicit written presentations of his theories and composing a book, the form of which would evidence how these theories functioned when applied. The two editors used the layout of the almanac as a "canvas" to try out the new ideas which to them concerned the future of the arts as well as a display of the relations between the arts. The book's statements and works were all by artists and these would be composed into an order by artists (not editors), thus creating the kind of purity that Kandinsky had wished for from the start.

While putting together the various parts of the book, the editors had had to adjust to the vagaries of the politics of the Neue Künstlervereinigung München (NKVM) and to drop commissioned works by Jawlensky and von Werefkin. They also had to change the plan of the book because of disappointments experienced with a number of artists from whom contributions had been expected.[19] All these factors are reflected in the make up of the almanac. The editors then improvised (perhaps one should use Kandinsky's term, "composed") to discover an order and a sequence that would express their theory of the relation of the arts while literally stating in prose the goals and achievements of (the state of) modern arts. The editors chose to exemplify by choice, position, and juxtaposition the variations of *Klänge und seelen Vibrationen* accessible to the reader in the works displayed. A great proportion of the almanac was planned so that a sequential effect will play upon the sensibility of the reader. In Kandinsky's language, the inner emotion of the artist in the reproduction will be communicated to the soul of the viewer. While I cannot very easily show how this happens, I will try to demonstrate that there are several consistent kinds of effects at work.

Franz Marc's opening essay suggests that the almanac will function by indirection and suggestion. "Geistige Güter," though, is full of misgivings: "Es ist wahnsinning schwer, seinen Zeitgenossen geistige Geschenke zu machen."[20] The author seems predisposed to accept as normal the fact that spiritual treasures are rarely recognized. Moving to examples of artists as spiritual kin, Marc discusses El Greco and Cézanne, since "both mark the beginning of a new epoch in painting. In their views of life, both felt the *mystical inner construction, which is the great problem of our generation" (TBRA,* 59). Finally, Marc mentions Picasso, writing that he "belongs to this sequence of ideas, as do most of our illustrations" *(TBRA,* 60). This introductory essay is deceptively understated, so much so that few readers will know what "sequence of ideas" Marc is referring to in the statement. For, in his essay, there is no sequence of ideas, properly speaking. Rather, there is a limpid flow from one vaguely stated idea to the next and then a claim made for Picasso, which might be acceptable in terms of El Greco and Cézanne as painters who mark "the beginning of a new epoch," but totally unacceptable if one wishes to include the notion of the "mystical inner construction."

However, Marc's casual prose is only part of the material presented in this section. The essay is illustrated by eight reproductions of a rather shocking variety. In the deluxe edition, the article is preceded by color reproductions by both Kandinsky and Marc. Both feature primary colors (reds, blues, yellows) clearly and brightly reproduced.[21] Both works might well serve as examples of the *Geistige Güter* of the article. However, because of the rarity of this edition, I will not examine these reproductions but instead proceed to the subsequent works: a German fifteenth-century woodcut from a series called "the Knight of the Tower" (1495), a Chinese painting, a Bavarian mirror painting of the Death of a Saint (1800), Pablo Picasso's painting *Femme à la guitare* (1911), and two children's drawings of figures. The editors juxtaposed this group with Marc's essay so that the items would appear radically unconnected by form, style, period, and subject matter. Second, the editors wished to apply the general theory of relation that Marc mentioned in his essay: "Most of our illustrations . . . belong to this sequence of ideas." This, of course, does not seem to constitute a theory just as Marc's essay didn't complete a sequence of ideas. The missing parts and the missing theory are only gradually revealed in *Der Blaue Reiter.* They make up a restatement of the ideas that Kandinsky brought to the almanac at its origin and they are stated (at least partially) in the concluding essays Kandinsky wrote: *"Über die Formfrage"* and *"Über Bühnenkomposition."* In this context, the reader needs to be aware of the "inner-emotions" and "inner-desires" that are awakened by works of art. Each work, the editors claimed, was chosen because it embodied a "spiritual treasure," and each work is comparable to the others, not because of external similarities but rather because of internal identities.

However, before the reader attempts a thorough analysis of each of these reproductions in search of its "internal merit," he should be warned that Kandinsky's manner of selection and placement is intuitive and experimental, rather than rational and certain. The effect of the works of reproduction is part of the experiment of *Der Blaue Reiter*. While there are occasions where analysis and explanation are useful, there are as many cases where the application of a critical method is beside the point. In certain cases, as soon as one grasps the diversity and range of work that is placed in the same context, he might well throw up his hands. Yet, the topic of the essay itself provides a thematic base. Like the Cézanne and the El Greco, these other pieces are not alike in appearance, but rather represent aspects of the range of painting that go beyond the expected in western European art. When Marc discusses the Picasso reproduction, it was, if not the newest, then surely the most modern of the paintings in the almanac and certainly worthy of further discussion. Yet, Marc merely points to its presence and comments that it, like the other reproductions, "belongs to this sequence of ideas."

Marc's brevity and his refusal to applaud or explain the presence of a completely new Picasso Cubist painting should not be seen as ignorance of the shocking qualities of the painting or innocence of its likely effect on readers. For it is especially here, at the beginning of the book, that the editors put their theory to its most severe test. No one will fail to notice the differences between these works. But will any audience be able to derive the underlying unity of a set of reproductions as diverse as this? Marc's argument projects a confidence that is difficult, even now, to imagine. As Kandinsky will argue explicitly in *Über der Formfrage*, all forms are equal in value. Discussion of the innovations inherent in the Picasso painting will be of interest only insofar as these discussions illuminate the inner-necessity of the artist. In this way, Kandinsky and Marc will insist that Bavarian mirror painting may express an inner-value equal to an early painting of Cézanne or a masterpiece by Picasso. This argument is implicit in each set of juxtapositions of reproductions and texts, and it is most surely evidenced in the choice of reproductions grouped together in *Geistige Güter*.

In the subsequent essay, Marc describes the new German art *(Die Wilden Deutschlands)* and discusses briefly *Die Brücke* in Dresden, *Die Neue Sezession* in Berlin, and *Die Neue Künstlervereinigung* in Munich.[22] With neither criticism nor advice, he describes the fate of each of the three movements in terms of their spiritual qualities, their innerness, and their openness to mysticism. Meanwhile, placed within the essay are three reproductions, the first two of which (i.e., a painting by August Macke, *Der Sturm* [1911] and a lithograph by Ernst Ludwig Kirchner, *Women Dancers* [1910]) seem to suggest an illustrative pattern wherein each of the German groups will be represented by a work of art.[23] However, instead of a third and completing illustration, the editors insert a reproduction of a piece of wood sculpture of a warrior from South Borneo. Once again, as in the first essay, there is an element of surprise in the juxtaposition of a primitive piece next to Macke and Kirchner. There are no observable relationships in subject matter, style, form, or any other exterior elements. Instead, the editors, without arguing their theory, simply insert the primitive work beside the two contemporary German works and await the effects of juxtaposition. The first kind of demonstration of the inner-relations of the arts is as simple as this. Experimenting with placement and juxtaposition, the editors attempt to show the relations of their illustrations by placing the illustrations in the same context.[24]

Marc's third essay attempts to elucidate this very point using two illustrations: in this case, an illustration from a nineteenth-century almanac (which Marc takes to be a representation of the popular art of love) and an expressionistic painting by Kandinsky of an abstracted horse and rider, entitled *Lyrische* (1910). With full awareness of the radical differences in form and format, Marc suggests the Blaue Reiter aesthetic principle of inner necessity by alluding to the "spiritual" which, he infers, can be observed and compared. In this way, *Reinhald das Wunderkind*, because of its pure "artistic feeling," can be compared to Kandinsky's work, where "the same spiritual artistic expression—even if not as easily enjoyed—is present."[25] For, he claims,

> if we wish to be wise enough to teach our contemporaries, we must justify our knowledge through our works and we must exhibit them as a matter of course . . . We will make that as difficult as possible for ourselves, never fearing the ordeal by fire that will result from placing our works, which point to the future and are still unproved, beside the works of older, proved cultures. We believe that nothing can illustrate our ideas better than such comparisons. Genuine art can always be compared with genuine art, however different the expression may be. (*TBRA*, 65)

In the illustration in question, the comparison takes place quickly and Marc moves on to another issue, the dawn of the new epoch. His three essays form a three-part preface to the book and expose the central ideas behind *Der Blaue Reiter*. His writing style creates a matter-of-fact and rather unpolemical tone and his essays are placed to contrast with the closing essays by Kandinsky, which further clarify the fundamental principles of the group and the book.

The central theoretical statement in the book is Kandinsky's *Über die Formfrage*. Will Grohmann declares that "*Formfrage* was written with poetic elan . . . [and] is Kandinsky's most mature contribution to the theory of art."[26] The essay is the clear statement of the fundamental assumption upon which both the almanac and its concurrent movement are based. It is also an explanation of the aesthetic principle involved in the composition and the effects of the book itself. By dismissing the importance of the conventions of form (in some cases Kandinsky seems to be addressing "style"), he permits himself free access to every historical period, rapidly breaking down the boundaries that traditionally provide the organization of the history of art. In his examples and illustrations, he also demands that the viewer take a second look at the relationships engendered by the composition of the book itself. In recollecting an ancient and somewhat mystical theory of art, the relation of the *"inner-klänge* and *inner-notwendigkeit"* to the spiritual, Kandinsky dispenses with the premise of the early modern "avant-garde." The competition to have done the latest, newest work must be modified and all the barriers between the arts removed so that the exterior qualities will appear in their true nature, as servants of the inner necessity of the artist.

Kandinsky's reflections make clear how he reaches his equation that *realism = abstraction* and *abstraction = realism*. By attributing degrees of abstraction and realism to every painting, he asserts that the relative relationship of the two depends upon the individual artist. Where the element of abstraction is diminished quantitatively in any painting, it is increased qualitatively.[27] Presumably, the reverse equation is also true. Hence, abstraction and realism are essential parts of the whole. Kandinsky concludes that the question of form is not a question at all. For if the equality of the two antipodes (realism and abstraction) places them on the same plane, then "it makes no difference whether the artist uses real or abstract forms. Both forms are basically internally equal."[28] The quest for forms and rules is attributed to art historians and art critics, whom Kandinsky finds lacking in creativity and thus of limited use to artists. "Abstrakt gesagt: es gibt keine Frage der Form im Prinzip."[29]

He closes with directions to the readers that bear not merely upon his essay and its illustrations, but upon the whole book:

> Wenn der leser dieses Buches imstande ist, sich seiner Wünsche, seiner Gedanken, seiner Gefühle zeitweise zu entledigen, und dann das Buch durchblättert, von einem Votivbild zu Delauney übergeht und weiter von einem Cézanne zu einem russischen Volksblatt, von einer Maske zu Picasso, von einem Glasbild zu Kubin usw. usw., so wird seine Seele viele Vibrationen erleben und in das Gebiet der Kunst eintreten. Hier wird er dann nicht ihn empörende Mängel und ärgernde Fehler finden, sondern er wird statt einem Minus ein Plus seelisch erreichen. Und diese Vibrationen und das aus ihnen entsprungene Plus werden eine Seelenbereicherung sein, die durch kein anderes Mittel als durch die Kunst zu erreichen ist.
>
> Später kann der Leser mit dem Künstler zu objektiven Betrachtungen zur wissenschaftlichen Analyse übergehen. Hier findet er dann, dass die sämtlichen gebrachten Beispiele einem inneren Rufe gehorchen—Komposition, dass sie alle auf einer inneren Basis stehen—Konstruktion.[30]

Just under the surface of Kandinsky's sentences, there is an undercurrent of the premise upon which his argument depends. By this time it should be no secret that Kandinsky assumes the power of the call of the spiritual in the work of art and puts his belief in the communicative power of the inner emotion of the artists as "embodied" in the works reproduced in *Der Blaue Reiter*. However, the first step the theory calls for is an interesting, almost phenomenological, suspension of the "Wünsche, Gedanken, und Gefühle" (a bracketing of those parts of the consciousness that are most likely to prevent perception) to allow the work of art to sound. According to Kandinsky, the initial mode for sensing the presence of the spiritual is inattention, such as the state of a casual observer "leafing" through the book to look at the pictures. This method is at least the beginning and it can be corroborated by a subsequent *wissenschaftlichen Analyse*. Marc and Kandinsky carry out this theory in their book both by literal, if disarming, statements of it and by their practice in the choice, position, and juxtaposition of the texts and reproductions. Kandinsky's statement appears to be an appeal to the reader to make an extra effort to understand the full meaning of *Der Blaue Reiter*. By bracketing the normal attributes of reading and viewing (i.e., desires, ideas, and feelings) and assuming a free-floating consciousness, the inner vibrations of the works, their harmony, and their counterpoint would be manifested.

As Kandinsky seems to have expected from his comments on art critics, the reaction of the "art world" to his books was mixed. Herwarth Walden, editor of *Der Sturm* and promoter of the avant-garde, thought the book an extraordinary effort at the leading edge of the modern. Other reviewers tended to treat the almanac as an art book and judged it with appropriate misunderstanding. Apparently it was one thing to paint "awful abstract" works (for these could be dismissed as the unimportant indiscretions of one of the *Wilden Russlands*) and quite another to create books, first in *Über das Geistige in der Kunst* and then in *Der Blaue Reiter,* which explicitly threatened the honored order and tradition of fine arts. Furthermore, both books make the inner necessities of the spiritual an accepted and fundamental part of the artist's world. Kandinsky's works make evident how strange the visionary claims of European Romanticism still were to most Europeans in 1912.

To the artists, the message of *Der Blaue Reiter* was twofold. First, it announced the ongoing effort to achieve unification and mutual support of the spiritual forces that hinted at the "great spiritual change." Second, the almanac served as an example of what could be achieved in the practice of the synthesis of the arts. Certainly in the history of modern art, no collaborative effort as improvisationally and rapidly accomplished has achieved as lasting and positive an effect. The great Romantic ideal of the *Gesamtkunstwerk* was revived and, to artists like Hugo Ball, Hans Arp, Herwarth Walden, and Thomas von Hartmann, the synthesis of the arts was no longer an idle Wagnerian dream. The actual project of synthesis was brought out before their eyes in the form of the almanac and especially in the *Bühnenkomposition.* These works demonstrated the validity of the goal of "Monumental Art," that dream of the synthetic, collaborative work that haunted a number of figures in the arts at the beginning of the "great epoch."

In the case of *Der Blaue Reiter,* it is not sufficient merely to explain the goals of the collaboration. One must, in fact, examine elements of the work itself to discover how the disparate kinds of art are related and then assess the degree to which these relationships can be evaluated. There are three separable kinds of relation between the texts and the reproductions. The first is direct illustration where reproductions serve to exemplify (as an example or else as the case in point) the arguments of the respective authors. Illustration is the simplest relationship, both in terms of its application and its observable effects. For with illustration, there is a direct and obvious connection between the reproduction(s) and the text. In Marc's "Zwei Bilder,"[31] the author discusses two paintings which are reproduced within the essay. His references to the nineteenth-century illustration *Reinhald das Wunderkind* are somewhat self-explanatory as are his rather brief comments about Kandinsky's *Lyrische*. Yet, Marc's bare assertions would be unintelligible without the illustrations. Then, in "Zwei Bilder," the theory of illustration is taken one step further. Accompanying the direct illustrations are two "indirect" illustrations wherein Marc's principle is implicitly demonstrated with a pair of wholly different works. In this case, a Bavarian mirror painting from the early nineteenth century is juxtaposed with a reproduction of Heinrich Campendonk's painting *Springendes Pferd* (1911). Marc's axiom: "Wie alles Echte: an seinem innern Leben, das seine Wahrheit verbürgt" is immediately tested.[32] If the "spiritual quality" of the first pair of reproductions can be compared, then the reader is prepared to see the second, unmentioned pair in the same light. If the principle of comparison is valid, it will function in both cases. Part of Marc's point here may be that the spiritual values can be observed but not explained, an attitude that follows Kandinsky's subsequent instructions to the "casual reader."

As applied in "Zwei Bilder," the use of direct illustrations to supplement and exemplify the text is certainly not unusual for the period, and examples of the practice varied from reproductions of *Jugendstil* art works in literary texts to more ambitious attempts at combining reproductions with texts, as in Raoul Dufy's woodcuts for Apollinaire's *le Bestaire* (1909). In fact, there are several other examples of direct illustration in the almanac. First, the straightforward reproductions of two works by Bernard Kahler introduce the forms and format of the little known painter. Then, in Erwin von Busse's essay "Die Kompositionsmittal bei Robert Delauney," two examples of Delauney's recent work (*St. Severin*, 1909, and *The Window on the City [La Ville]*, 1911) are reproduced and then discussed in the text.[33]

Roger Allard's essay, "Kennzeichen der Erneuerung in der Malerei," on cubism and modernism in French painting is accompanied by six illustrations. The fact that none of the paintings reproduced for Allard's essay is cubist may appear to break down the normative expectations for direct illustration. Even a very loose definition of cubism (and there were a number of these in 1911) would not be likely to include either Matisse's *La Danse* (1910) or the children's mural (*TBRA,* 108). To have selected Cézanne would have made excellent sense according to contemporary tradition in art history, but both paintings reproduced are so early and so uncharacteristic of the painter's late works that it is hard to trace direct connections with cubism. Even Le Fauconnier's *Paysage lacustre* (n.d. c. 1909–10), which might be considered mildly cubist, must then be compared to the historical development of the cubist forms rather than to the actual cubist practices of 1909–10.[34] He seems, in this painting, to be working toward the full development of an analytic cubism. The best explanation of these reproductions must go beyond earlier commentators who declared that all these paintings are cubist (as Allard's text suggests).

First, as is the case in all the other essays, Allard had no say in the choice and placement of the reproductions. Second, although there is some truth in his judgments of cubism, it does not suffice to explain the editor's choices. The principles of illustration were those of "spiritual kinships," complementary patterns rather than direct correlations of style. Certainly in this sense, Paul Cézanne, as the spiritual father of Picasso and Braque, is an appropriate choice to illustrate the discussion of cubism even if his paintings do not specifically represent the formal questions relevant to the development of the cubist aesthetic. The inner-effect of Cézanne's early work, however different in "style" or "form" from the concepts of cubism, still manifests a positive spiritual benefit, according to Kandinsky's theory. In fact, given the paucity of information available to Kandinsky concerning the influence of Cézanne's late works on the development of cubism, the evocation of the spirit of Cézanne is an impressive piece of intuition.

Similarly, both Picasso and Braque subsequently confirmed in interviews and their own works that they learned from Henri Matisse. The early distortions of form and perspective in the Fauvist exhibitions (in 1904–5) as well as the experiments with pure color were vital counterpoints to the innovations of Braque and Picasso during the crucial period before they achieved a full expression of their cubism. Furthermore, *La Danse* presents a motif that had fascinated first Cézanne, in late works such as *Les Baigneurs* (1890), *Les Grandes Baigneuses* (1898–1900) and *Les Grandes Baigneuses II* (c. 1900), then both Braque in *Le Grand Nu* (1908) and Picasso in *Les Démoiselles d'Avignon* (1907). Matisse's *La Danse* comments upon a convention carried through from classicism in which naked female figures are gathered in a primordial situation in nature to enact ritual activities. The space for such activities is generalized and abstracted in the works of Cézanne, Matisse, Braque, and Picasso, and attention is focused on the shapes of the human figures, the rhythms of their forms in space, and the geometrical organization of the group (a circle, a triangle, a diagonal line). In each of these paintings, the attention is directed away from the representation of natural reality and toward the painterly expression of human forms abstracted from realistic context, hence abstracted from previous conventions of painterly representation. Within this larger context, Le Fauconnier's *Paysage lacustre* presents the abstraction of nature without the presence of human figures (in a manner reminiscent of Braque's *Maisons à L'Estaque*). Yet, the parallels between the paintings of Cézanne, Matisse, Le Fauconnier, and the silk embroidery of the beheading of St. John (see *DBR*, 85) are internal and suggestive rather than illustrative and parallel.

It could clearly have been otherwise, for, as the almanac itself suggests, the editors could have provided historically direct examples of cubism from reproductions at hand. The Picasso painting reproduced with one of Marc's essays, "Femme à la guitare" (1911), would have constituted an excellent, direct illustration of the state of cubism at the time Allard was writing his essay.[35] Furthermore, the painting *L'Abondance* (1910) by Le Fauconnier (which is located within an essay on "Die Freie Musik") could also have served as appropriate direct illustration of the cubist modernism had the editors chosen such a method.

Instead, two views of cubism are juxtaposed. The first comes from the text of Allard's essay, which advocates a kind of avant-gardism in declaiming vague new worlds and reporting the roll of advanced honor. The other view, which is complementary to the first, is intuitive and is implied by the choice and position of the reproductions. The function of the illustrations is, nonetheless, to support and expand the views of the author. Thus a second relation between text and reproductions is developed in the almanac. It is also illustrative, but in this case, the connection between text and artwork (and, in some cases, between the reproductions themselves) is indirect since the illustrations work either by association or by analogy.

The editors accompany August Macke's essay, "Die Masken," with a series of sculpted forms and masks. However, in spite of the title chosen by the editors, the essay is not at all about masks, but rather is a lyrical evocation of the general value of difference. Macke develops a loose and rather freely associated series of paragraphs praising as many forms as he can name, from Gothic cathedrals to a still-life by Cézanne (82), then a cavalry attack, the war paint of the American Indians, and the masks and stage productions of the Japanese and the ancient Greeks. While this listing suggests the "forms" mentioned in the essay, it by no means exhausts either their range or variety. The editors take Macke's process of association one step further by providing a series of illustrations of examples within one form (thus adding a paradigmatic series within Macke's syntagmatic list). However, the series of reproductions of "masks" from Brazil, Easter Island, Cameroon, Mexico, New Caledonia, Alaska, and a drawing of Arabs by Lydia Wieber are not attempts to draw direct associations with the text. The variety of sculpted reliefs, masks, and ceremonial objects merely demonstrates one direction of Macke's opening thought. By attending to the process of the mind of the author, the editors create a describable interrelation by association. It might thus be inferred that the title of the essay as well as the selection and order of the reproductions were the editors' part of the collaboration.

Another example of the "indirect" relation between text and illustration occurs in the essay on "Scriabin's Prometheus" ("Prometheus von Skrjabin" by L. Sabanejew).[36] Here the editors apply the principle of analogy, juxtaposing art works to certain passages of criticism where a parallel effect can be suggested. Thus, Sabanejew's opening words describing Scriabin's "positive mystical action that leads to an ecstatic experience" (*TBRA*, 127) are placed opposite a reproduction of Cézanne's still-life, *Pommes, poivres et raisin* (c. 1890–96). Because of the absence of an obvious or "direct" connection between the text and the reproduction, it is not immediately apparent that these two are related, much less how they are related. However, the overriding consistency throughout *Der Blaue Reiter* of the correspondences and relations between conventionally unlike forms is useful in this case. The editors first evoke the spiritual calls of contrary works of art, then insist upon Kandinsky's distinction between the inner and the outer (interior and exterior) qualities of art works. Once observable, formal differences are devalued, other distinctions take on a new importance. In this case, the relation that the editors attempt to establish is between the reproductions and the music of Scriabin (which is the subject of the text). Cézanne's explorations of the relation between inner vision and outer perception are thus brought out in the context of a verbal description of Scriabin's musical invocation of visionary, ecstatic states of mind. However, because the text does not mention Cézanne, the analogy suggested by the juxtaposition of the painting and the description of the effects of the music must remain implicit. Furthermore, while the editors are free to refer to the possibilities of these "effects of juxtaposition," it is not clear how far the reader can proceed since analogies built upon "inner sounds" tend to be free rather than restricted and thus difficult to make clear in a *"wissenschaftliche Analyse."* There is a leap involved in Kandinsky's theory of composition that goes beyond logical discourse and, perhaps, beyond the analysis of the forms themselves. At least, that seems to be the argument in *Über das Geistige in der Kunst,* and that is the argument that is demonstrated here.

The principle of the comparison of contraries (in the sense of works similar neither in their exterior qualities nor in kind) is continued on the following pages of Sabanejew's essay. The next example does not initially concern the text, but rather two reproductions placed side-by-side. The first is a bas-relief of a German knight from a fourteenth-century tomb while the second is a relief of a Benin warrior (n.d.). Certainly, in these two sculptures, there are superficial similarities since both are armed warriors with swords, shields, helmets, and armor. However, the forms employed are considerably different. The slender, idealized figure of the fourteenth-century knight contrasts sharply with the squat, powerful stance of the Benin figure. While both are accompanied by their respective religious signs, the iconography of the Christian European (i.e., the black swan, the cross, and the heraldic signs) creates a meaning for European viewers who share a common tradition. On the other hand, the traditional stance, the inlay of the Benin shield, and the intricate signs carved on the breastplate of the African work are meaningless except to those anthropological investigators who happened to have worked with the Benin. The small, spiritual figure that appears at the side of the Benin warrior invokes again a portion of the mythology of the tribe but this meaning, like almost all other symbolic aspects, is inaccessible to the reader of 1912. Indeed, part of the meaning of the juxtaposition depends upon the unfamiliarity of the one in contrast with the other. For both figures are warriors of the sacred and both are represented with the signs and symbols of their mythology. Their juxtaposition, which cannot reveal this similarity through the outer forms, is posed so that the inner necessities of the artists and their work can penetrate the reader. Whether the reader senses this "inner-relationship" would depend upon the efficacy of Kandinsky's theory. In this set of examples, the juxtaposition of these two figures purposefully attempts to overcome the exterior differences so that an "inner-identity" can reveal itself.

Two pages later, the editors place photographic reproductions of Gauguin's wood relief *en face* with an anonymous Etruscan bronze relief of the Gorgon. In Gauguin's work, a Polynesian figure peers at the sacred falls in the moment of discovery of the primeval source where the amorphous form of the god is revealed. The saving quality of the talismanic flower in the hand of the voyeur serves as a charm. The unknown Etruscan artist recreates a moment in the Greek mythology of origins (or, at least, in a myth borrowed from the Greeks) wherein the Strong One, Sthenno, establishes her reign over the animals, birds, and plants. The obvious differences in form and format are once again overcome by an essential comparison of the iconography of two distinct myths presented by artists outside the myths. As Mircea Eliade writes:

> sacred time is indefinitely recoverable, indefinitely repeatable. . . . With each periodical festival, the participants find the same sacred time—the same time that had been manifested in the festival of the previous year or the festival of a century earlier; it is the time that was created and sanctified by the gods at the period of their *gesta*, of which the festival is precisely a reactualization. . . . The participants . . . meet in it the first appearance of sacred time, as it appeared *ab origine, in illo tempore.*[37]

The juxtaposition of representations of mythic occurrences marks the differences between mythologies and artistic conventions as well as the similarities among the essential, "original acts" that are paradigmatic.

At the end of Sabanejew's essay, during which the author has described the musical effects and innovations of Scriabin's *Prometheus* (again, a choice of theme that is paradigmatic), the editors arrange consecutive pages of reproductions by Emil Nolde and Kandinsky. Nolde's watercolor, *Bühnenskizze* (1910), stands next to, but not opposite, Kandinsky's early abstract painting, *Entwurf zu Komposition Nr. 4* (1911), which, in the original editions, was reproduced in color.

In all of these examples, a comparison and contrast of the works placed together is implied (if not actively called for) by the arrangement of the reproductions in the text. In all three pairs, there are certain superficial similarities (whether in media, two sets of reliefs, one set of paintings, or in theme). In some art journals, these exterior likenesses might suffice as explanations of the presence of reproductions, if explanations were required (and they rarely were). But, in all these reproductions, there is another relationship that the editors establish by selection and placement which can be overlooked if one attends too closely to individual reproductions without weighing the particular context provided by the text and surrounding works. The context supplied by Sabanejew's text is controlling in all three pairs of reproductions for the text invokes the key themes that are played upon each other in the reproductions. The fact that Kandinsky chose to end the article with a full-color reproduction of his *Entwurf zu Komposition Nr. 4* suggests two compositional ideas: First, to allow the viewer to pass from Cézanne through medieval and primitive relief forms to modern and ancient versions of mythic experience, thence to Nolde's sketch of the stage, and finally to Kandinsky's own abstract work. Second, Kandinsky attempts to provide an experience analogical to that of Scriabin's *Prometheus* as it is described by Sabanejew. Thus, the effect of the illustrations would be to surround Scriabin's music of ecstasy—a music that "leads to an ecstatic experience—to ecstasy, to the perception of more elevated dimensions of nature" (*TBRA*, 127) with parallel examples from the plastic arts. It is not accidental that Kandinsky's color reproduction should occur in the context of a discussion, however abbreviated, of Scriabin's theories of the relation of music and color. Inferences from Scriabin's color theory can thus be applied to Kandinsky's painting. This confrontation creates a comparison between the explicit color concepts of the Russian composer and the color theories implicit in *Entwurf zu Komposition Nr. 4*. For the adept reader, this comparison can be expanded by reference to the outline and explanation of the effects of the colors in *Über das Geistige in der Kunst*. Nor need one suppose that the juxtaposition of Kandinsky's painting in the book with several passages of Scriabin's music was merely coincidental. This parallel suggests further general relations between abstract painting and music, with color as the middle term.

The one other clear example of "indirect" illustration in the almanac occurs within N. Kulbin's short essay-manifesto entitled "Die Freie Musik," which attempts to describe a new music.[38] The author calls for a liberation from the norms of classical music and the adoption of a free tonality by which he means the use of quarter and eighth notes as well as the conventional full and half notes. Kandinsky and Marc insert four reproductions of works within the text that serve as graphic analogies of the freedoms and innovations recommended by Kulbin. The first illustration is Max Pechstein's stylized *Badende* (*Badende III*, 1911), a color woodcut in the original edition wherein both shape and perspective are distorted to distill a multi-leveled experience into one landscape with figures. The motif is much the same as that evoked in Matisse's *La Danse* and Cézanne's *La Grande Bain*, yet here foreground, middle ground, and background are created by the advances and recessions of the primary colors rather than by line and plane. The areas of pure color create a movement reducing the figures to a single, temporal image whose space is organized by the relation of shapes and by the force and strength of the colors.

Henri Le Fauconnier's *L'Abondance* (1910), the next reproduction, blocks volumes of the canvas into small planes that are recognizably cubist and influenced by the earlier experiments of Braque and Picasso (i.e., *Tête de Fernande* [1909] and *La Femme aux Poires* [1909], or Braque's *Nature morte avec compotier* [1908–9] and *Carrières Saint-Denis* [1909]). This painting creates a new visual experience by distorting the conventions of perspective and form in a way analogous to Pechstein's *Badende III*, though the paintings are certainly not alike in appearance. Le Fauconnier's cubist reorganization of the painterly conventions of volume and perspective achieve an impressive sense of solidity and weight in the central figure. Both of these works share qualities that are analogous to Kulbin's central theses about the new composers and their music: (1) the new music breaks down conventions of form; (2) the new music creates new forms by freeing the art of its constrictions; (3) the composers and the music define themselves and are defined by their attachment to modernism (i.e., here we must assume Kulbin means the avant-garde or the various modernisms that Kandinsky and Marc attempt to bring together in *Der Blaue Reiter*). In each of Kulbin's major points, the analogy between "modern" music and "modern" painting (or, if you will, between *Neue Musik und Wilde Kunst*) is straightforward and needs no elaboration. Each of the points could have come from the writings of painters in *Die Brücke, Cubism,* or *Der Blaue Reiter.* It is left, though, for the illustrations themselves to make or, at least, to suggest the analogies.

In this way, the legacy of *Der Blaue Reiter* in the arts is difficult to trace in art history, for, unlike *Die Brücke,* futurism, or cubism, *Der Blaue Reiter* had no common stylistic goal, no mutual agreement on elements of form or media, and no communal innovations to promulgate. While many of the individual participants (i.e., Kandinsky, Marc, Macke, Gabrielle Münter, Paul Klee, Hans Arp, André Derain, Robert Delauney, Arnold Schoenberg) subsequently gained international recognition, few historians attribute their fame to the brief prewar movement. Of the artists associated with *Der Blaue Reiter,* only Marc and Macke depend upon their association for recognition and, even then, any potential artistic development ended with the untimely deaths of both men in the First World War. For many of the young artists who exhibited with *Der Blaue Reiter,* the exhibitions constituted their first major showing and most of these continued long thereafter to praise their early affiliations with the movement. The single remaining evidence of the ways in which Kandinsky's association of artists was both effective and influential in synthesizing the arts is this curious composite work, produced by the collaboration of the editors and the artists. Examining the relations of the several arts in *Der Blaue Reiter* thus shows not merely that relationships can be established, but also that the interrelations were supported by a general theory and applied in a thoroughgoing, if unsystematic way.

FOUR

THE RELATION OF THE TEXT
Herzgewächse

I N the preceding chapter, I discussed certain relationships between the reproductions and the texts in *Der Blaue Reiter*. By examining the documents surrounding the creation of the almanac, the texts themselves, and the placement of the illustrative material, I was able to deduce the presence of direct, indirect, and complementary relationships. Furthermore, I was able to show how both direct illustrations and indirect illustrations exemplified Kandinsky's claim of the overriding importance of the inner necessities. I also suggested some ways in which the reproductions selected for the almanac might serve as models for further explorations of the essential relations of the arts. While this chapter continues this exclusive attention to *Der Blaue Reiter*, in this case I shall explore the relations of a single text, "Das Verhältnis zum Text," with its accompanying musical example.[1] I want to make clear how a different kind of relation between the arts functions in *Der Blaue Reiter* by studying the relationship to the text in Schoenberg's setting of a poem by Maurice Maeterlinck, *Herzgewächse*.

In Schoenberg's essay, "Das Verhältnis zum Text," he states two contradictory ideas that are only resolved in his music. He writes, first, that there is no clear relation between (literary) text and music that can be grasped outside a rare capacity for "pure vision."[2] Furthermore, the extreme rarity of this capacity serves to elevate the external parallels between the two arts above all common comprehension. Second, Schoenberg insists that there are "higher" inner-congruences between poetry and music, but that these very congruences are beyond the scope of language in the same way that "pure music" is beyond the scope of music criticism. These are indeed paradoxical responses for a composer much of whose work between 1908 and 1914 was based upon literary texts.[3] However, both views are fundamentally in accord with Kandinsky, whose influence Schoenberg explicitly admits in this essay:

> So sind das Symptome für eine allmahlich sich ausbreitende Erkenntnis von dem wahren Wesen der Kunst. Und mit grosser Freude lese ich Kandinskys Buch 'Über das Geistige in der Kunst' in welchem der Weg für die Malerei gezeigt wird und die Hoffnung erwacht, dass jene, die nach dem Text, nach dem Stofflichen fragen, bald ausgefragt haben werden.[4]

The way that Kandinsky shows is toward the same "inner-congruences" (die innerische Übereinstimmung) that Schoenberg names, but does not attempt to describe. Instead, the composer's argument is a somewhat defensive protestation against what others do in the name of music and music criticism. Given the restrictive relationship between music and text, those who pretend to write texts on music might well reexamine their assumptions. Schoenberg accuses music critics of thinking that music with texts is somehow more accessible than pure music: "In absoluter Hilflosigkeit steht er der rein musikalischen Wirkung gegenüber, und deshalb schreibt er lieber über Musik, die sich irgendwie auf Text bezieht: über Programmusik, Lieder, Opern etc."[5] Schoenberg's distrust of music critics goes further than his particular distaste for the ways in which they have misunderstood his music. He attacks the very notion of "parallel effects" in the study of the relationships between music and texts since he finds that such parallels are nearly always "external" and based on a simplistic notion:

> In Wirklichkeit kommen solche Urteile von der allerbanalsten Vorstellung, von einem konventionellen Schema, wonach bestimmten Vorgängen in der Dichtung eine gewisse Tonstärke und Schnelligkeit in der Musik bei absolutem Parallelgehen entsprechen müsse. Abgesehen davon, dass selbst *dieses* Parallelgehen, ja ein noch viel *tieferes*, auch dann stattfinden kann, wenn sich äusserlich scheinbar das Gegenteil davon zeigt, dass also ein zarter Gedanke beispielweise durch ein schnelles und heftiges Thema wiedergegeben wird, weil eine darauffolgende Heftigkeit sich organischer daraus entwickelt, abgesehen davon, ist ein solches Schema schon deshalb verwerflich, weil es konventionell ist. Weil es dazu führte, auch aus der Musik eine Sprache zu machen, die für jeden "dichtet und denkt."[6]

Here, the composer undercuts any notion of absolute parallels by suggesting (in line with Kandinsky's practice of indirect illustration) the effectiveness of contrapuntal (opposing) effects. While any such notion of opposition implies the presence of a conventional expectation, the fact that the opposite effect is just as powerful demonstrates the arbitrariness of the earlier, "banal" convention. Schoenberg's resistance to any method that would appear to make music accessible to "everyone" is consistent with his assertion of the rarity of "purely musical" comprehension.

The most important illustration of Schoenberg's argument is also the most well hidden. By its very position in the book (i.e., its placement in relation to the text for which it serves as an example), it is the most obscure and, if one were to believe Schoenberg, the most difficult to assess. The composer had finally sent his essay to Kandinsky after much hesitation and, apparently, from his own comments, considerable deliberation. Along with his essay, he sent a score that he had just completed as well as two scores by his students, Alban Berg and Anton Von Webern.[7] The music in this case is Schoenberg's *Herzgewächse;* Berg's *Aus dem Gluhenden* von Alfred Mombert; and Webern's *Ihr tratet zu dem Herde* after a poem by Stefan George. The three scores seem to be appended somewhat as an afterthought.

However haphazard the inclusions of the musical examples may appear, their presence is no accident. Kandinsky and Schoenberg had agreed in their correspondence that Schoenberg should write an article.[8] Schoenberg, on his part, had promised to try to provide music as well that would be representative (in his mind) of what Kandinsky and Marc were trying to create across the arts. Schoenberg had, rather at the last minute, changed his subject and then, even later, sent the editors a third essay, "Das Verhältnis zum Text," along with the musical scores.[9]

It should not be surprising that the musical scores might serve as illustrations of Schoenberg's own ideas about the "purely musical point of view" and the paradoxical relations of text and music. While the possible collaborations are twofold—composer and poet (music and poetry) as well as theorist and composer—there is no effort made in the presentation of either the essay by Schoenberg or the musical scores to demonstrate any distinct or preordained relationship. The reader discovers Schoenberg's text, then the music, much later, reading serially, following the last page of the Bühnenkomposition, *Der gelbe Klang,* where it is appended.

The unstated connections thus imposed would conform to Schoenberg's own expectations. His stated premise that the essence of music cannot be translated into criticism is, in this case, carried to its logical conclusion. The scores are simply reproduced with neither introduction nor analysis. In fact, of the three scores, Schoenberg's is in autograph facsimile that is difficult to read, even in the first edition of the almanac. For Schoenberg, this would seem to be a case of reserving the music for those who can readily make it out.[10]

I dwell on the peculiarities of placement in part because it is a vital aspect of Kandinsky's art in *Der Blaue Reiter*. In the case of Arnold Schoenberg, however, there is another, more explicit reason for the positioning of the composition. The musical example he composed and sent to Kandinsky happens to be an excellent direct illustration of his central ideas in "Das Verhältnis zum Text." He bases his composition on a symbolist poem by Maurice Maeterlinck ("Feuillage du Coeur") from *Serres Chaudes*.[11] The poem (which is reproduced here in both the original French and the German translation used by Schoenberg) begins with a purposeful entry into the refined, almost decadent world of symbolist *correspondances*. The original version is written in a highly conventional, eight-syllable line in quatrains rimed *abba cddc effe ghhg*. Maeterlinck's poem stresses interior rhymes and rich musical associations of vowels and consonants. As a short lyric, it is a fitting example of the seemingly simple poems of the symbolists that achieved a complex set of effects from the melodic suggestiveness of the language. Certainly, the intentional mysteriousness of this set of symbols, having accrued value from Nerval and Baudelaire through Verlaine and Mallarmé, must have attracted the composer. Terms like *"le cristal bleu," "les lasses mélancholies," "les vagues douleurs," "végétations de symboles,"* and *"[la] mystique prière blanche"* all have their celebrated parallels in symbolist poets who preceded Maeterlinck.[12] Such poetic diction virtually guarantees the poet a certain tone through repetition. And, similarly, it enriches the range of choices available to the composer as he recommences the text.

Feuillage du Coeur

Sous la cloche de cristal bleu
de mes lasses mélancholies,
Mes vagues douleurs abolies
S'immobilisent peu à peu:

Végétations de symboles,
Nénuphars mornes des plaisirs,
Palmes lentes de mes désirs,
Mousses froides, lianes molles.

Seul, un lys érige d'entre eux,
Pâle et rigidement débile,
Son ascension immobile
Sur les feuillages douloureux

Et dans les lueurs qu'il épanche
Comme une lune, peu a peu
Elève vers le cristal bleu
Sa mystique prière blanche.

Foliage of the Heart

Under the bell of blue crystal
Of my melancholy weariness
My vague abolished pains
were, little by little, immobilized:

Symbolic vegetation,
White water lilies sad with pleasure,
Slow palms of my desires,
Cold mosses, indolent lianes.

Alone, one lily rises among them,
Pale and stiffly weak,
its immobile ascent
Over the mournful foliages

And in the beams that it discharges
like a moon, little by little
rises toward the blue crystal
its mystical white prayer.

Herzgewächse

Meiner müden Sehnsucht blaues Glas
deckt den alten unbestimmten Kummer,
dessen Ich genas,
und der nun erstarrt in seinem Schlummer.

Sinnbildhaft ist seiner Blumen Zier:
Mancher Freuden düstre Wasserrose,
Palmen der Begier,
weiche Schlinggewächse, kühle Moose,

Eine Lilie nur in all dem Flor,
bleich und starr in ihrer Kränklichkeit
richtet sich empor
über all dem Blattgeword'nen Leid

licht sind ihre Blätter anzuschauen,
Weissen Mondesglanz sie um sich sät
zum Krystall dem blauen
sendet sie ihr mystisches Gebet.

The Fond Heart

My weary longings of blue glass
guard the old unnamed sorrow,
from which I recover,
and which now grows numb in slumber.

Full of symbols is its floral profusion:
The waterlily darkens many joys,
Palms of desire,
Soft swaying creepers, cool moss,

Only one lily in all the flora,
Pale and motionless in its sickliness
Stands erect aloft
Over all leafbecoming grief

Light appeared its petals,
White moonbeams it sows around it
Up to the blue crystal
It sent its mystical prayer.[13]

In the German translation that Schoenberg used, the speaker complains of his "müden Sehnsucht blaues Glas." In symbolist conventions, this line expresses the artist's impossible yearning for transcendence.[14] He declares that he has almost defeated this temptation ("dessen ich genas") when he is suddenly attracted to the world of plants that surrounds him (a world not unlike Baudelaire's *"fôret de symboles"* in the poem "Correspondances"). However, in "Herzgewächse," the forest metaphor has been narrowed to "seiner Blumen Zier," a floral profusion. We might note here how much the German version has refined Maeterlinck's purposefully suggestive phrase, *"végétations de symboles."* The speaker begins the second stanza by remarking that all the blooms have become *"Sinnbildhaft."* This transfiguration is the key to the symbolic action of the rest of the poem. Naming mysterious forces in the flowers, the speaker enumerates a series of identifications between plants and human feelings. These identities set a tone and an expectation for the reader. *"Wasserrosen," "Palmen," "Schlinggewächse,"* and *"Moose"* (waterlilies, palms, lianes, mosses) are all names with personifying adjectives, thus evoking the symbolic meaning of each. Yet, in the second stanza, the associations (symbolic meanings) of the plants are merely juxtaposed, leaving the dominant tone of the poem to suggest the lines of correspondence. In the third stanza, the speaker singles out one flower from all the others and makes it his symbolic example.

Unlike allegory, wherein the reader is given a direct scheme of transference from the literal to the allegorical, the speaker here refuses to make clear the meaning of the miraculous vision of the single lily. Ambiguity is the profession of the symbolist and one assumes that the transcendence of the lily is a paradigm of beatific vision enacted in a world that is fully *Sinnbildhaft* (wherein we may interpret the flower as representing an ideal). In its saintly paleness, the lily transcends its immediate reality to reach the pure light of the mystical. The transcendence is also a symbolic representation of the spiritual experience of the speaker. In the latter case, both the flower *qua* flower and the flower as visionary correlative of the mystical experience are upheld in the poem. In either case, the function of the symbol in standing both for itself and for what it symbolizes sustains an ambiguity that is essential to the full meaning of the poem. It is possible, in this sense, to associate the lily with Christ, since the overlapping Christian symbolism is obvious (as are the allusions to palms, if not *Palmen der Begier,* as well as the singularity of Jesus' Resurrection), though there is no necessary reason why the image of Christ need be invoked in place of a number of other saints and mystics. It is one advantage of symbolist procedures that the experience of transcendence can take precedence over the identity of the one who transcends. Whether one prefers a Christian reading or a different mystical stance in which the *blaues Glas* and *Krystall den Blauen* are part of *l'azure idéel* of a Mallarmé, the poem breaks into distinct movements and Schoenberg uses this rhetorical division to organize his setting of the poem to music.

The first part of the song corresponds to the first quatrain of the poem. Schoenberg sets the voice and mood of the speaker before beginning the symbolic description. At this point, the music is tentative and the composer "positions the voice (a high coloratura soprano [to *F* in alt], with celesta, harmonium, and harp) in the low to

Example 1.

Mei - ner   mü - den Sehn   -   sucht blau - es   Glas   -

Example 2.

deckt den al - ten un   -   be - stimm-ten   Kum   -   mer,

Example 3.

und der nun er - starrt   in   sei - nem   Schlum - mer.

middle range register" which could be said to fit the meditative, melancholy tone evoked by the text.[15] The controlling mood of the first
quatrain is melancholia, and the musical attention that is paid to
words in phrases like *"müden Sehnsucht blaues Glas," "alten unbestimmten Kummer,"* and *"und der nun erstarrt in seinem Schlummer"* creates a
darkness in tone and mood that is enhanced by the tempo and by
the relatively small intervals.[16]

The second part of the musical organization (which corresponds
to the second quatrain of the poem) recreates the movement of transition in the poem wherein the speaker shifts from what is primarily
an evocation of a state of mind to a declaration of the essential du-
ality of the world of the poem. The language of the poem moves
from the self to the landscape, represented by the foliage through
metonymy. The first assertion ("Sinnbildhaft ist seiner Blumen Zier")

Example 4.

links the speaker's perception with the perceived in a special relationship. Musically this perception is expressed both as literal and as freighted with another, implied level of meaning. Schoenberg accentuates and punctuates the key word *(Sinnbildhaft)* by isolation, but does not dramatize or attempt to imitate the meaning musically.

Example 5.

- ser - ro - se,   Pal   -   men der Be - gier,

   The symbolic names are likewise punctuated and annunciated by
the vocal *gesang* without intervention or counterpoint on the part of
either harmonium or harp. The third line of this quatrain, *"Palmen
der Begier" (Palmes lentes de mes désirs),* however, evokes a significantly
greater range in the setting, and the vocalist must execute intervals
that introduce the widening range demanded in the score (see example 5). For Schoenberg, these demands in range and quick interval
changes were not entirely new since the most startling and innovative sections of Stefan George's *Das Buch der Hängenden Garten,* Op.
15 (1909) and Marie Pappenheim's *Erwartung,* Op. 17 (1909) had
already introduced rapid and extreme intervals to express the emotional force of particular sections of text. In the setting for *Herzgewächse,* there is a gradual buildup of these demanding sections from
measures 10–11 through measures 16–19, 21–22, and 23–25. This
expansion is climaxed in the final vocal measures (27–29; see examples 7, 8, and 9).
   In none of these cases is there a melodic repetition. Nor is there a
distinct motivic device. Rather, the music is created in an ordered
series of shapes that gives the setting an emphasis centered on the
developing inner-drama symbolized in the speaker's vision in the final two quatrains of the poem. The poem itself, while incorporating
three movements, is neither highly stressed nor dramatic. A recita-
tion of the poem, either in German or in the original French, would
normally remain subdued to the end since the symbolic action
achieves its effect without emotiveness. The music, though, exposes
and then parallels the inner-drama of the ascent of the single lily.

Example 6.

Example 7.

Schoenberg's music creates, by analogy rather than imitatively or programmatically, the inner-drama of the action through the tension of the dramatic leaps of the soprano. The contrapuntal movements of the harmonium, celesta, and harp underscore the shapes of the vocal part without creating conventional harmonic accompaniment. For example, in measures 24 and 25 (ex. 8), the harp first descends, then ascends as the vocal part works toward the spectacular high notes of measures 27 and 28 (ex. 9). The sense here of the separate parts is not to create harmony but rather to balance a movement. While the harp counterpoints the vocal part in these measures, its downward direction prepares the listener for the ascending notes of the soprano in measure 27 and the descending notes in measures 28 and 29. Thus the accompaniment anticipates the dramatic changes in the vocal part and suggests a feature of the movement of the last notes of the setting. Yet, these features do not conform with the previous conventions of the art song.

Such measure-by-measure analysis of the setting shows that Schoenberg's use of the text is neither that of the musical illustration nor a close accompaniment. How, then, can I claim that,

Example 8.

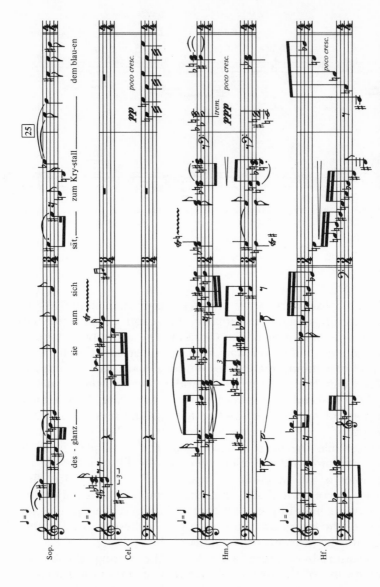

in this short song, Schoenberg's method of composing is nonetheless based on the meanings and values of the text? While avoiding the appearance of strict adherence to the word-by-word or line-by-line interpretation of the text, Schoenberg does create a complementary interpretation of the text which functions as a collaborative effort in the presentation of the composite work. In *Herzgewächse,* in spite of its position in Schoenberg's *oeuvre* and its brevity, the readers of *Der Blaue Reiter* were given an exemplary score of the new music. They were also presented with yet another model of collaboration. If the setting is still somewhat strange and difficult for the contemporary listener, how much more so it must have seemed to listeners in 1912. However, the composer's choices, first of a text and then of the manner of composing, were not so random as his critics have claimed.

While one effect of the music is to create the higher inner-congruences the composer writes of in "Das Verhältnis zum Text," another is to make use of the theoretical base for music that has dispensed with the conventional bases of tonality and harmony. The relation in this case between music and text is not so much that of adding an art form to an art form as it is using two forms to create a whole. As Schoenberg was later to explain, during the crucial period of his experimentation (1908–15), poetic texts were the necessary source of structural ideas for his music:

There are of course various means of different value with which to produce formal cohesion within a piece of music. One of these means, tonal harmony, with its emphasis on tonal centers, guaranteed not only cohesion, but also made for clarity of design by articulating the constituent parts. By not using this device in the new direction that my music had taken, I was compelled, in the first place, to renounce not only the construction of larger forms, but to avoid the employment of larger melodies—as well as all formal musical elements dependent upon the frequent repetition of motifs. It seemed at first impossible to find pertinent substitutes for these through musical means. Unwittingly, and therefore rightly, I found help where music always finds it when it has reached a crucial point in its development. *This, and this alone,* is the origin of what is called Expressionism *(Expressionismus):* a piece of music does not create its formal appearance out of the logic of its own material, but, guided by the feeling for the internal and external processes, and in *bringing these into expression,* it supports itself on their logic and builds up that. No new procedure in the history of music!—at each renewal or increase of musical materials,

93

Example 9.

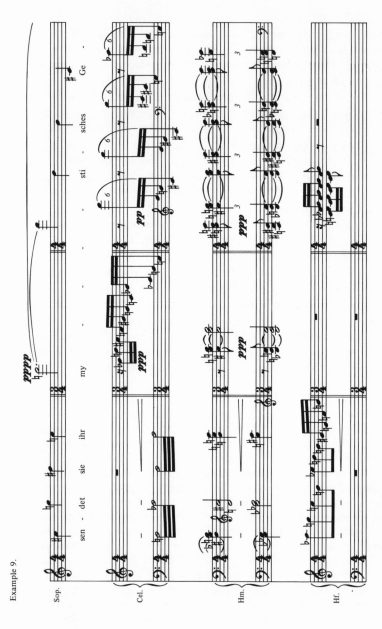

Example 10.

it is assisted by feelings, insights, occurrences, impressions, and the like, *mainly in the form of poetry*—whether it be in the period of the first operas, of the lied or of program music.[17]

By consciously depriving himself of the very methods needed to organize his music, Schoenberg was forced to resort to nonmusical elements to provide cohesion to the composition (as a poet might introduce outside elements such as a series of paintings or photographs to accompany his poem).[18] He describes his operations as guided by feeling around the framework of his own response to the outside element: the poetic text. Speaking of the period 1908–15, he writes, "I continued to prefer composing music for texts, and I was still dependent purely upon my feeling for form.[19] The selection is also a necessity, although Schoenberg's preference for literary texts rather than paintings, monuments, or pictures at an exhibition distinguishes both his practice and his resulting compositions. His explanations clarify the necessity of the text in his works (and these comments should be juxtaposed to those in the essay "Das Verhältnis zum Text"): "As always during the first decade of a new style of composing, music theory has in this case not progressed nearly far enough. The other consideration, however, is that compositions for texts are inclined to allow the poem to determine, at least outwardly, their form. To be sure, this tendency can generally be noted less in songs than in dramatic or choral music. Yet here, in my Opus 22 it appears conspicuously for the above mentioned reasons."[20]

From Schoenberg's comments as well as from his practice, one might wish to conclude that the function of the text is qualitatively different for those composers who are involved in radical innovation than for others. Where the innovator rejects the fundamental organizational patterns of his form (in this case tonality, tonal harmony, and the emphasis on tonal centers), he must in the interim give more value to the form and meaning of the text than might heretofore have been expected. Yet, the value given to the text will not necessarily be reflected directly in the composition.

The new style of composition emphasizes new musical relationships between the notes and the elements of the setting. It fragments and reorders the traditional expectations of both the harmonic structures and tonal patterns. The relation between the music and the text cannot be like that of earlier, traditional examples since the base of any such relationship is necessarily in question. Thus, where earlier ideas of setting may have included melodies, tonal centers, harmonic relations, repeated fragments (motifs) and various attempts at musical imitation or illustration, the new method Schoenberg employs eschews all the traditional methods of marking and emphasizing the text (whereby the setting normally makes clear its musical relation with the text in lieder, opera, and program music). Instead, the composer works to express his "feeling for form" by means of the text. Schoenberg is purposefully vague on this point both in his letters and in this lecture, but his reference on several occasions to

Expressionismus is rich in its associations.[21] He connects the larger movement explicitly with his own procedure and implies that his own creative process, in his search for radical innovation in form, results in an approach to each work that is intuitive. He stresses the Expressionist emphasis on the "inner-congruence" of feeling, a balance of the outer (musical, logical) with the inner (spiritual, emotional). If such a procedure strikes the reader as something of the old ideal of the balance between the classical and the Romantic, it should be remembered that the composer, during the period in question, kept his faith in his classical instinct and his musical logic while casting himself adrift from the formal order of the tradition. Schoenberg's works and his comments show him seeking the new musical expression through his feeling, his inspiration, and his intuitions (in his mind a kind of *Expressionismus* that does not throw reason or the classical tradition overboard). The adventure may sound conservative when paralleled to those of Kokoschka, Trakl, Marinetti, or Scriabin, but in the larger context of European Expressionism, there is much to compare in Schoenberg's formal innovations and those of Wassily Kandinsky, Frank Wedekind, George Kaiser, and Mary Wigman. Schoenberg's achievements make the most complete sense when seen in this larger context. The attitudes and feelings of his friends, many of whom were seminal figures of Expressionism, are present in the writings, the works, and the reminiscences of the composer. From Stefan George and Richard Dehmels to Julios Hart, Kandinsky, Kokoschka, Adolf Loos, Busoni, and Berg, there are, among his friends, numerous examples of creative people who worked simultaneously toward new means of expression in the several arts. The curious figure of Arnold Schoenberg, the Expressionist painter (1910–13), is important as evidence of the composer's part in the Expressionist outburst. Yet we value these paintings not for their quality but rather for what they do to fill out the image of a conservative, somewhat academic, music teacher who dared to break the mold and exhibit hauntingly naive oils full of those very emotions and energies that he recalls in his backward glances.[22] Kandinsky's elimination of questions of form served no better purpose than the resultant praise of Schoenberg's work, a praise greater than a mere gesture of friendship, a praise of the spiritual. Where, in the world of music, Schoenberg's remarks concerning the crisis he felt in music and his difficulties in working his way through it might be seen as symptoms of a self-induced revolution, from a different perspective, they appear in the context of *Der Blaue Reiter* in concord with the larger cultural trend that Schoenberg recognized, retroactively, as Expressionism.

The larger relation between music and the Expressionist movement is not at issue here, for the problem of defining requisite analogies between the formal innovations achieved by the arts of Expressionism would necessitate a work beyond the scope of this book, much less this chapter. However, Schoenberg's works during his crisis (1908–15) and the methods and procedures he developed during this period do suggest at least discernible and important relations between a man, his music, and the most vital cultural phenomenon of his time. The possibility that he is the greatest composer of the Expressionist movement is only qualified by the fact that he may be the only composer for whom an adequate case can be made.

FIVE

THE STAGE COMPOSITION
Der gelbe Klang

T HE 1982 premiere of Kandinsky's "color opera," *Der gelbe Klang,*
brings into question once again the nature of collaboration in
the painter's work.[1] There can be no doubt that the Solomon
Guggenheim Foundation went to extraordinary lengths to see the
obscure stage work performed for the first time ever and, judging
from the wealth of Kandinsky's works that the Guggenheim museum
has documented and exhibited since its inception, one might well
have expected an extraordinary effort in the theatrical production.
Thomas de Hartmann's heretofore lost music makes a whole performance out of what otherwise had always been a collaborative work
with one part absent. In fact, Gunther Schuller's organization of
Thomas de Hartmann's fragmentary score, his original composition
of the missing parts, and his orchestration of the combined scores
did not merely add an element to the *Bühnenkomposition,* they made
the complete performance of *Der gelbe Klang* possible.[2]

The effect of this music in *Der gelbe Klang* is remarkable. The orchestral parts are here established as integral to the performance, so
that we can no longer imagine the *Bühnenkomposition* without the
musical element. Yet, two-thirds of that contribution belongs to
Gunther Schuller. (Future performances will have to credit the music
to two composers.) We may never know whether de Hartmann completed a full score for *Der gelbe Klang.* The fragments discovered in
the de Hartmann papers may have been all the composer ever finished. If that is the case, we have a new understanding of why no
score was published with *Der gelbe Klang* in *Der Blaue Reiter* even
though different scores by Schoenberg, Webern, and Berg were appended. It may even be clearer now why Stanislavsky could not understand the work when de Hartmann suggested it for the Moscow

Art Theater in 1914. We also understand why it would have been so difficult to perform the play at the *Volksbühne* in Berlin in 1922 or later in the Bauhaus under the direction of Oskar Schlemmer. In all likelihood, there was never a completed score. Yet the format and movement of the work depended on the integral effects of orchestral and choral music. Kandinsky's comment explaining why he turned down the *Volksbühne* offer in 1922 is absolutely literal. It was not the musical direction of the composer that he (still) needed; it was a score. De Hartmann had never finished his part of the collaboration. As I shall show in my analysis of *Der gelbe Klang* as collaborative form, the work is built upon two primary effects: the visual and the aural. To subtract one of these (or the most important part of one) leaves the viewer with nothing. It will be Gunther Schuller's lasting contribution that he re-created and reintroduced the missing part for the *Bühnenkomposition*. Schuller's collaboration with de Hartmann more than compensated for the weaknesses that critics found in the Guggenheim New York production of *Der gelbe Klang*. He deserves much credit for resurrecting Kandinsky's apocalypse. Future performances will correct whatever minor defects in lighting, sets, and choreography might have detracted from Kandinsky's ideal performance.

In any case, this production of Kandinsky's "color opera" demonstrates an enduring interest in avant-garde works that combine the arts even if these art works are obscure and reputedly unproducible. Certainly for those who have studied Kandinsky's career, *Der gelbe Klang* has held a special attraction since its first publication in *Der Blaue Reiter* in 1912. Kandinsky evidently thought it a model of what he called "stage composition" (*Bühnenkomposition*) and composed a special, introductory essay, "Über Bühnenkomposition," to prepare readers of *Der Blaue Reiter* for his synthesis of the arts.

Kandinsky first wrote of the possibilities for combining the arts as an aside in *Über das Geistige in der Kunst,* a book he wrote in 1910. While there was no necessary connection between the theory of abstraction he was working toward and the actual collaborations he was, at the same time, composing, the subject of the relations of the arts was clearly a natural outgrowth of the painter's interest in the spiritual. Moreover, once Kandinsky declares (as he does in the title of *Über das Geistige in der Kunst*) that his topic is art and not just painting, he characteristically draws on examples from all of the arts (music, dance, sculpture, poetry, drama, painting). In the same text, he suggests that the relation of the arts is fundamental to all the arts and that this relation is best demonstrated in works that incorporate more than one art. "The various arts," he writes, "have never been closer to each other than in this recent hour of spiritual crisis."[3] He seems to sense a new direction for all the arts when he declares, "In each expression (in each art) there is the seed of an effort toward the nonrepresentational, abstract, and internal structure" (CSA, 39). The original thrust toward the nonrepresentational is his own, though he projects it upon such other artists as Matisse and Picasso.[4] Kandinsky's idea of abstraction in the arts—he speaks of dance and music as well as painting—is unique in 1909 and yet, remarkably enough, it is difficult to tell whether abstraction (as it is described by the painter in these passages) originates in Isadora Duncan's dances, Arnold Schoenberg's string quartet (No. 2, Op. 10, 1908), or in painting. Instead of attempting to make one art (such as he nearly does with music) the touchstone for all the others, Kandinsky bases his vision of the relations of the arts upon the inner-necessity of the artist. The demands of the "internal" then become the underlying assumption of all his judgments. Similarly, what had begun as an aesthetic argument changes into a religious (almost theosophical) treatise complete with hints of prophecies and dark warnings of spiritual crisis.

At the end of his essay, he turns to examples of how the arts are related as his final demonstration of the spiritual in art. "The painter naturally seeks to apply the means of music ('the least material of the arts today') to his own art. And from this results that modern desire for rhythm in painting for mathematical abstract construction, for repeated notes of color, for setting color in motion and so on" (CSA, 40). Each of these phrases was literally applied in the Bühnenkompositionen of the same period, for it was in these works rather than in his painting that Kandinsky first tried out the lessons of the spiritual in art. The composition of Der gelbe Klang and two other Bühnenkompositionen (Der grünen Klang and Schwarz und Weiss) occurred, as far as we can tell, before the completion of Über das Geistige in der Kunst.[5]

The central comparative term in Kandinsky's analysis of the arts is the German word Klang, which means both "tone" (a musical note) and "sound" (with broader connotations that range from vocal or instrumental sounds to speech and noises). While this choice emphasizes a musical analogy (part of Kandinsky's claim that music is "the most advanced art"), the Klänge of paintings, poems, and dances (or, more specifically of colors, motions, points, lines, and sounds) are described as the essential inner-connections between the arts. For

Kandinsky, the medium of relation is the soul of the perceiver. The *Klänge* of the different elements of the arts, either singly, or in combination, strike receptive chords in the soul of the observer (literally create "Seelenvibrationen," vibrations in the soul).

Kandinsky notes that "comparison of means among the arts and the learning of one art from another can only be successful when the application of the lesson is fundamental. One art must learn how another uses its method, so that its own means may then be used according to the same fundamental principles, but in its own medium" (*CSA,* 40). For Kandinsky, the term *fundamental* is here equated to the spiritual. All other matters in the arts must follow from that equation. The object of comparing the arts, then, will not be to seek out minor analogies or parallel structures. The "inner" is invoked on all occasions where the spirit and the emotions of the artist strive to find adequate expression. While Kandinsky understands the external differences between the arts, he declares that all the arts are responses to the same spiritual necessity. To him, this makes all the arts identical at the level of the spiritual and creates the internal identity of all forms. This step opens the way for the abstraction of these forms, which before had not seemed possible to him.

Following a careful elucidation of the *Klänge* of the different arts, Kandinsky presents, at the end of the essay, an outline of what he calls *"Monumentalkunst"* (the "monumental art work"), which, he predicts, will be the future form of the arts. His own introduction to this form proposes that the synthesis of the *Klänge* of the different arts would create an entirely new effect. The origin of this notion may have been the effect of Isadora Duncan's dances:

> In search for more subtle expression, modern reformers have looked to the past. Isadora Duncan forged a link between Greek dancing and the future. In this she is working parallel to those painters who are looking for inspiration in the primitives. In dance, as in painting, this is a stage of transition. In both mediums we are on the threshold of a future art. The same law, utilization of pure motion, which is the principal element of dance, applies to painting too. Conventional beauty must go, and the literary element, "story-telling" or "anecdote" must be abandoned. Both arts must learn from music that every harmony and every discord that springs from internal necessity is beautiful (i.e., functional) but it is essential that they spring from internal necessity alone. The "ugly" movements of modern dance become beautiful and

emanate an undreamt-of strength and living force. At this point the dance of the future begins. (*CSA*, 50–51; *UGK*, 107–8)

Kandinsky's interest in Isadora Duncan is informed by his awareness that the purity of her motion in dance is analogous to that of motion in painting. The belief that both dancers and painters might profit from the study of the structures of harmony and dissonance in music supports his earlier claim that music is further advanced toward abstraction in the pyramid of the arts.[6] He then concludes with a preliminary definition of the *Monumentalkunstwerk:*

> The dance of the future, today on a level with music and painting, will help to realize stage composition, the first form of a monumental art.
>   Composition for the new theater will consist of these elements:
>   (1) Musical movement
>   (2) Pictorial movement
>   (3) Dance movement
> Regarding pictorial composition everyone will understand the threefold effect of the inner movement (stage composition). Just as the two main elements of painting (drawing and pictorial form) may exist independently, each speaking its own language, as from a combination of these elements painterly composition arises, so it may be possible on the stage to organize the above three movements into an harmonious or contrapuntal composition. (*CSA*, 72; *UGK*, 108–9)

This is the earliest mention in Kandinsky's published writings of the "stage composition," i.e., *Bühnenkomposition*, and it corresponds exactly with his early experiments in the form. Although he does not elucidate how or in how many ways the three movements (i.e., art forms) can be combined, he does return to musical terminology to suggest that the separate forms may either be used to create a composite harmony or a counterpoint (either a combinative effect or an off-setting effect). The *Klänge* of the separate arts will then combine in ways analogous to combinations of notes and chords in music or of colors in painting. It remains for the artists of the *Bühnenkomposition* to derive the rules of combination.

While it may have seemed at the time to have been wishful prophecy, particularly when the quoted passage virtually completes his reference to the new form, two factors explain both Kandinsky's presentation of the concept of monumental art and the abruptness of that presentation. First, the idea is an extension of his argument through the entire book. For, if the arts are linked by an inner identity, then the *Klänge* of each of the arts might very well be composed to work together. Second (and here Kandinsky follows his normal practice of achieving the first example of his innovation before suggesting its theoretical possibility), he had already written at least two *Bühnenkompositionen* before completing *Über das Geistige in der Kunst* in 1910. Hence, what might have seemed to some readers to have been ideal speculations were in fact the first hints of a new form, already created in several versions.

The first two stage compositions, *Schwarz und Weiss* and *Grüner Klang* were written in Russian in 1909 and never published.[7] In Kandinsky's notebooks at the Städtische Galerie in Munich are two handwritten manuscripts of plays in German from the period 1909– 10. One of these plays is titled "Bühnenkomposition III, *Schwarz und Weiss*" and is a transcription into German of the earlier play. The other was given only the title "Bühnenkomposition I."[8] It is difficult to date Kandinsky's writings with great accuracy since he wrote in both Russian and German during this period and most of his Russian manuscripts have been lost. He apparently rewrote *Der gelbe Klang* several times between its inception (c. 1909), calling it during this period *Die Riesen,* and its publication in early 1912, when it came out under its present title. He chose to revise *Die Riesen* when he found that he might actually be able to publish a collaborative book. Although he subsequently published one section of the other play he wrote during that period (*Violett* [1914]), *Der gelbe Klang* is the only fully published stage composition.[9] It also served in *Der Blaue Reiter* as the single example of his theory of the *Bühnenkomposition:*

> In a perfected stage composition both elements will be increased by the third, endless possibilities of combination and individual use will be opened up. The external can be combined with the internal harmony as Schoenberg has done in his quartets. In them we see how much internal harmony gains in force and significance when outer harmony is used in this sense. It is impossible here to develop this idea. The reader can apply for himself the principles of painting already stated to the problem of stage composition and can have the happy dream of the theater of the future. (*UGK,* 109; *CSA,* 72)

Considering the minimum attention that monumental art was given in *Über das Geistige in der Kunst,* it might have ended as a "happy dream" (*der glückvolle Traum* [*der Zukunftsbühne*]). However, the publication in *Der Blaue Reiter* of the essays "Über die Formfrage" and "Über Bühnenkomposition" as well as *Der gelbe Klang* served to bring reality to the reader's dream.[10]

Both essays expand Kandinsky's views about combining the arts. "Über die Formfrage" attempts to shock the reader of 1912 by destroying the traditional importance attached to the concept of form. The argument of the essay, though, is not to destroy form, but rather to establish the equivalence of all forms, thus making the question of form a nonissue.[11]

The second essay, "Über Bühnenkomposition," serves a more prophetic purpose by elucidating the remarks about monumental art as stated in *Über das Geistige in der Kunst.* In this essay, Kandinsky reiterates his contention that the traditional divisions between the arts have become unimportant in light of their internal identity. Given the diversity of the modes of expression (tone, word, color, line, motion), he argues for a more powerful and more complete expression (as in monumental art). Combining the separate forms (whether in a harmony or in a dissonance) expresses their identical spiritual base more fully. Only where the arts (and here Kandinsky thinks of his own *Bühnenkompositionen*) are composed together and then organized in performance will monumental art occur. He dismisses the Wagnerian pursuit of the *Gesamtkunstwerk* as merely historically interesting, though a failure. In Wagner, the nineteenth-century arts (drama, opera, ballet) were juxtaposed according to their "external effects," a fact that limited their combined potential. For Kandinsky, a broad spectrum of potential interactions exists between the extreme poles of realism and abstraction: "Eine Reihe von Kombinationen, die Zwischenden zwei Polen liegen: Mitwirkung and Gegen Wirkung."[12] The chords, overtones, and counterpoints create a new work from the collaboration of the separate arts. Each form strengthens and grounds the others so that the effect of the whole is different from that of the additive parts. This much of Kandinsky's theory of combination was written after the two preliminary plays (*Grüner Klang* [1909] and *Schwarz und Weiss* [1909]) and after the first *Bühnenkomposition (Der gelbe Klang)*. Given its place in *Der Blaue Reiter*, "Über Bühnenkomposition" quite literally explains the goals of *Der gelbe Klang.*

However, in both his theories of painting and his theories of monumental art, Kandinsky had reached a level of abstraction for which there were no extant models. Like the generation of physicists who were his contemporaries, he compensated for the absence of concrete examples by creating an ideal model. The *Bühnenkompositionen* were composed as "ideal" works in which the predicted interactions of the elements of the theater were projected in the mind in much the same way that the physicists imagined the interactions of the atomic particles in "ideal experiments."[13] Ideal drama is the projection into the future of interactions on a stage that is not yet invented.[14] For Kandinsky (and for the stage of 1910–12), certainly propositions concerning an "infinite horizon" and three or four different, but simultaneous lighting depths were ideal projections. The physical projections of spots and colors, giants that float and increase in size, and vague shapes that change hue and vanish seem fantastic even today. In *Der gelbe Klang,* pictured events alter swiftly and mysteriously. Kandinsky's deletion of the plot and his "suppression of the anecdotal" (in fact, of all external contexts for sense-making) render the work even more difficult to stage. It should not be surprising, then, that it should have taken more than fifty years to produce an accurate premiere performance. Even fifty years after the play's composition, certain effects that Kandinsky contrived through the interaction of the different elements of the *Bühnenkomposition* were not effectively produced.[15] At critical moments in his scenario, his directions (if taken literally) exceed the capacity of even the most modern theaters of Europe. There is a simple explanation. Kandinsky's theater was of the mind, not the stage. The *Bühnenkompositionen* were first "poetic" theater whose allegiance was to no material stage or performing hall. They cannot be treated like the plays of Strindberg or Wedekind, for they have little literary value. They remain a curious combination of painting, opera, choreography, and poem to be danced upon a stage whose depths and heights are as expressive as any single motion on the stage.

And when modern critics remark about the several "failures" to produce the play, they should recall the fact that Kandinsky did produce an impressive number of avant-garde activities on several fronts and in several fields in the brief time he was in Munich. From the Phalanx to the NKVM and the books, paintings, exhibits, and sundry collaborations of *Der Blaue Reiter,* he seemed remarkably competent at accomplishing his goals. That he never produced *Der gelbe Klang* is not purely accidental. It was not just that the music was never quite finished. The physical production of the *Bühnenkompositionen* was never really necessary. Each of the compositions was an exploration in the relations of the arts that allowed Kandinsky the freedom to try out the new ideas he had discovered in his paintings.

As we can see in *Über das Geistige,* his was an expansive mind and his ideas at this time seemed to go beyond the canvases he was painting. The stage compositions were the necessary bridges between the lessons of his new painting and the other arts.

In the following interpretation, I shall describe the events in *Der gelbe Klang* and link them to Kandinsky's theories.[16] In so doing, I want to try to reconstruct the ideal experiment and explain how it was to work both as a stage production (using the recent production as a model) and as an illustration of the ideal of the *Monumentalkunstwerk.* In *Der gelbe Klang,* the approaches and retreats of the *Innerklang* of the colors, music, lights, movements, and sounds combine before the viewer and the reader to produce a moving picture in real space.

The composition begins with a "Prelude for Orchestra, Choir, and Tenor Voice." This overture is followed by six consecutive "pictures" (*Bilde*) which function as short scenes. The cast features five yellow giants (left from the original text, *Die Riesen*) who move without touching the floor. Accompanying the giants in the second picture are a dozen red figures having the abstract form of "birds." Through all of the succeeding pictures, there appear colored forms sometimes referred to as flowers (even though they change their shape and color) which hover in the inner recesses of the stage. Other forms— the mountains, rocks, small figures, and humans, for example—combine the functions of sets, props, and characters. These forms also move, change color, and cover one another at times. In the later pictures, there are also several groups of life-sized human dancers (in pictures III, IV, and V).

As he suggests in *Über das Geistige,* Kandinsky conceives his *Bühnenkomposition* along the lines of "the modern dance of Isadora Duncan."[17] There is no plot, no exterior controlling structure, and only a minimal cause-and-effect relationship between the events that are described as occurring on the stage. Moments of dramatic potential are integrated into the larger rhythm of destruction and renewal. The motion of the composition is thus one of rapid fluctuation between combinations and subsequent negations of these combinations. This structure, in turn, is based on a musical analogy. The brief thematic statements in the prelude and the first pictures are then given new development through repetition and variation. Kandinsky composes from the full palette of the arts, however, and any theme can therefore be stated in a number of ways provided the theme is "fundamental." The composer can choose from words, movements, colors, lighting intensities, choral music, and instrumental music to restate or vary his themes.

The staging itself presents a particularly difficult problem for readers and producers alike. Parts of Kandinsky's work appear to make impossible demands upon the physical stage. Yet, some of those very elements that appeared impossible to produce in 1912 are now within the capacity of numerous theaters. Technical advances in lighting and projection since that time have made the presentation of the yellow giants, the red flying figures, the changing hues and colors seem almost the normal fare of multimedia theater. Numerous contemporary productions of light and sound, of film projections, and of multiple lighting combinations make Kandinsky's visions almost conventional.[18] Even so, the most difficult proposition of *Der gelbe Klang*, the idea of the stage itself, still resists solution. The newest theater in Munich in 1909 when Kandinsky composed this work was the Munich Artists' Theater; even though it was considered a model of the latest concepts in stage production, it was constructed with strict stylistic limitations. Like most conventional stages of the time, it was a three-sided box, elevated somewhat in front of a larger space for audience seating. The major difference between the Munich Artists' Theater and the other, "conventional" theaters in Munich and other German cities was the shallowness of the stage.[19] In this aspect, the Artist's Theater followed the ideas of the most celebrated prewar stage designers, Adolph Appia and Gordon Craig. However, even this innovation did not fundamentally change the shape or alter the limitations of the stage.

The most impressive subsequent example of Expressionist architecture and stage design, the *Grosses Schauspielhaus* in Berlin, did little more to alter the essential presuppositions of stage design in spite of the enormous increase in seating capacity and an impressive decorative effect in the interior of the theater itself.[20] The stage of the *Grosses Schauspielhaus* was not appreciably different, except in size, from the opera houses and theaters built in the previous centuries. Kandinsky's stage (as described in *Der gelbe Klang*) is not merely an adaptation of existing stages. He proposes instead a painter's stage in which he creates the same abstract four-dimensional space implied in his canvases during this same period: "Die Bühne muss hier möglichst tief sein. Ganz weit hinten ein breiter grüner Hügel. Hinter dem Hügel glatter, matter, blauer, ziemlich tieffarbiger Vorhang."[21] The first aim of these directions is to dematerialize the dimensions of the stage. They occur at the beginning of *Bild* 1, the first point in the composition where the stage is fully visible to the audience. The three-dimensioned box that constituted the realist stage is here immediately superceded. There will be no depth created by the usual placement of objects on and around the stage, since no such objects—chairs, windows, curtains, or carpets—are onstage to suggest familiar space. Instead, colors—the green of the hill and the blue of the backdrop—are to create through their psychological effects intermediate planes of action. There is no limit to the depths to which the blue of the backdrop can recede. Hence, the effect of infinite space.

This much of the spatial illusion of the *Bühnenkomposition* is paralleled in Kandinsky's paintings of the same period. He had rejected the traditional painterly illusions of perspective at the same time that he turned to nonobjective elements in his canvases. Thus, as his paintings became less and less figurative, he found he had to apply new techniques to re-create the illusion of space and depth on the flat canvas. In his stage directions, as in his paintings, Kandinsky creates a different technique for suggesting the visual planes perceived by the viewer. He replaces the traditional "open box" stage with the idea of the "open window" stage through which the audience views the stage space as through a picture window (beyond which the illusions of distances and depths are vastly enlarged). On the stage, these illusions are created through multiple planes, lighting, and stage movements.

Kandinsky suggests new spatial dimensions without using foreshortening and without attempting any of the realistic conventions for suggesting space (i.e., a large painted set or a scenic backdrop). Instead, he creates several planes of depth on the stage by means of a series of spaces juxtaposed against the infinite background of blues and blacks. By controlling the lighting effects and color changes at certain depths of this setting, Kandinsky reinforces the complex spatial illusion. He increases the feeling of expanded space by placing the orchestra and choir behind and off the stage so that neither group of performers can be seen. The audience perceives sounds, colors, lights, and forms moving in and out from in front of a large, open window as selected examples of a large and infinitely more complex spiritual universe. Only in the final pictures (in *Bilde* 4, 5, and 6) do we have a sense of the window-stage becoming the local space for significant action.

When in *Über das Geistige in der Kunst* Kandinsky wrote of the ways an "ideal plane may be created" in front of the material plane of the

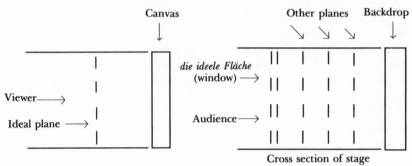

Fig. 11.   Fig. 12.

canvas,[22] he describes an effect parallel to that he hoped to create with his stage composition (figures 11 and 12). Through the movement of color, line, and form, this illusion (the ideal plane) is where the painting seems to exist for the viewer. The painter takes advantage of the retreating and advancing properties of the different colors to create multiple planes in the painting, yet all of these planes act off the base or "ideal" plane. In other words, the color planes represented in the illustration (figure 13) are variations upon the depth of the ideal plane. This latter base exists between the surface of the physical canvas and the mind of the observer. In the stage composition, the ideal plane is identical to the open window through which all action is viewed. The variable planes of color, form, and movement are based, as in his paintings, on this plane.

In addition to the open-window concept, Kandinsky adds other original directions in *Der gelbe Klang* that are essential in understanding the total effect of the *Bühnenkomposition*. However, to approach these more "painterly" stage directions, one also needs a clear idea of their creator's developing theories of color, movement, and space as implemented in his painting. Much of the collaborative effect of this composition is predicated on the same painterly theories he discussed in *Über das Geistige in der Kunst*.

The actual positioning and coloring of the set "in a deep space . . . as deep as possible" functions in much the same way as these elements (color and line) do in the paintings between 1910 and 1914.[23] Several important aspects of his use of color, space, and movement in *Der gelbe Klang* anticipate developments in Kandinsky's

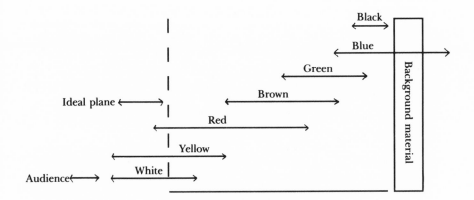

Motion of color planes in *Der gelbe Klang*

Fig. 13.

paintings during the following twenty years.[24] In the latter cases, it is curious that Kandinsky should apply a complex theory of color in a completely new form before he achieved these effects in paintings. Perhaps a great innovator in one art form is less cautious, more willing to attempt the raw version of his vision in another, less fully defined format.

In any case, in *Der gelbe Klang* Kandinsky creates a complex spatial-temporal scheme that is like nothing written or produced on the stage before the First World War. By the simulation of infinite depth (space) on a shallow stage, he uses his own idea of the ideal plane to create numerous contrasting color planes. A number of moving figures such as the giants and the bird-like beings cannot be fixed at any base plane in the picture, but instead hover as if unimpeded by the physical limits of the stage. These relative axes of objects and apparitions combine with the complex set of planes created through the manipulation of color and lighting to provoke two separate effects: (1) the illusion of almost chaotic complexity, and (2) a sense of liberation in which both the colored objects (apparitions) and the colors themselves melt on and off the stage without apparent cause. Finally, and perhaps most strikingly, the normative expectations of the audience are upset by the unexplained expansion and diminution of several figures on the stage. A green hill grows and changes color in front of the dark background. The shape, motion, and hue of the giants also undergo radical changes, followed by expansions and contractions of the apparent objects themselves: the people, the flowers, the distances viewed.[25]

Many of the effects here described lead to one central idea: the expansion of the spatial and temporal dimensions of the conventional stage into the world of the supernatural. Kandinsky's planes of interaction suggest the cosmos itself.

The crucial element in the creation of these planes is the systematic use of color to create depths, movements, and emotions. In *Über das Geistige in der Kunst,* Kandinsky draws upon his long apprenticeship in painting to discuss colors and their psychological effects. Paul Overy has shown that Kandinsky made occasional use of several, more extensive color theories in his studies, and that echoes of Goethe's *Farbentheorie,* the Young-Helmholz theory, the Hering theory and the Ladd-Franklin theory enter into his research into the psychology of color.[26] Though Kandinsky rarely mentions the specific sources of his own technical study of color, Overy's examination of his writings and paintings shows that "it is fairly obvious . . . that Kandinsky was familiar with the psychological research on color that was widespread at the end of the nineteenth and at the beginning of the twentieth century, particularly in Germany."[27]

Kandinsky simplifies the relations between colors and effects of pure colors by creating a wheel of antitheses based upon four major contrasts (see figure 14).[28] Of these eight colors, only orange is left out of *Der gelbe Klang.* Each opposed pair of colors is antagonistic and functions as a contrary.[29] These same color antitheses form the basis for Kandinsky's ideas about emotional correspondences. In his discussion of the synesthetic reactions to the colors and the effects of their juxtaposition, blue, for example, is a retreating (withdrawing) color that is neither angry nor depressive, but cold and elevated above the ordinary. It is the primary color of the spiritual (*UGK,* 77–79). Yellow is opposite blue on the color wheel. It is lively and advancing. It creates the impression that it is moving toward the viewer, eager to jump out of its container (*UGK,* 76). In *Der gelbe Klang,* yellow is consistently juxtaposed against blue, as in *Bilde* 1 and 2. In this example, playing one color against the other accentuates the outward growth of the giants and their eccentric (centrifugal)

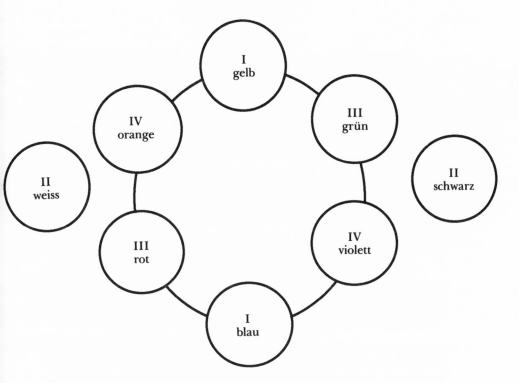

Fig. 14.

motion against the concentric (centripetal) motion of the blue background.

Kandinsky adds to these contrasts by playing white light against the blackness of the stage at the pauses, ends of actions, and between pictures. According to his own speculation, there is a distinct affinity between yellow and white (as exemplified in *Bilde* 3 and 5) and between blue and black (as in *Bilde* 1, 2, and 5). The presence of black and white in Kandinsky's color theory is explained by his own requirements in painting, in which both black and white are colors on his palette.[30] During the performance of *Der gelbe Klang* the yellows and whites are fused in two scenes and, on several other occasions, both colors grow beyond their respective forms.

Against these combinations of white and yellow (the warm and aggressive tones) Kandinsky alternates blue (spiritual, elevated) and black (nihilistic, empty). Black is first projected in interludes to mark an indefinite period of visual loss, with each pause a temporal and spatial negation. However, through repetition, black comes to have a symbolic meaning. Every picture concludes in a sweeping closure of total darkness and, according to Kandinsky's theory, this always implies a tragic, if not nihilistic tone. These are the major color values of the play. The other colors are present, but their effects, individually and in contrast to their opposites, are not emphasized by placement or repetition. Thus, the uses of green, violet, gray, and red (as in *Bild* 5) are projected according to the same theory as the central colors, but tend to be played in a minor (supportive) key.

The prelude contains nearly all the verbal components of the play and even there the use of language is more properly emblematic than literal. Words are sung by different sections of a choir behind the stage. The voices are introduced at the beginning as if to appeal to the familiar expectations of the audience. The lines and chants, however, form an oracular, but not particularly intelligible discourse. They introduce the audience to the abstract (inner) tone of the production through the most conventional medium. Some of the statements allude to events that will take place in the following *Bilde* (in this sense, they are roughly analogous to titles and captions in paintings):

> (Tiefe stimmen:)
> Steinharte Träume . . . Und sprechende Felsen . . .
> Schollen mit Rätseln erfüllender Fragen . . .
> Des Himmels Bewegung . . . Und Schmelzen . . .
> der Steine . . . [31]

Others evoke the emotional vibrations that are to be expressed by other media:

> (Hohe stimmen)
> Tränen und Lachen . . . Bei Fluchen Gebete . . .
> Der Einigung Freude und schwärzeste Schlachten.[32]

Abstracted from the context of the performance, these lines appear to contain an oblique reference to an uncanny situation. In its proper context, each fragment serves as an invocation and, like the opening measures of the overture to an opera, introduces important thematic elements of the composition. In this way, the passages sung by the bass voices create an apocalyptic mood. The things themselves are behaving in strange ways.[33] The feelings of mystery and terror evoked by these verbal paradoxes should prepare the audience for the parallel *Klänge* that are to follow from the other arts. Thus, when the full chorus sings

> Finsteres Licht bei dem . . . sonnigsten . . . Tag
> Grell leuchtender Schatten bei dunkelster Nacht!![34]

the contraries named here suggest the uses of white and black that follow on the stage. Each fragment prefigures one of the fusions of contrary colors, motions, and feelings that are subsequently presented in the composition.

Every element of the prelude reflects the same mood of mystery, uncertainty, and imminent catastrophe. Yet, no single part, not even the dramatic role of the chorus, is in itself sufficient to make sense of the section. Nor is there any attempt at exposition. The prelude suggests, with much the same brevity, quickness, and symbolism as *Bild* 6 the movement (motion) of infinite expansion in the midst of finite closure. Where the words merely insinuate catastrophe in the prelude, in the last *Bild* the silent physical expansion of the abstract figure symbolizes the last gesture. Between the allusiveness of the prelude and the symbolism of the last scene, Kandinsky coordinates a rich, collaborative inner-drama. The purposefully fragmented and abstracted elements of the different arts interact to create a nonrepresentational stage work (except for an almost realistic interlude in *Bild* 4). Pictures 1 through 3 present four-dimensional images which are literally pictures that change and move upon the stage.

In the first picture, the interaction of the color blue with the orchestral sounds is broken up by the emergence of five yellow giants. These yellow figures are juxtaposed against the changing hues of the blue backdrop. Before their appearance, the parallel movement of the orchestra and the color had dramatized the inner chords of that color (*die blauen Klänge*). The initial domination of blue is broken by its contrary color. Then, the tension between these contraries is halted by a sudden, sweeping darkness that brings all light and all sound to a halt.

All the pictures are punctuated with these pauses. Certainly every such closure sets off each sequence from the next. In this sense, the audience accepts the blackness of every pause as it would accept a scene change. However, the frequency of these pauses adds another, darker possibility. Every fragment of light, color, and action is surrounded temporally and spatially by the engulfing black. On the simplest level of interpretation, the physical tones of yellow, red, and green seem to have no continuity.

After the first pause, the yellow giants reappear upstage to sing a wordless song. Just as abstraction dispenses with the visual representation of reality, so these giant abstract shapes need no words. At the end of their song, they fade and the mountain in the background grows, moves forward, and then consumes the stage in a display of brilliant white. The color white dominates the yellow that remains where the yellow giants were. To emphasize this effect, this color grows in space and intensity. The picture ends as the orchestra is heard to "conquer" the chorus, thus eliminating the only human presence in the work thus far.[35]

However, the demise of the only recognizable human feature, spoken language, serves a positive function because it opens the stage to the full abstraction of the inner-drama. And, where the prelude and the first picture introduce the themes as expressed by color, figure, movement, sound, and language, the following pictures (*Bilde* 2 through 6) restate these same primary conflicts and themes with some variation. Picture 2, for example, recreates the major conflict of the spiritual forces in terms of the crisis of yellow, the core of *Der gelbe Klang*. The interactions of yellow with sounds in space and with the various abstract and human figures lead to a clear dramatization of these conflicts on both a literal and a spiritual level. Single tones are swallowed into one larger sound. Single colors are engulfed by more powerful hues. Subsequently, a flower blooms, assumes its yellow color, and then responds to an appropriate yellow sound. This staging prepares for the entry of a large group of dancers attired in different colors. Like the white objects in Kandinsky's paintings, the white flowers they carry seem to aspire to yellow. The dancers perceive a limited, silent universe covered with flowers. They have brought, one by one, examples of their world with them. In unison and then separately, they chant over and over the simple song of their belief:

> Die Blumen bedecken alles, bedecken alles, bedecken alles.
> Schliess die Augen! Schliess die Augen!
> Wir schauen. Wir schauen.

Bedecken mit Unschuld Empfängnis.
Öffne die Augen! Öffne die Augen!
Vorbei! Vorbei![36]

Consistent with their naive view of the world, they will not look at reality. In the middle of threatening tones of terror and death, the dancers portray the innocent blindly groping for a wished-for world.

Kandinsky deflates this simplistic belief with irony. The dancers quickly become victims of the larger conflict. Their sightlessness suffices only to deliver them from consciousness of their defeat, and their naive song directly contradicts all the other events on stage. In addition, they ignore the contrapuntal effects of the distant figures, the colors, the lights, and the sound, which further undercut their credibility. While they are onstage, the notes of the orchestra drown out the singers' rondo. Gray-green figures appear at a distance on the hill, driving the yellow flower to a frenzy and finally causing it to give up its color, i.e., its identity. This event, analogous to a sacrificial rite, leaves the dancers entranced. As if asleep in the world, they repeat their chant by rote, imitating unconsciously the incantations associated with ritual activity. They do not awaken until the transformation has occurred. For, as soon as the large flower has lost its color, their small flowers change to yellow and then appear to be covered with red. In their frame of reference, this change signals a blood sacrifice. They tremble in terror, incapable of expressing themselves (in dance or song) before they are swept away into blackness at the end of the picture.[37]

By the end of this scene (*Bild* 2), each of the original contraries of *Bild* 1 has been reintroduced in several forms. A cycle of repetition commences in picture 3 when the five yellow giants reappear, whispering at the rear of the stage. They seem uneasy and communicate great anxiety. They respond to the violence of what follows: "In schneller Abwechslung fallen von allen Seiten grellfarbige Strahlen (Blau, Rot, Violett, Grün wechseln mehrere Male). Dann treffen sich alle diese Strahlen in der Mitte, wodurch sie gemischt werden."[38]

Recalling Kandinsky's theory of color, we can no longer see this as a random light show. All of these colors—the darker, more withdrawn hues—are related and none is contrary to any of the others. Their emotional, inner values range from the spiritual coolness of blue to the restful earthiness of green. Yet, each plays upon yellow as part of a series of high contrasts. As the stage is filled with a fast sequence of colored lights, the onslaught of contrary emotions overwhelms the target color.[39] The giants fade and darkness follows.

After a period of total blackness, a small yellow light appears. The intensity of this light grows and floods the stage. In a reverse parallel, the color grows stronger and the orchestra's chords become deeper until the orchestra is silenced. The very color that had previously been destroyed in the attack on the giants is here symbolically reborn.

As the new yellow consumes all things on the stage, it opens the way for the return of the giants.[40] But they return alone; the rocks and the mountains have vanished. The giants have grown noticeably. For Kandinsky, this small transformation is one example of the process of rebirth and change that is the constant promise of the spiritual. In various actions from the first through the fifth picture, the giants are threatened by symbolic counterforces represented in the paintings of this period by noncomplementary colors, discordant sounds, and opposing objects. In each action, the yellow figures are overcome by the violence of these conflicts. They disappear into the void that marks the beginning and end of every *Bild*.

In a parallel way, the orchestra's notes foreshadow the obliteration of the positive figures. The tone of such destruction is apocalyptic. Each time the stage is overcome with black, the spiritual colors (the blues) vanish and the life forces (the yellows, reds, and greens) are obliterated. Time stops with each black pause and the terror of the end of time is projected. It is against the total destruction symbolized by each of the pervasive black pauses that small counterpoints are repeated. Every period of blackness (except the end of the composition) is followed by a regeneration of movement, color, and *Klänge* on the stage. The rhythm of rebirth is regular, but inexplicable. Thus, when in picture 3 the pure yellow light breaks through the darkness, conquers the dissonant orchestral sounds, and resurrects the yellow giants, no rational explanation is given. Rather, like the creation of something out of nothing—the archetype of the myth of origin—the process of renewal is merely asserted. The whole of the *Bühnenkomposition* functions as a serial display of this process.

The next picture (*Bild* 4) is a pastoral interlude which contrasts with the abstract quality of the preceding parts. A little boy rings a bell. This sound stands out in the silence as an isolated call for the spiritual in the profane world. The ringing, though, is weak, for the boy is still small and the bell is cracked. "A very large man . . . dressed entirely in black" commands "Silence." The picture ends as the ringing stops and darkness fills the stage. This brief scene is a parallel to the action of the abstract *Bilde* 1 through 3 and is inserted as a restatement to clarify the audience's understanding. The authoritative voice, which represents the black hand of evil, stops the weak call. On the simplest level, innocence is dashed when the force of negation overcomes the faint projections of spiritual hope. Though brief, this naturalistic scene represents and simplifies the more abstract presentations of the other pictures; in fact, it may over-simplify the earlier scenes.

With the fifth picture, the composition returns to the symbolic enactment of spiritual conflict. Picture 5 opens by repeating the action in picture 3, with one significant variation: a pure white light replaces yellow as the color of deliverance. Kandinsky thus demonstrates his theory of the internal relation of white to yellow by showing how white can produce similar effects. In this instance, the yellow giants return and grow in the white light. Then, like the flowers in picture 2, the giants convulse at the sound of the dissonant "intensified music" ("*allmählich greller* [*Musik*]" *DBR*, 226). A completely darkened stage marks a pause in the action.

In this picture, however, the entry of the dancers breaks the black spell. Their costumes are of different solid hues—gray, black, white, then colors: green, blue, yellow, red. Each group of dancers distinguishes itself from the others by characteristic movements. Individual dancers are described doing different things; for example, one walks, one stretches, one leaps joyously, and so on. Even though the dancers are together on the stage, there is little sense of harmony or community. After an extended solo dance by a white-clad dancer, individual dancers respond to individual chords from the orchestra, each dancing a chord until it ends. Before the relation between music and dance can be developed, however, a powerful sweeping red light closes down music and movement. The dancers are swept off the stage by the color. The giants in the background tremble. Various lights and shrieks fill the stage to dramatize the violence that the red has engendered. As part of the great confusion, the dancers cross and recross the stage, blending individual and group movements. "At the moment of greatest confusion in the orchestra in movement and light, it suddenly becomes dark and silent" (*TBRA*, 224).

The yellow giants are again devoured by black. By the end of the fifth picture, the central conflicts represented by the music, the movement, and the light have again been presented and negated. The forces of black have won. As described in Kandinsky's scenario, each of the following abstract elements has produced an effect and many of these have occurred in combination with several other elements: the abstract yellow giants (color, form, movement, sound); the dancers (color, movement); the voices (sound, music, words); the orchestra (sound, music); and the colors (colored lights projected on stage). All these evaporate at the end of picture 5 as the theater of illusion is suddenly emptied.

There remains only a brief apocalyptic finale. One of the yellow giants is brought back to enact the rite of symbolic (spiritual) expansion. The giant appears to expand until the stage is filled vertically. Without whispering or motioning, it overcomes the physical limits of the stage space. One last gesture, done for the sake of the audience, reinforces the spiritual significance of the *Bühnenkomposition*. The giant forms the silhouette of a man on a cross. This final picture transcends the conflicts of the previous pictures and implies, on a mythical or theological level, a meaning to the struggles expressed on the stage. Kandinsky was not above hedging, even in a so-called abstract synthesis of the arts.

The mythic pattern of rebirth and renewal suggested in the symbols in picture 6 are present in other pictures as well. But in every other instance, the resurrection of the spiritual is achieved through Kandinsky's color symbolism. Thus, in picture 3, the rebirth of the yellow giants from the void of the stage can be interpreted as an allusion to the eternal return of the spiritual, but such a reading is neither self-evident nor necessary. The sign of the cross given by the expanded giant in picture 6 is less ambiguous. Nonetheless, our interpretation of this picture (and our interpretation of *Der gelbe Klang*) depends upon how we interpret a symbolic gesture whose basis might seem to be outside the terms of the work itself. In spite of much dogmatic criticism to the contrary, religious symbolism can be ambiguous when applied out of context. For example, without a specifically Christian context, the silhouetted crucifix may signal merely another in a series of sacrifices in the *Bilde*. Throughout the play, the repeated rhythm of presentation and destruction has implied, spatially and temporally, a final destruction, a rhythm R. W. Sheppard seems to have applied to the work, declaring the tone and meaning of *Der gelbe Klang* to be dark and pessimistic.[41]

On the other hand, as soon as the work is considered in a Christian context, the significance of both the last scene and the production as a whole changes radically. Rose Carol Washton Long has pointed to the prevalence of Christian themes in the apocalyptic symbols and motifs in Kandinsky's paintings from 1910 through

1914.[42] Her analysis uncovers an iconography of figures of Christian symbolism in a number of relatively nonfigurative paintings. Her analysis and categorization of these signs in the paintings (such figures as St. George, the Horsemen of the Apocalypse, numerous saints, and other figures from Genesis and the Book of Revelation) have provoked a necessary reinterpretation of this period in Kandinsky's career. Her work also affects the way readers can interpret this stage composition. For, when seen in the context of his paintings as well as his theories, the sign of the crucifix is completely complementary to the rest of the play. The giant signals a spiritual self-sacrifice: in imitation of Jesus, he gives himself for the world. But such an action should not be imagined even symbolically as self-destruction. Paradoxically, the Christian context insists that the Crucifixion is celebrated on a note of expectancy and joy. The sign of the cross is the symbol of Christ's victory over death, and resurrection must surely follow. The crucifixion of one giant leaves four others remaining. These may be interpreted in the apocalyptic mode. Yet even in this mode, a point amply discussed by Washton Long, the promise of the eschatological is not death, but a new life. Kandinsky's visions of the end, complete with the horsemen, the patriarchs, the saints, trumpeting angels, mysterious seals, and Armegeddon-like battles between the forces of materialism and the spiritual, prophesy a renewal of the spiritual. The unstated theme of every apocalypse is the advent of the new Jerusalem after the last Judgment.[43]

Without a knowledge of Kandinsky's early paintings or an understanding of his experiments in color theory, harmony, counterpoint, and movement, early viewers would doubtless have found his work bizarre, if not bereft of any meaning at all. His paintings of the same period (1910–13) also evoked dismay and indignation from viewers in several parts of Germany.[44] If, in fact, one can imagine that his associates in the *Neue Künstlervereinigung München* rejected his painting *Composition V* in the jury for the Third Exhibition in November 1911, then it will not be difficult to guess the kind of reception *Der gelbe Klang* might have enjoyed.[45]

As previously indicated, *Der gelbe Klang* was not performed during Kandinsky's lifetime. The advent of the First World War soon after the second edition of *Der Blaue Reiter* cut off all possibility of Kandinsky staging his experimental *Gesamtkunstwerk*. There were, however, several attempts before the war to do just that. The first was that of Thomas de Hartmann, who wrote that he tried to persuade

Stanislavsky to perform the work at the Moscow Art Theater.[46] De Hartmann had collaborated with Kandinsky during the period following the original draft of *Der gelbe Klang* (a sketch of the composition called *Die Riesen* is in GMS 415 in Kandinsky's hand, dated from 1909). Jelena Hahl-Koch and Susan Stein present interesting evidence that Kandinsky revised and expanded the original text during the two years that elapsed between the composition and its publication under a different title in *Der Blaue Reiter.*[47] An offprint text of *Der gelbe Klang* discovered among de Hartmann's papers indicates that he and Kandinsky were still working on their collaboration in early 1912.[48] Kandinsky wrote in musical directions and timings for almost all of the sections of the composition.

Further evidence of the date of de Hartmann's contribution to *Der gelbe Klang* comes from the fragments of de Hartmann's score for the composition. Each of the parts that de Hartmann left in his papers (rediscovered by Peg Weiss in the Yale Music Library's de Hartmann collection) follows the precise timings suggested by Kandinsky in the annotated text. This implies that he wrote down what we have of his score after receiving the version of the text that remained in his collection, in other words, after the spring of 1912.[49]

Prior to the rediscovery of de Hartmann's music, all attempts to produce Kandinsky's *Bühnenkomposition* were destined to fail, though not always for lack of a score. Hugo Ball, the founder of the Dada movement in Zurich in 1916, shared Kandinsky's vision of a synthesis of the arts and had even introduced Kandinsky's text of *Der gelbe Klang* to the Munich Artists' Theater in 1914 for possible production. It is not clear if Ball had access to de Hartmann's score or even knew about it, but with Kandinsky in Munich at the time, the musical part should not have proven difficult to obtain. However, after 1 August 1914, the whole world changed and those artists' plans that had grown in Munich were forgotten in the chaos of war. Kandinsky himself was declared an undesirable alien and forced to leave Germany. Ball exiled himself to Switzerland.

Subsequent attempts to produce the play by the *Volksbühne* in Berlin in the early 1920s and by Oskar Schlemmer at the Bauhaus later in the same decade failed. As Kandinsky later wrote to a friend:

Wissen Sie, dass mir 2x eine Aufführung angeboten wurde? Das erste Mal dicht vor dem Krieg—die Aufführung musste im Spätherbst in München stattfinden. Das zweite Mal in Berlin ("Volksbühne") 1922. Und dieses zweite Mal stand nicht der Krieg im Wege, sondern mein

Kompoist, Th. v. Hartmann, der damals unerreichbar war. So musste ich ablehnen. Ich erinnere mich plötzlich, dass es auch noch ein drittes Mal gegeben hat: Schlemmer wollte das Stück aufführen. Es kam aber wieder ein Strich durch die Rechnung. . . . Solche Dinge haben eigene Geschicke.[50]

After the Second World War and Kandinsky's death in 1944, the text of *Der gelbe Klang* was mentioned far more frequently by music historians and art critics than by those in literature or theater. Several incomplete attempts at production have been recorded but the absence of reliable descriptions and reviews makes it impossible to speculate about the nature of these performances. Will Grohmann records a performance in Paris in 1956, produced by Jacques Polerei using a musical score composed by Jean Barraque. This work, *La Sonorité jaune,* disappeared without further comment.[51] Peg Weiss notes a production called *The Yellow Sound* which was performed by the Massachusetts School of Art at the Guggenheim Museum in New York in 1972. The production company (Zone, Theater of the Visual) apparently presented their version of the play without music, though dancers, lights, and sets were included. This production also received little comment.[52] So it was that in 1982, the Ian Strasfogel production of *The Yellow Sound* claimed with some justification that its performance of the color opera under the instigation of Peg Weiss and with the collaboration of a director, a composer, a choreographer, and two creators of stage effects was the world premier of the *Bühnenkomposition.* The attention I have devoted to Kandinsky's collaborative work is not justified merely by its premiere. Rather, it has been my contention to show how a work as brief and apparently obscure as this one can manifest an ideal that remains as appropriate now as it was at the time of its first publication in 1912. Kandinsky's vision of the underlying unity of the arts led to his composition of several collaborative works and *Der gelbe Klang* remains a model of his theory of combination. As I have already pointed out, this work exemplifies the function of one rule of collaboration: the law of nonsubtraction. This should surprise no one, since Kandinsky himself suggested the basic rules of nonsubtraction in his article "Über Bühnenkomposition." Further claims for the unity and limitations of the *Gesamtkunstwerk* are derived from my examination of the combined effects of the movements, colors, sounds, and objects projected into the ideal space of Kandinsky's "open-window" stage. However, my attention is not directed toward the historical accounting of Kandinsky's notions, i.e., the sources and influences on Kandinsky as discussed by Peg Weiss and Rose Carol Washton Long among others, but rather toward an understanding of how the different, abstracted values of the parts of *Der gelbe Klang* express, through harmony and counterpoint, the combinative effects Kandinsky predicted in his notebooks and other writings.

The fabled *Gesamtkunstwerk* is merely a more complex case of the combination of any of the arts. As such, it must abide by the same set of expectations and limits as any other combination of the arts. The number of arts involved then does not increase in any incremental or significant way the range of effects, the limit of expectations, or the potential power of a work of art. However, this formulation (one of the limits of collaborative forms) does not take into account the one factor that does change with the number of parts added to any work: the level of difficulty. I mean first the difficulties for the creating and performing artist or artists, and second a similar level of difficulties for audiences. Collaborative forms begin at a formidable level of difficulty. It is harder to combine music and poetry than it is to compose either one or the other individually. The artist who wishes to put together three arts assumes an even more difficult task. The study of the *Gesamtkunstwerk* convinces me that the degree of difficulty inherent in combining the arts increases exponentially rather than incrementally. Thus, in terms of the difficulty posed for the artist, the difference in theory between a work that combines two arts and a work that combines three arts is significant. In practice, the rule of difficulty places a high price in effort and in talent on multiple combinations of the arts. Yet, this rule implies more than a common-sense appreciation of the *Gesamtkunstwerk* and its rarity. It also defines a problem for the criticism of such works. For proof of these claims I will turn next to a small collaborative production that took place at the same time as the composition of *Der gelbe Klang*. Oskar Kokoschka's *Mörder, Hoffnung der Frauen* was first performed in 1909, but it was one of the earliest examples of what came to be called Expressionist drama. My final chapter will then introduce a contemporary master of collaborative form, Alwin Nikolais. Although his works are well-known to audiences of modern dance, his contributions to Total Theater can best be appreciated in the context of collaborative form.

SIX

DER STURM
Mörder, Hoffnung der Frauen

FOLLOWING the demands for a fusion of the arts in Symbolism and Jugendstil at the turn of the century, Expressionism continued the search for a synthesis of the arts in several notable directions. As we have just seen, in 1909, Wassily Kandinsky explored the abstract relations of the arts in his stage compositions. In the same year, in Vienna, Oskar Kokoschka organized and performed his own version of composite art. The ideal of combining the arts became one of the cherished goals of a number of Expressionist artists. While Kandinsky's essays "Über die Formfrage" and "Über das Geistige in der Kunst" played a crucial role in opening, if only briefly, the traditionally closed paths between the arts, other artists from different centers of German Expressionism also pursued composite forms in theory and in practice. During the great period of Expressionist activity before the First World War, one can read of collaboration in the writings of Ernst Ludwig Kirchner, Paul Klee, Franz Marc, Arnold Schoenberg, Anton Webern, and Alban Berg, among others.

This development of Expressionism was first announced in the publication of Herwarth Walden's weekly journal of the arts, *Der Sturm,* in 1910, and subsequently echoed in Franz Pfemfert's bi-weekly review, *Die Aktion.* It was in these loose-leaf magazines that the seemingly esoteric notion of making something new out of the relations between the so-called "sister arts" became, once again, a central rather than a peripheral goal in European cultural history. The goal itself was expressed by the *Sturmkreis:* to create a fusion or synthesis of the several forms. Walden pushed and paid to sponsor an ideal that in retrospect looks very similar to the work that Wagner, in his most Romantic phase, might have called the *Gesamt-kunstwerk.* Though this word may now appear to overstate any combination of the particular artistic productions of the period, it was nonetheless a perfectly appropriate creation of an epoch that best expressed itself in apocalyptic visions.

The earliest example of this phenomenon in the Expressionist movement was a small and mystifying performance given one summer evening in the *Gartentheater* at the *Wienerkunstschau* in 1909, when Oskar Kokoschka, a young painter, produced and directed his composite art work, first titled *Hoffnung der Frauen*. It has been called the first pure example of Expressionist drama even though it incorporated other art forms in ways that the traditional Expressionist plays rarely did.[1]

Kokoschka recounts that he had originally been interested in the idea of performance. His notions of the proprieties and conventions of literary drama were as vague as his memories of any other of the subjects that had been force-fed in the Wiener *Realschule*. Only as he began rehearsals did he begin to add lines for characters to augment their movements and actions. He tailored each speech, each fragment of language to the other fragmentary motions, symbols, and acts that were invented for the stage. In fact, it was not until the first and only full rehearsal of the performance that he wrote out the entire script along with the complete stage directions he had envisioned as the work had taken shape.[2] This rather extemporaneous method of creation explains the fact that the script for the work as published resembles nothing so much as a shooting script for a film production. The text, which filled two folio pages in the original publication, has more lines of stage direction than of dialogue.

Mörder, Hoffnung der Frauen is a painter's play and makes demands on the visual imagination like few other modern plays. It is filled with the color, movement, and intensity of a series of Expressionist paintings. The characters on stage are both more and less than human. They do not develop; they simply reenact. None of the characters (there are effectively only four voices) is developed in any of the conventional ways in which playwrights work out characterization. They are given, instead of whole and interesting selves, symbolic colors to wear and ritual movements to perform as they dance through archetypal patterns and perform a carefully choreographed ballet on a tilted stage. The set itself is functional, minimal, abstract: a tower, a door to a cage, torches. The dialogue is full of imprecise evocative literary and mythic allusions. Sources like the Bible, Ovid, Jung, and the cabala are suggested, but none of these structures provides a satisfying explication of the action. The fragmented lyric statements serve only as parts of a larger whole.

The choreography of the chorus begins the performance in ways much closer to dance than to drama. The forces and effects of the colors used in the performance also assume a crucial part in creating the desired effects of the performance. Kokoschka painted his sets and chose bright hues for the costumes of two central characters to make their contrary natures visible, a convention not unusual even for the stage in Vienna in 1909. But the artist also literally painted his actors: the man's face and hands are stark white, the woman's skin is red, then completely white at the end of the play. The two choruses are lined with black paint at every point where skin shows. The effect was surreal.

Critics objected to the unearthly colors and found the dialogue incomprehensible.[3] Yet the individual spoken lines create a series of counterpoints to other movements in the play. The language of the play is intentionally fragmented; those lines that are most cryptic create an abstract vision of the whole. The overall effect depends on the interaction of words with dance, color, and song. For this reason, most of the attempts to explicate the power and originality of *Mörder* as lyric drama have failed. Yet, the claim that *Mörder, Hoffnung der Frauen* makes rather little sense as a work of literature is beside the point, for few have yet treated the whole work as conceived and performed.[4] Consequently, the importance of Kokoschka's contribution to avant-garde theater has been underestimated.

It is conceivable that one could ignore the influence of the play even after reading of the scandal that ensued from the single performance in Vienna. After all, "What happened in Vienna (Krakania)," as Robert Musil wryly remarked during this epoch, "could scarcely be fool enough, of itself, to happen elsewhere." Though the intellectuals of Vienna attended this performance en masse, thinking it to be one of those rare occasions that provide conversation in Viennese cafes for decades thereafter, these notables, including Musil, Adolf Loos, Karl Kraus, Egon Schiele, and Gustav Klimt, among others, would not have carried the drama to the young dramatists of Berlin, Munich, Dresden, Paris, or Milan. In fact, had it not been for a fortunate postponement of the first scheduled performance, which gave the painter time to run off a hundred lithograph *affiches* to advertise his "show," no one but friends of the cast would have attended.

Fig. 15. Kokoschka's poster for original production of *Mörder, Hoffnung der Frauen* (Copyright 1990 ARS N.Y./Cosmopress)

However, Kokoschka's poster (see figure 15) was so bizarre, so ghoul-ish, and so brilliantly colored that crowds came just to see what production could inspire such a strange *affiche*. Posters for art exhi-bitions were not unusual, yet this poster was unlike any contempo-rary example. The intellectuals responded and the theater was filled to overflowing.

But it is quite another event that placed Kokoschka's small work at the head of the Expressionist movement and made its influence on subsequent works certain. In the following year, the text of the play was published in its entirety on the front pages of the most impor-tant journal of the avant-garde in Germany, *Der Sturm*. Accompany-ing the text in this publication were four etchings reproduced from drawings that Kokoschka had made for the play since the 1909 per-formance. Thus, on 14 July 1910, in Herwarth Walden's enterpris-ing revue, the ground was broken not only for the drama of the following years but also for the concept of collaboration in the arts. In combining *Mörder, Hoffnung der Frauen* (a work that implies the interaction of several forms) with the drawings that were created to go with it, Walden began his impressive career in support of all the arts, whether separate, as in the *Sturm* painting exhibits, or together, as in the larger, collaborative shows sponsored immediately before the First World War.

The play begins as a man appears in the midst of a savage crowd. He is dressed in bright blue armor and his face is painted stark white. He is astride a large horse (which would have made the play an appropriate addition to *Der Blaue Reiter Almanach*), and has an unexplained wound in his side, which he covers with a red kerchief. The men of the chorus are painted with black-and-white lines across their faces and arms to accentuate their strangeness and to make vi-sual a radical differentiation between them and the blue rider.

Without a word, the chorus begins to circle around the rider and then directs its attention toward the center (where, according to Mircea Eliade, the Holy stands out and the sacred events take place).[5] Their attentiveness is manifested by unified, orchestrated gestures. This choreographed geometry of the mythos places the man in the center of all the lines of force that the painter creates on stage. His position is reinforced by the lines of attention that are focused on him from outside the microcosm of his followers. The chorus of women, forming a half-circle on the opposite side of the stage, si-lently rivets its attention on him and creates a second set of lines that intersect the first like the beams of the half-moon intersecting

the sun. Thus, through formation and gesture, Kokoschka establishes elemental lines of force on the stage.

Once the symbolic forms are completed, violent gestures break
them apart. To the accompaniment of bells ringing, torches flaming,
and strange deafening noises (*Getöse*), the men creep in on the rider,
closing the circle to contain him. But they are lethargic (*müde, unwil-
lig*) and lack sufficient will to hold back his motion. Though they pull
his horse to the ground, nothing seems to affect the man's method-
ical progress. He breaks the circle and stalks on toward the women
opposite him. As he crosses the stage, his defenders commence a
low-pitched incantation that builds to a crescendo:

> Wir waren das flammende Rad um ihn,
> Wir waren das flammende Rad um dich,
> Bestürmer verschlossener Festungen![6]

The first lines of the play are spoken in the imperfect tense and
serve to announce the end of the chorus's role as protector of the
Holy. The self-description given by the chorus as the flaming wheel
is visually appropriate, since the men's torches are lit and form a
circular pattern. The passion of their chant reflects their helpless-
ness, for the *Bestürmer* has broken through the fortress as easily as a
man walking through water. Yet, without the nonverbal levels of action that precede these lines, the hysteria of the men would make
little sense. In the full context, the fragmented incantation both
punctuates and clarifies the motions and forces evoked by the figures
on stage.

The next set of "line-forces" is created by *die Blicke*. Two looks are
directed on stage by the gestures of the head and body, and they
assume ritual significance when considered in conjunction with the
choreography and the dialogue. Everything stops during the exchange of looks by the man and the woman when they meet. At the
moment of confrontation, the two choruses merge and circle the
static pair, drawing attention to *die Blicke* meeting at center stage.
From this simple exchange come strange events. Such a clash,
though silent, must be set off from other action: throughout a
lengthy pause, the couple are locked in their staring and the circling
chorus stops. Once again, the ritual place of the sacred event is the
physical center of the microcosm. Here, the focus of action is directed inward to force a suspension of attention and a virtual stop-
page of time (as defined by the plot).

The first result of this duration in sacred time is the awakening of the man and the woman, both of whom profess ignorance of the changes taking place. Questions are asked as if memory had been obliterated:

Frau: "Wer war der Fremde, der mich sah?"[7]

Shortly thereafter the man utters his first words:

Mann: "Bin ich ein Wirklicher, was sprach der Schatten!"[8]

The woman's questions are direct, while the man's point outside the normal limits of the apparent situation. Both express a kind of wonder that is explained only by the force of the stare. "Sahst Du mich an, sah ich Dich?"[9] the man cries out, first as a question of the reality of what happened and then as a query of his own perception. Does he speak to shadows, or is he already thinking of the woman as a mere shade? The text is obscure.

Kokoschka's drawings of this scene add several elements to the text (figures 16 and 17). Both figures are cross-hatched with small, busy lines that represent outlets of nervous energy: great tension is evident. The male figure's head seems to look away although his body is directly facing the woman. The artist creates a simultaneous reduction of the profile and the full face, adding both spatial and temporal perspectives in order to represent simultaneously both the cause *(der Blick)* and the effect (the assertion of superiority). The other figure is drawn larger and is recognizably female only because of the size of her breasts and the length of her hair. She is posed below the male and seems to retreat from the encounter. Her expression is blank and is shown from only one temporal perspective. The lines of force here favor the male. The cryptic signs drawn on him are on the ascendant, even though he is struck directly by the rays of the sun, the woman's sign.

Without an exchange of identity, recognition has occurred, and the two figures (both in the play and in the drawing) recoil from the event as if they were trying to deny the force that pulls them unerringly together. In the text, three separate members of the female chorus voice alarming and mysterious presentiments to the woman; then, contrapuntally, three voices from the male chorus answer all the charges of *die Mädchen:*

Himmlische und irdische Liebe
Zeichnung von Oskar Kokoschka

Fig. 16. Kokoschka's illustration from *Mörder, Hoffnung der Frauen* from *Der Sturm* (Copyright 1990 ARS N.Y./Cosmopress)

Oskar Kokoschka
Zeichnung zum Drama: Mörder, Hoffnung der Frauen

Fig. 17. Kokoschka's drawing from *Mörder, Hoffnung der Frauen* from *Der Sturm* (Copyright 1990 ARS N.Y./Cosmopress)

Wir Sahen, wie er das Feuer heilen Fusses durchschritt.
Tiere martert er, wiehernde Stuten erdrückte sein Schenkel.
Vögel, die vor uns liefen, mussten wir blenden, rote Fische
im Sande ersticken.[10]

All clues indicate a fearful identity, but neither chorus is capable of discovering it from the parts. Each male voice amplifies rather than contradicts the previous rumors. While the women scream headlines, the men calmly chant the worst news in monotone. The difference is sexual. The women are terrified by the rumors of irrational acts. The male figure strikes an emotional chord (one sister died for want of him), threatens spiritual faith (slaughtering defenseless maidens at prayer in the temple), and evokes mythic awe (he *is* the *"Singende Zeit"* and the *Raum* where *niegesehene Blumen* exist). The men recognize him as a mysterious force, which they follow. Like disciples, they have seen the miracles and have projected themselves into the deeds while grasping only the violence. They seem incapable of perceiving the whole range of sensibilities represented in the feminine visions. Ironically, the males chant, in their pride, of gratuitous bestiality, unaware that each strange act alludes to ominous mythic patterns. This *bleichmann*, like Achilles in the *Iliad,* is known by his epithets. He squeezes horses to death with his thighs. He is beyond normal human reactions and, like an Eastern holy man, walks on fire unaffected. Like no mythic or literary forebear, he commands his legions to pitifully small acts of sadism. Blinding birds and stifling fish in the sand may seem a rather insignificant rebellion, but at the symbolic level both acts are crucial signs of the identity and the function of this mysterious figure. In Homer's Greece, birds were the sources of insight into the future, and the bird-interpreters were considered seers. Blinding the birds ends their flight, makes it impossible for them to recognize their tormentor, and cuts off their response accordingly. Stuffing fish in the sand is more than cruelty; it is symbolic of an unmitigated war declared against all life forms, for the fish are red with roe. The Man in Blue orders them annihilated at precisely the time they are spawning in shallow water, standing thus against sex as against all procreative acts. His own men, although ignorant of what they say, pronounce truths about him that are more essential and more terrifying than anything the women charge. The men's murders are not specific; they are total. From these fragments of dialogue, the destroyer *(Bestürmer)* is revealed at the moment in which a ritual is about to be repeated.

The woman, on the other hand, represents the life force. She is temporal, sensitive, feminine, and perhaps a seer. She reacts emotionally, yet her acts are explicable. While the confrontation between the two leaders might look like a battle between the sexes, symbolically the stakes have risen to the eschatological. She speaks for life itself when she asks:

> Warum bannst Du mich, Mann, mit Deinem Blick, fressednes Licht,
> verwirrst meine Flamme, verzehrendes Leben
> kommt über mich, *Flammenende.*
> O nimm mir entsetzliche Hoffnung ———
> und über dich kommt die Qual ———[11]

While speaking explicitly of the Blue Man's powerful masculinity as if she were bound by simple sexual responses, she simultaneously asks the primordial questions about death and of death. She senses the *Flammenende* even though she cannot clearly grasp her dilemma. In front of the *bleiche Gesicht* of death, her force is devoured *(verzehrendes Leben)*. Hope becomes terrible *(entsetzliche)* and nothing remains but the curse.

From this point in the play, violence overwhelms language. The branding of her living flesh is performed as a rape. The unmistakable gestures of the lusty and bestial group of men change the literal branding into a sex act, sadistically perverted by the mark of death branded in the victim's flesh. Her response is immediate and appropriate. She tries to murder murder itself, to kill death as personified in the man. The cycle yawns open like a wound. Bleeding profusely, the man sings the song of eternal recurrence in answer to his own assassination. It is more a refrain than the statement of a theme.

The stabbing is illustrated in the etching shown in figure 18, in which both figures are nearly nude. The woman's dress is torn to her waist and she has already been marked (one notes the "OK" on her leg). As she stabs, the man turns toward her, more curious than surprised, more angry than afraid, and more perplexed than expectant. She stabs the same spot where, at the beginning of the play, the man had bandaged his side to protect the "original" wound. Events begin to be repeated; the lines of force at the man's right seem to project him with great velocity toward the woman's knife. Neither figure is excited. Their expressions reflect a disinterest that describes for both their ambivalence toward the ritual repetition taking place.

The man is covered with the minuscule signs of his own tension. His torso exerts itself to receive the knife. He grips her arm with his

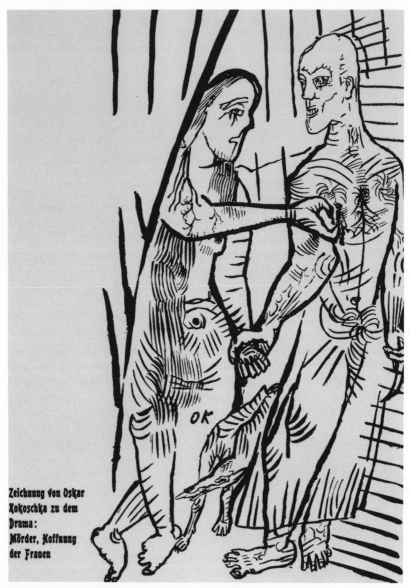

Zeichnung von Oskar
Kokoschka zu dem
Drama:
Mörder, Hoffnung
der Frauen

Fig. 18. Kokoschka's drawing from *Mörder, Hoffnung der Frauen* from *Der Sturm* (Copyright 1990 ARS N.Y./Cosmopress)

hand as if to help her, to steady her aim. They are posed like dancing partners as the music ends. She strikes backhanded, off-balance. She seems in her disproportion to be curtsying while thrusting. The curtain-like lines of her left force her out on the stage to commit her act.

In both the drawing and the text, the man accepts the blow with great compassion before moving off by himself to sing a solo ("singend mit blutender sichbarer Wunde"):

> Sinnlose begehr von Grauen zu Grauen,
> unstillbares Kreisen im Leeren.
> Gebären ohne Geburt,
> Sonnensturz, wankender Raum.
> Ende derer die, mich priesen.
> Oh, Euer unbarmherziges Wort.[12]

While scarcely appropriate for someone who has just been fatally stabbed, this song demonstrates the distance that has opened between the two figures at the center of the stage. This is no ordinary mortal. To him (for he speaks from outside human time), the whorls of space gather into a form to be repeated. Thus, he is able to make visible the invisible mythos, even though the fragments of oracular imagery are neither completed nor explained. The *Kreisen* stay *Unstillbares . . . im Leeren*. Like one of Nietzsche's *Übermenschen,* he sings the song of the eternal return, which takes the shape, on stage, of a horror story forever told and forgotten in the telling.

His death throes, too, seem endless. The chorus sticks to the well-worn script for disciples by denying him as the cocks crow. Yet, unlike the fearful Apostles, these men treat the master's death as a liberation and quickly propose marriage to the *singende Mädchen*.

At this point, the woman begins her ambivalent dance:

> (Sie schleicht wie ein Panther im Kreis um den Käfig.
>   Sie kriecht neugierig
> zum Turm, greift lüstern nach dem Gitter, schreibt ein
>   grosses weisses
> Kreuz an den Turm, schreit auf.):
> "Macht das Tor auf, ich muss zu ihm!"
> (Rüttelt verzweifelt.)[13]

As the corpse is prepared with accompanying signs of death (a coffin, crosses), she dances to indicate her recognition of necessity; she must stir life out of death. Her subsequent acts succeed in giving birth to death, for she resuscitates her "savior" with her own blood.

Light appears in the background like dawn breaking over midnight. The prowling woman grows sadistic in her frustration. She reaches through the bars, and goads the "permanent wound" with "geil böswillig keuchend, wie eine Natter."[4] Finally the revived man responds to her unorthodox approaches, adding, through his elliptical and fragmentary song, to her frenzy and confusion:

> (Der Mann drinnen, schwer atmend hebt mühsam
> den Kopf, bewegt später eine Hand, steht dann
> langsam auf, immer höher singend, entrückend):
> "Wind der zieht, Zeit um Zeit, Einsamkeit, Ruhe
> und Hunger verwirren mich. Vorbeikreisende Welten,
> keine Luft, abendlang wird es."[15]

His solo voice rises in both pitch and volume as his body is resurrected to this song. His voice moves up, note by note, bar by bar. Each word is sung as one note and the lines describe the linear expansion of his strength. While the idea of singing gods may be Wagnerian, in this the year of *Erwartung*, Op. 17, the musical sense is much closer to Schoenberg.

Die Verwandlungsszene is played as a duet and the change of roles is choreographed so that each character moves independently toward the consummation. From the body of death on stage, there suddenly appears a strange light: "(Frau beginnende Furcht): So viel Leben fliesst aus der Fuge, so viel Kraft aus dem Tor, bleich wie eine Leiche ist er."[16] But what is apparent to her is not real. He seems to her *wie ein Leiche* at the moment when he is described as rising in the cage and growing mysteriously larger against the bars ([er] . . . *wächst langsam*). He appears to swell up and out within the confines of the cage where he looms, an unstable form behind the door. As she creeps up the steps, she emits a shrill scream. From this point on, all of her questions are behind the time and go unanswered. Hypnotized by his presence, she moves toward the door to cover him with her body. But as she approaches, he responds, anticipating her acts: "Bin ich der Wirkliche, Du die tote Verfangene? Warum wirst Du blässer?"[17] He cryptically predicts the ensuing reversal of roles. Once more the privileged standpoint of the eternal obliterates any sense of the plot as a sequence or progression. The cocks crow again, punctuating the atmosphere and introducing the man's song of the living mythos:

Sterne und Mond, fressende Lichter, Frau!
Versehrtes Leben, im Träumen oder Wachen
sah ich ein singendes Wesen.
Atmend entwirrt sich mir Dunkles.
Wer nährt mich?[18]

Here he names his signs and his savior (the stars, the moon, light, and the woman). He sings of the truth of eternal recurrence, a truth that only he can act on. *Ein singendes Wesen* leads him to the revelation of the dark things *(die Dunkles)* whose necessities he seems to sense.

As he regains color—by front lighting—the woman turns pale. Blended in a momentary union, the motifs of sexual intercourse and birth are suggested by the obscene *Döppelgänger* they form on either side of the bars. The entire cycle of procreation is compressed into one moment on the stage. She mates him, gives him (re)birth, and ends by nursing him. His question, "Wer nährt mich?" cannot be answered, for in the time it takes to ask, the *Verwandlung* has transpired. Her role as executioner, savior, and victim deprives her figuratively of identity and literally of life.

The two drawings that treat this scene and the final scene are made from pencil sketches for the 1909 production of the play (figures 19 and 20). Both drawings differ considerably in style from the drawings discussed earlier. The second was made into an etching for publication in *Der Sturm*, while the first was only a charcoal drawing for a poster at the *Wienerkunstschau*. This drawing shows the woman's regenerative acts as she holds the man's somewhat transposed head. The dog found in nearly all the drawings forces his way between the two figures, while the sun and the moon vie for supremacy in size and brightness. The unique value of this sketch is that it was drawn during the period (June and July 1909) when Kokoschka was composing and rehearsing the original version: it represents the pretextual state of the *Verwandlung*. Neither figure is as cruelly nor as nervously represented here as in the later, more symbolic drawings. The artist had not yet added the small-line, transparent nerve endings in the skin or his double-plane perspective. Hence there is great simplicity in both sketches and a kind of serenity in the scene, which counters the frenetic pace of the play up to this point.

The drawing of the final scene (figure 21) was also completed in 1909 and then reproduced by a line-engraving in the two early *Sturm* publications. The style is less lyrical, cruder, and more primitive than

Fig. 19. Kokoschka's charcoal drawing for poster of *Mörder, Hoffnung der Frauen* (Copyright 1990 ARS N.Y./Cosmopress)

Fig. 20. Etching of *Mörder, Hoffnung der Frauen* made for *Der Sturm* (Copyright 1990 ARS N.Y./Cosmopress)

the earlier pencil draft, and thus more appropriately matched to the final moment of the play. The resurrected man breaks open the cage door, tramples the woman who had given back his energy in the form of her blood, and sets out to finish his appointed tasks.

What follows is the relentless and nauseating slaughter of the chorus, as isolated members run back and forth like chickens awaiting the hatchet. Though symbolically they have profaned the Host, and thus may deserve their roles as victims, the actual staging of a massacre, even though filled with allusions and images of apocalypse,

Fig. 21. Kokoschka's drawing for the first page of *Der Sturm* (Copyright 1990 ARS N.Y./Cosmopress)

overwhelmed the first audience. As red light suffused half the stage and bleeding bodies lay contorted in their death agonies, the tensions erupted in fist fights among the startled and outraged spectators. As the sacred warrior stalked off into the lighted distance where the last cock was crowing, real-life soldiers from nearby barracks, who had wandered in to see the show, drew swords and charged in to break up the combative audience. A new day is born and the world is ended to the *Getöse* of what one might call "a collaborative audience." The last line of the play takes on a new (and accidental) significance in the context of the performance: " . . . verlören!"[9]

In Kokoschka's first version of *Mörder*, the effects of poetic drama, dance, painting, and song combine to announce the apocalyptic meaning of the work. Each element adds to strange fervor that pervades the piece, removing it effectively from the conventions of naturalism. Where many viewers have suspected Kokoschka of simply trying to shock the Burghers of Vienna, on examining the interactions of the arts that make up the performance, it seems clear that the author uses the parallel actions of the separate arts to capture a specific effect: the other-worldliness of ritual reenactment. The effect, then, of the choreography of the men and the women at the opening of the work is to signal a mythic enactment while carrying out the relationship of the principal characters. The singing voices of the man and woman project a further distance from reality and add to the strange sense of incantation that is first announced by the cadence of speech of the choruses of men and women. Finally the starkly painted bodies and the bright but barren set parallel the symbolic meanings of the speech, dance, and song.

Each element reinforces the central theme and adds levels of meaning through displacement and symbolism. The sum of these effects is a collaborative form, but, we should remark, the simplest kind of collaboration of the forms. Each element is directly linked to the theme and where this is the case, the parallel actions are not difficult to follow. Of all the methods for creating a *Gesamtkunstwerk*, this is the most direct. The traditional flaw in such parallel actions is that the separate arts tend to spread their effects rather than unify them. Kokoschka solves this problem by compressing and condensing his work (it can be played in about twenty minutes) and by minimizing each form; thus, the speech fragments are brief and elliptical, the dance movements simple and unconventional, and the singing momentary. He accomplishes in a short work what Wagner and others were often unable to do in longer works. For example, in the full-length opera of Ring cycle, Wagner's parallel effects tend to lengthen and separate the theme instead of unifying it. In isolated scenes, these effects can be stunning. (In defense of Wagner, each of these "isolated" scenes is longer and more completely achieved than Kokoschka's brief entry in staging.)

There is, however, another method of achieving the *Gesamtkunst-werk,* as already exemplified here first by Wassily Kandinsky in his stage composition, *Der gelbe Klang,* and then by Alwin Nikolais in his dance theater production of *Triad.* In both cases the technique is that of "abstraction" where the artists "abstract" certain elements from the several arts and then recombine them in such a way that the elements remain disassociated from their conventional formal contexts. It is to the latter that we turn next.

SEVEN

THE SACRED AND THE PROFANE
Triad

R ECENT performances of early modern collaborative works are
one way of demonstrating a continuing interest in combinations
of the arts. Such revivals as *Der gelbe Klang, Parade,* and *Le Sacre du
Printemps* are not a sign of a renewal of the avant-garde but rather a
reflection of present sophisticated expectations for such performances. It has become commonplace among art critics and reviewers
to say that the avant-garde is dead. The argument against the idea of
an avant-garde is, itself, a wondrous example of intellectual and cultural complacency. An epoch that is sure that it has seen all possible
permutations of change in the arts is an epoch that has forgotten
that it, too, is a historical period, defined by the very limitations that
it calls its advantages. If it is said that art can no longer shock its
public, it may be that the public is no longer looking at art.
Strangely enough, in an age that claims to have seen everything, collaborative artworks remain as rare as ever. In spite of theories about
mixed media, synesthesia (in rock shows, theater, and dance), and
chance combination (John Cage and Merce Cunningham), no great
number of collaborative works were produced during the years following World War II. Thus it is all the more noteworthy that, while
critical arguments raged in the various centers of the "avant-garde"
about the possibility of Total Art (from the mid-1950s through the
1970s), Alwin Nikolais improvised, staged, and then carried around
the world a complete collaborative dance theater that satisfied the
very demands for Total Theater that were elsewhere predicted but
never produced. His choreographies exemplify the best and purest
collaboration of the arts, and serve as our final example of the form.

Nikolais incorporates in his works the major elements of the *Gesamtkunstwerk* as envisioned by Richard Wagner in the mid-nineteenth

century and subsequently created by Kokoschka, Scriabin, and Kandinsky before the First World War.[1] Although Nikolais does not claim to carry on the ideas of the *Gesamtkunstwerk* (however vague one's sense of both the meaning and the pretension of the term might be), he, more than any other contemporary American artist, has succeeded in developing and successfully performing collaborations of the arts in his Dance Theater. In doing so, he has extended and given concrete examples of the collaborative form.

Nikolais began his career as a dancer with Trudy Kaschmann in 1938. He subsequently worked for nearly ten years as choreographer (1952–62) with his first company, the Henry Street Playhouse Dancers. During that time, he explored the ways choreography, sound, light, and objects could be combined for performance. During this term, he molded a viable dance company to respond to the demands of his choreographies. By the time he formed an autonomous company to tour and perform, he had enlisted Murray Louis (of the Murray Louis Dance Company), Phyllis Lamhut (of the Phyllis Lamhut Dance Company), Carolyn Carlson (of the Carolyn Carlson Dance Company) as well as Michael Ballard, Gladys Bailin, and Bill Frank. The combined excellence of these dancers added to the excitement of Nikolais's early works.

It was perhaps to Nikolais's ultimate advantage, as he pointed out, to have been relatively unknown during the initial period of the company.[2] His obscurity resulted in ten years of freedom from complex tour arrangements and sink-or-swim New York seasons. A lesser-known company can experiment more freely and survive occasional failures. Thus, during this crucial period (1950–62), Nikolais established the foundations of his Dance Theater. He experimented with every aspect of his theater and learned to build a variety of dance structures—from the short skits of *Masks, Props, and Mobiles* of 1952 to the longer, major pieces of the 1960s—in which motion was composed upon space-time coordinates. He tried out the expansion and contraction of these forms and mastered each stage of the process. At the same time, Nikolais persisted in working within his own conviction that the vital center of his dance theater was the company of dancers. No amount of collaborative excellence can cover up weak dancing. However, in the Nikolais Dance Theater, it is also the case that if any of the other elements of the performance is out of sync, the dance is also likely to fail.[3] One difference is then created. Critics seemed able to tell the dancers from the dance and, consequently, it was Nikolais who was applauded or hissed instead of his dancers.

The concept of "Total Theater" demands absorption of the individual dancers into the whole. It requires both a sacrifice of the individual to the unity of the whole and a willingness on the part of the dancers to forego the usual identity with the dance. In one sense, the dancer exchanges the self-conscious control of the effect of the dance for a control of the dance which is a part, first of a larger danced portion and then of the still larger, whole work. The major difference between the dancers in Nikolais's company and dancers in other companies does not concern their particular talents, strengths, and ambitions as dancers but rather their convictions as dancers and as artists that they are collaborators in a major, formal experiment.[4] In this sense, they contribute not only performances, but also ideas, movements, and improvised parts as the dance is created. They share in the combined creative activity that leads to performance and thus they go beyond the pure role of dancer.[5]

The components of Alwin Nikolais's dance have been traced briefly by Nikolais himself in *Nik: A Documentary* where he recounts, in fragments from his own writings, how he developed his idea of a dance theater.[6] Nikolais's origins are profoundly entwined with certain key figures in the development of modern dance. He first served as assistant to Trudy Kaschmann, a disciple of Mary Wigman.[7] From this heritage comes the principle in Nikolais's works that in dance, one creates motion in space. The discovery of elements that added new dimensions of motion and enhanced the illusions of space did not replace the premise that the dancers were the essence.

Nikolais's definition of dance as "motion in space" is an abstract description of dancers on a stage and of a wider range of effects, a range originally thought impossible for modern dance. Composite effects are used to emphasize, clarify, and make memorable the fundamental variations of movement that most "modern dance" shares. Thus, while the effect of Nikolais's work may be visionary, ritualistic, or abstract, the fundamental elements are as simple as human movement, light, and sound.

However, the actual structures and timing of the components of Nikolais's dance theater are complex and require a complicated coordination of dancers, props, sets, lights, projections, sounds, and "movement." The projected images on the stage are those of collaborating forms creating and decreating relatively simple conceptions. That the forms appear to be abstract should not create a difficulty for contemporary audiences. Nor should it try an audience that the specific sources of Nikolais's collaborative effects are hard to identify (i.e., it is difficult for the spectator to distinguish how certain total effects are brought about).[8] Dance critics often attest to the success of Nikolais's performances by writing of the ways in which his work forces viewers to reexamine their preconceptions. The range of explorations has varied from the use of stretch bands lowered from overhead (in "Tensile Involvement" from *Masks, Props, and Mobiles* [1953]); and covered aluminum extensions of limbs ("Mantis" from *Imago*, [1967]); to great stretch sacks that completely cover each dancer (where prop becomes costume in "Noumenon" from *Masks, Props, and Mobiles*), and the stretch-jointed, caterpillar-like forms of the "Trio" (from *Vaudeville of the Elements* [1965]). From these simple transformations, Nikolais has expanded to more abstract and dance-filled explorations of a pedestal (*Temple* [1974]), variations on sections of a ladder (*Tower* [1965]), and the slide projections of body parts on dancer's bodies (as in *Scenario* [1971]).

Nikolais combines elements in ways that blur the distinctions between sets, props, and costumes. One example occurs early in the Nikolais Dance Theater when, in *Vaudeville of the Elements,* the dancers begin to explore a unit of cylinders painted bright silver which resemble open-ended cans. By extending arms and legs through the prop, the dancers turn it momentarily into a large costume (see figure 22). This kind of transformation had occurred earlier in "Tensile Involvement," where the props are changed, in sequential steps, into abstract designs (a set) and then into appendages of the dancers (costumes), and finally back into a complex set of props whose geometrical relations are developed by the dancers' movements (with, within, between, outside, and wound-up in, among others).

A third variation on the theme of transformation is developed around the change of a prop-like device into a costume. Here, the motion, if deprived of prop/costume, might not develop great interest. For example, the dance "Trio" (from *Vaudeville of the Elements*), if stripped of the interesting and unusual device which all three dancers wear, would be a fairly plain series of movements. However, given the potential of the form of the prop/costume in which the three dancers are enveloped, the dance is, instead, a short introduction to the visual imagination of Nikolais's choreography. In "Trio," three female dancers dance inside triple jointed, ringed, and striped costumes. Their movements project a series of inhuman shapes as these exhibit the qualities of their props/costumes and no more. After a number of circular patterns are developed, the dancers turn upside down, create another set of shapes (these include visually rec-

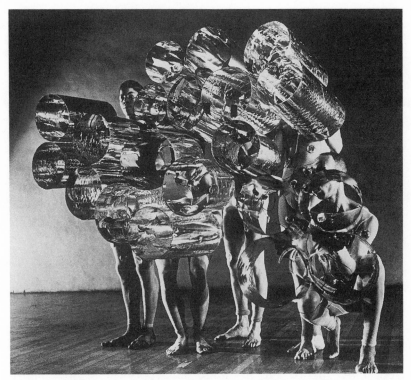

Fig. 22. Nikolais's prop turned costume, *Vaudeville of the Elements* (Photograph: Greene)

ognizable shapes, such as rising caterpillars). The dance makes no emotional statement. Instead there is a lightness, a quickness, and a wit that makes this section of *Vaudeville* deft and refreshing.

The fusion of props and costumes is not always presented in so light a mode. "Noumenon" (from *Masks, Props, and Mobiles*), for example, marks Nikolais's first use of stretch material. The dance presents three shrouded figures whose shapes are developed through the articulation of the material by a dancer hidden underneath it. Every movement is organized around the prop/costume, and the forms become archetypal and mysterious. A re-creation of this motif occurs in the section of *Grotto* (1973) called "Triple Duet," in which only two of the pairs of dancers are covered by the banded, stretch

Fig. 23. "Triple Duet" from *Grotto* (Photograph: Caravaglia)

material (see figure 23). All three pairs perform identical movements. The two covered pairs are mirrored by the uncovered pair.
The viewer is thereby given an occasion to compare the elements of
movement with and without the stretch material. One is led, in this
way, to judge the extent to which the effect of the dance is attribut-
able to a prop. In this case, the prop clearly seems to highlight and
accentuate the forms created by the choreography. The simultaneous action of the semi-nude dancers and fully covered forms adds
variety and an ironic double awareness as the trio of pairs builds
shapes and works through a continuous flow of body sculptures. The
mystique of the abstract shapes projected from the prop/costume is
mirrored in the barren simplicity of the uncovered dancers.

Yet another variation upon the theme of the fusion of sets, props,
and costumes occurs in the group dance from *Sanctum* (1964) where
each dancer is shrouded by a wide band of stretch material (see figure 24). The opening movement (subtitled "Water Study") creates
the illusion of light playing over water. The dance opens with the

Fig. 24. Group dance from *Sanctum* (Photograph: Ken Kay)

performers lying on their backs on the floor of a darkened stage. As lights sweep the stage horizontally from different directions the individual dancers raise their limbs and torsos in rapid extensions that are briefly caught by the light. These movements are syncopated to a quick rhythm, yet appear to occur in a random sequence like sunlight flashing off waves. The undulations seem both liquid and abstract. As the dancers work through the first set of movements, it becomes obvious that what seemed a stage set was really a group of dancers manipulating props. This impression is further modified by the movements of individuals who subsequently transform the props into costumes in which the body of each dancer can be seen. Nikolais's attention to these visual metamorphoses forces a radical shift in our understanding of the usual distinctions between the sets, props, and costumes.

A large part of Nikolais's mastery of stage design comes from those elements of the Total Theater that are frequently left to technicians. Nikolais experiments with every aspect of his stage composition. He continues to create, manipulate, and choreograph the lighting, projections, film, and music that constitute the "other elements" of his dance theater. Some dances (*Noumenon,* for example) require special spot and flood changes with minimal color, while other pieces combine the normal angles and lighting changes with multiple positions (front high, front low, footlights, side low, medium, high angle, and back lights) as well as special spots for scrims, props, and positions. All this lighting is in addition to the standard overhead spots and floods in varied colors.[9] A number of Nikolais's works ("Group Dance" from *Sanctum, Vaudeville of the Elements, Galaxy* [1964], *Totem* [1960], *Echo* [1963], and *Tent* [1968]) are choreographed to complex and unusual lighting effects from combinations of spots, back and side floods, color placement, projections of designs, colors, and slides (and even a symphonic play of light as design and motion). Nikolais also superimposes projections of solids and designs onto the dancers and the sets to produce the abstract effects and sensuous harmonies that are brought together in the movements of the dance. In several of these works, the dancers are made to dance to the light (for example, *Galaxy, Triptych* [1965], *Echo,* and *Somniloquy* [1967]) and in doing so add surprisingly original effects to the spatial dimensions of the theater.

The addition of scrims gives Nikolais another effective technique for modifying the space of the stage and the relative movement of the dancers. He positions the scrims to catch and reflect projected light and places them at sides, rear, and front of stage. In *Somniloquy,* the scrim reflects abstractions in colors and patterns. In *Echo,* the scrims project the illusion of multiple depths when Nikolais divides them into different areas. These effects are composed just as surely as the dances are choreographed. The principle Nikolais applies in these stage compositions is self-consciously that of collaboration of the different forms. Thus the dancers' motion is combined with the props, the light changes, and the rhythms of the music to create the larger unity of the work. Nikolais balances the spectacular with the ordinary; he works to make every effect (light, sound, motion, space) complementary.

Nikolais's theory makes dance move toward spectacle. This theory is translated into Nikolais's practice. Instead of choreographing dancers on a stage, Nikolais orchestrates his company, moving within moving light (in colors, designs, and film projections) to the movement of electronic music. His light experiments have extended beyond those already mentioned to include the use of rapid projections and the creation of slide works that function almost as independent designs; he also includes multi-faceted, fast-lighting events such as strobe lights. Yet, in each case, the "light show" is composed to complement and "make strange" the motion of the dancers in the space defined on stage by the lights themselves.

From the beginning works with the Henry Street Playhouse Dancers, Nikolais has provided his own accompanying musical scores. In the early pieces of the 1950s, these compositions tended to be built around taped percussive arrangements with some semblance of musical scoring. He also borrowed scores which he mixed, spliced, and edited on tapes to form a sound track for a particular dance. As he began to explore the possibilities of sound mixing and editing on tape, however, he developed his own version of *musique concrète* to accompany his works. He subsequently was introduced to the Moog Synthesizer with which he could create sound without all "the mess and bother of mixing, splicing, and editing the eight miles of tape" that usually confronted him.[10] Since the mid-1960s, Nikolais has composed all his sound for the synthesizer and has prepared "electronic sound" to complement his choreographies. Just as he has increasingly abstracted light to allow for the full range of effects from plain spotlights to colored projections and strobe effects, so has he pursued "electronic sound." The compositions in the Nikolais repertoire are now nearly all original tracks, some of which are adaptable enough (and attractive enough) to merit inclusion as sound for the dances of such other choreographers as Murray Louis. Nikolais provides a partial explanation of his own concept of "sound" when he writes:

> we are closer to the art of music [now] than [at any time] since the primitive times of musical art. Primitive musicians selected sounds, not methods. They had no choice of methods, they had only choice of sound. In effect, they went directly to their art source: the sound itself.[11]

Nikolais seeks the origins of art not just in his music, but in each of the elements of his dance theater. He often strives to represent primordial experiences—that is, he creates effects that are imaginative reenactments of "first things." His dancers appear to work through the kind of human responses that we might expect of an early (or original) people faced with situations for which there is no precedent. In this sense, whether the "new" is a prop, a set, a mask, a series of sounds, or all of the above, the dancers express their responses as choreography rather than as mime or spoken expression. The shock of the original (or the "new," as Robert Hughes once put it) leads to a carefully orchestrated investigation of the ways in which the new is experienced by one or more dancers. The structure of such dances is often based upon a set of learning experiences. Thus, what might begin as danced reactions of fear and flight may end with the dancers learning to get used to and finally to use the very element that had, at first, terrified them. This process is analogous to the process of myth which tells the story of how things first happened and what the gods or first people did. In dance, though, the story is enacted through movement and the viewer is left, as it were, to tell the story. Nikolais creates the props, sets, mobiles (those tents, triptychs, ladders, platforms, triads) to expand the possibilities of the dance. They attract the attention of both audience and dancers and provoke a common sense of engagement. The dancers respond to visible and audible elements on the stage rather than to the unseen and unseeable inner emotions. In this respect, Nikolais's choreographies are somewhat more abstract than earlier modern dance and, for the same reason, less obscure. The dancers' responses to the mysterious presence—the shapes, props, lights, sounds—are at least partially shared by an audience that also experiences something unfamiliar.

Thus, when I say that often Nikolais invokes preconscious experience, I do not mean that his dances are "preconscious." Far from it. Certainly on one level, the collaborative level, his dances are daunting in their complexity and sophistication. I refer instead to his means of representation of experience and to the illusion of the primordial that he achieves with the combined effects of unusual and striking elements such as sets, props, music, and light, and of the choreography. This characteristic may explain Nikolais's predilection for primordial experiences and primitive sound in such works as *Tower* (1965), *Grotto* (1973), *Temple* (1974), *Tribe* (1975), *Styx* (1976), and *Triad* (1976). It may also explain why many of his titles point toward dream, rite, ceremony, and myth (i.e., *Somniloquy, Sanctum,*

Totem, Styx, Tribe, Temple, Grotto, Echo, Triad, and *Galaxy* to name a few).[12]

There is, in addition, a related issue in the Nikolais Dance Theater that is both more complex and more centrally a part of the aesthetics of modern dance as developed in the works of Mary Wigman, Ruth St. Denis and Ted Shawn, Martha Graham, Charles Weideman, and Doris Humphrey. A dance that is a representation of preconscious experiences in that it partakes in original acts is best enacted in innocence. Nikolais's dancers move with the blank faces of those who cannot know in advance the results of their communal experience. This aspect of a dance like *Triad* adds to the illusion that the performance is, as it were, original with the dancers. The dancers act as if they see the sets of props and each other for the first time. In some scenes, a trancelike reaction is offered in response to the indefinite menaces suggested in the sound and light projected on the stage, signals of the terrors of the unknown that are truly unknown. The normative muteness of dance reinforces and may, to some extent, be responsible for this quality in performance: the illusion of the primordial.

Looking individually at the development of each of the constituent parts of the Nikolais Dance Theater serves to introduce the separate parts of the whole and to emphasize the continuous process of discovery on the part of Nikolais as he pursued nondance effects to enhance his choreographic ideas. However, the combinatory effects and qualities of the choreographer's work can only be shown by examining in some detail a whole work in which the fusion of the parts creates the whole that, in theory, might be different from its parts. During the past decade, Nikolais has created and performed more than a dozen such works, all of which introduce unique collaborative forms.

Triad is the most recent of a number of dances based upon the permutations, shapes, and combinations of the number 3. The triad comprises both the numerical meanings and the geometrical studies inherent in the figures and shapes on the stage. While in dance, trios might be thought no more distinguished than quartets, duets, and solos, in Nikolais's work there is a preponderance of success with trios that has outlived the other basic dance units. Beginning with "Noumenon" from *Masks, Props, and Mobiles,* through such successful revivals as the trio from *Vaudeville of the Elements* in 1972–77, Nikolais went on to develop a series of whole works upon the structure of

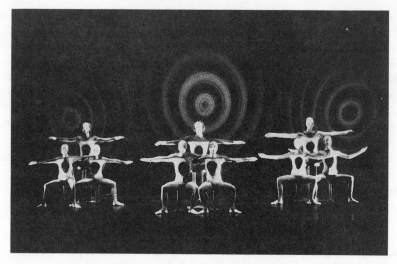

Fig. 25. Trios from *Temple* (Photograph: Caravaglia)

three: *Grotto* (containing the section entitled "Trio"), *Tower, Temple, Triptych,* and *Triad.*

In *Tower,* the group breaks down into three essential parts whose conflicts function to prevent immediate synthesis. In the formal conflict, the dancers struggle to find the structure of the Tower that they seem intent on putting together without language. The "Triple Duet" in *Grotto,* and the whole of *Temple* are similarly founded upon the multiples of the triadic unit. Each is danced by three groups of three, choreographed as simultaneous movements, flowing in and out of body sculptures with each moment of each shape held and mirrored simultaneously.

Temple places three pedestals in formation on the stage and opens with three dancers arranged upon each pedestal in an identical pose (see figure 25). The formal structure of the dance is built around each of the pedestals. The structural basis of this dance is the movement of the three dancers in relation to each other and the pedestal, which forms a solid platform for the dance as well as a prop to support the dancers. At any time in the dance, each of the trios is reflected by the other two as their movements are developed, with the resulting effect of doubling and redoubling of motion. A second effect is created by the unity of the three trios as they can be per-

Fig. 26. Trio from *Temple* (Photograph: Caravaglia)

ceived, not merely as one trio mirrored by two others, but as a group dance in unison, wherein each dancer is dancing a part of the two other parts (see figure 26.) The dance breaks back and forth from the illusion of threes to the illusion of the whole, then back to threes. This alternation forces attention sequentially to each dancer, to each trio, to the triad, and to the whole.

The natural economy of three in dance and its concomitant ease of division into duets and solos (even within these tightly choreographed, mirrored body sculptures) leads to a continuous formation and dispersion of shapes and releases from three to nine to two to two plus one, and so on. Nikolais's extension of the investigation of the possibilities of the trinity-triad-triangle-trio motif in *Triad* uncovers unexpected variations available to small numbers. At the same time, we find ourselves instructed in the mysteries of the origin of mathematical reason since the Pythagorean triangle is evoked symbolically in *Triad*.

In this dance, the fundamental numerical mystery is abstracted from the dancers, as it was in the trios and structure of *Temple,* and

Fig. 27. Dancers enter props in *Triad* (Photograph: Schaaf)

presented in the triple multiplication of the triangular shapes aligned in the center of the stage (see figure 27). The shape of each prop is essentially triangular. However the three props are given spatial depth by the illusion of perspective. Each form first appears in alternating front and back lighting, making the initial appearance of each prop mysterious. The inner surfaces of each structure pick up and reflect the lighting. Every lighting effect is multiplied whether the light is of low intensity or whether, as later in the work, the light is composed of bright-colored spots. The viewer's puzzlement is only gradually relieved as the motion of the dancers reveals the nature of the set by their progressive explorations.

For, as the dancers appear behind the triangular openings, the set itself is transformed into a prop.[13] The audience must remain aware of the prop, recognizing its real properties as well as its function in the dance. Nikolais makes it appear that the dancers are in the act of exploring physically and spiritually the possibilities of the "things" they have encountered. In this case, each set/prop is complex and, in fact, is used to create certain central visual effects. Each triad is com-

Fig. 28. Mirrored images in *Triad* (Photograph: Schaaf)

posed of three flat surfaces tilted toward the audience; each is made
of mirror-coated lucite. The three surfaces are formed in a triangle
that uses the floor as base (see figure 28). The configuration of each
of the "triads" creates an area of reflection inside and immediately in
front of the structure. There is thus a front and a rear opening in
each triadic form, and both can serve as entrances. The space between these openings becomes a threshold that is not immediately
apparent since, in the early portions of the dance, a scrim at the
back of the triad conceals the rear opening.

The dancers are first seen as silhouettes moving behind the triads.
As they approach the rear of the opening into the triadic space, they
are backlighted behind the scrim. When the scrim is lifted the audience sees the dancers' shadows again, backlighted, as they repeat
movements of the shadow dance (still upstage). Rhythmically, to met-
ronomic sounds, the dancers advance toward the opening. They
make progressively more complete revelations of themselves through

the triangular holes. Their explorations of the doorway follow the same pattern. First, they pass by each opening in groups of three; then they begin to thrust hands, feet, and heads through the imaginary spatial barrier created by the geometry of the triangular mirrors. Each of their penetrations into the triad is mirrored outward to the audience. This adds three images to each penetration of the inner-space (each of three mirrors in each triad picks up an image making four of one). The final movement before actual entry into the space of the mirrors is particularly suggestive of the playful quality of the figures moving on the stage. In each of the three spaces formed by the triads, two dancers (one holding the other from behind) work to execute (in unison with two other pairs) a somewhat antiritualistic proof that one-half makes a whole. Three dancers are lifted and extend one leg, one arm, their head, and part of their torso into the space where the mirror reflects the movement. In each triad there appears a playful illusion of another half. The precision and simultaneity of the movements provoke a moment of visual wonder as halves are made whole in all three spaces. However, the choreography suggests not magic, but spontaneity, a tone that is sustained throughout the work, as if the choreography were consciously working to preserve an element of consciousness and wit to balance out any unilateral interpretation of this dance as merely mythic experience. This part of the dance presents the ultimate partial penetration of the space of mirrored light. That is, in this case, there is an illusion of playful, whole penetration without the actual achievement of it. The trick implies a clever way to test the mysterious zone of space and light without complete commitment, as if the dancers project a fictive exploration just to see what would happen.

The dancers then move into the threshold of space between the front and back of the mirrored space. Each entry clears the way, as it were, for passage and exit as they break through the opening to the front of the stage. There they perform brief explorations of their freedom (again a testing out of the new space) and then reenter to disappear behind the brightly illuminated triadic forms.

The structure of the first half of the dance can be described as a movement from upstage through the threshold of the triangles, then downstage and back. Yet these parts of the dance, both upstage and downstage, have shapes, motions, and patterns that are interwoven, repeated, and varied in ways that defy any formula of spatial organization. Each section of the dance reenacts an exploration of the unknown. Each, for the most part, is completed in a spatially logical way since the dancers progress from upstage to the rear opening of the mirror structures, then pause for specific movements behind, at the back, into, then through the mirror-space. In the second half of the dance, the dancers display movements and shapes that suggest ways of changing the mysterious "hallowed" mirror-space into a prop. What was, at first, treated as "sacred space" becomes, through Nikolais's rapid and closely ordered time reduction, merely doors for the dancers' rapid entrance and exits.

Nikolais superimposes a variety of quick and witty movements on top of the fearful explorations of the dancers to overcome any suggestion of that heavy-handedness often found in modern dances that treat mythic experiences.[14] The whole work begins with the archetypal (that is, the terror of reenacting first things) and then moves toward the abstract, making universal the particular. Nikolais's dancers avoid the ponderous emotionalism of early modern dance in which the *Gestalten* of mood and experience were acted out as psychodrama.

Seen in rehearsal, danced, as it were, as parts without props or sets, the movements of *Triad* are curiously serial and somewhat static until the dancers begin to break through the scrim and move downstage. Placed in their full collaborative context, these serial routines come alive in the mystery of backlighted dancers on a darkened stage, advancing and retreating behind the dim triangular portals. These initial movements for trios (times three) are portrayed as oblique approaches to barriers which can only be seen through the barriers themselves. The direct light and backlighting effects bring about a simultaneous illumination (from the back) of the dancers behind the threshold/opening, which is itself illuminated.

There is, in *Triad*, an element of quickness and a minimum of repetition that keeps each step of the ritual of initiation vibrant and alive. Each approach to the threshold, each crossing and entering, each breakthrough downstage is achieved with vivacity. The dancers' final act demonstrates their mastery of the triad, the sign of the sacred and of the structure of the dance. The dancers, instead of harboring dramatic moments of terror, trepidation, and triumph, express the pure joy of expansive movement. They hold small triangles high and step quickly through the patterns that were set by their earlier gropings. Refusing priestly repetitions, the dancers become, like primordial humans, capable of original experience. They dance as if they, like all original humans, cannot be fully aware of the meaning of actions performed for the first time. The choreography emphasizes, in its rapid shifts and quick rhythms, movement rather than emotion.

The dance, by this time a group dance, ends with the two circles of dancers weaving into and through the triadic thresholds holding golden triangles, each having taken over the miniature sign of the penetrated mystery. Caught, as these dancers are, in the serrated action by blinding flashes of strobe lights, they synchronize with the music. They are stopped in the act of a free overtaking of the whole triangular form upon which the dance itself has been based. At the end, the giant, triadic props have been rendered ordinary by the dance. The mystery of the triangle, the basis of both the form and structure of the dance, has been revealed and divided into many small replicas. More abstractly, the dance has transformed the imposing image of the form of rationality itself. The first step was naive exploration of the form, then pure experience of it (its penetration), and finally its use: in this way, the mystery of reason itself (as the Pythagoreans once held it) has been brought to earth and made common. The triplification of each of these stages abstracts and makes formal what otherwise might seem overladen with mythic significance. *Triad* achieves the visual effect of mirroring light without repeating movement. The motions danced become progressively more complex in a serial way to demonstrate the greater capacity of the human figures as they work through an enigmatic and somewhat inhibiting triad of props.

While the structure of the dance suggests a primordial experience, the continuous changes that take place between the props and the dancers create ambiguity. These changes both reinforce the structural interpretation and suggest another accompanying meaning. The spatial progress of the dancers downstage is matched by the lessening significance and mystery of the triadic forms. In the final sections of the dance, these triads, so striking and ominous in the beginning, have been reduced to mere "openings," the entrances and exits of the dancers. The dancers, in effect, have taken over the entire stage in their progressive occupation of all centers of attention and in their encompassing and exploratory élan.

In the last section, the dancers run full speed in circles in near darkness, intertwining two moving circles in and out of the small "doors." The intricacy of the final group dance, which is performed between blinding light and total darkness, serves to demystify the space and, more vitally, to reemphasize the apparent lightness and ease with which the dancers celebrate their victory. The function of the dance, in its abstractness and in its refusal to specify or emote, is more closely that of the parable than the moral or philosophical allegory. Unlike some other model forms, the parable suggests several interpretations and resists any singular solution or facile simplification.

The Nikolais Dance Theater creates an art wherein the analysis of any single part is only that of a part and not the whole. The analysis of the combination of the parts (with a view of retaining the significant contributions of the dancing, the sets, or the lighting to the whole) still must bring the whole into view. Only with difficulty can the total effect of such a moment be recaptured. The dancer, the lover of dance, and the critic of dance content themselves by accounting as best they can and, no doubt, differently, for their common experience, knowing that the truth of performance must fade with the last curtain. If it were only a question, as Yeats wrote, of knowing the dancer from the dance, then we might more easily compare Nikolais to his contemporaries. But in the choreographies and dancers of the Nikolais Dance Theater, we are thrown back to artificial divisions between the dancer and the dance (as well as between the dancer, prop, music, light, and motion) simply to reach an adequate basis for judgment. Yeats's question will become equally applicable to Nikolais's dances when reviewers, critics, and viewers are able to see how Nikolais has expanded the field of unity.

THE THEORY OF
COLLABORATIVE FORM

WITH the preceding study of Alwin Nikolais's *Triad,* I show how a contemporary form of the *Gesamtkunstwerk* functions in the theater and how it combines the arts of dance, music, painting, and light in performance. Nikolais has composed and performed more than a dozen different experiments in collaborative form. Each of these works surpasses any such facile description as "multi media." The combinations of the arts that he projects on the stage are necessary to the effects he achieves. His performances are convincing displays of virtuosity that transcend the limits of modern dance. As Nikolais continues to create collaborative works, he demonstrates to other choreographers, dancers, and dramatists the vitality of the concept of total theater.

His work is the most recent of the variety of works that I have examined in this study. I have tried to suggest some of the variables in the manifestations of collaborative form in the twentieth century. As I stated in my introduction, my selections are representative of simple and complex combinations of the arts rather than of periods in the history of collaborative forms. I chose this set of works specifically to illustrate some of the different variations upon a single problem. While each work has been shown to be significantly different from the others, there are, nonetheless, certain common properties. For example, three of the works (*Lettera amorosa, A la santé du serpent,* and *Der Blaue Reiter*) are primarily textual where the arts in question are combined on consecutive pages and the reader must, as it were, "perform" the works for himself. The remaining works (*Herzgewächse, Der gelbe Klang, Mörder, Hoffnung der Frauen,* and *Triad*) are all intended for stage performance. The rarity of performances of *Der gelbe Klang* and *Mörder, Hoffnung der Frauen* should not detract from our interest in them even though every critic is compelled to return to the text and to historical accounts to understand the work. While there are, thus, superficial similarities, it should also be evident that these works represent six completely different permutations of the arts in combination. They do not exhaust the possibilities of collaboration of the arts in combination. No set of examples could be said to do that.

The underlying unity of this set of examples should, though, by now, begin to be evident. All of these works are attempts to combine the arts to create an unusual form, which I have called collaborative form. In doing so, they have all followed certain implicit principles. For the artists, these principles were discovered in the act of creating and performing their works. The fact that each of the works follows the same set of rules is surprising only if one is unaware of the common goals of any collaboration. Once the rules are induced from the set of works, the task of collaboration and the work of analyzing collaborative forms should be made easier. I have not attempted to argue these principles in my discussions of the respective works because the analysis of the works themselves must precede any statement of the rules of collaborative form.

At the beginning of any set of rules, a clear definition is in order. I begin then by restating the definition of collaborative form and I intend this definition as a premise:

A collaborative work of art is composed of more than one art.

This is the simplest definition of collaborative form. The subsequent rules are developed from this statement. For the purposes of this definition, I assume that each of the arts is distinguishable from the others. While I have not discussed the essential elements of any of the individual arts, I have accepted the conventions and traditions of each art as stated in the criticism of that art as a sufficient starting point. For the purposes of this study, I have treated poetry, music, dance, painting, drama, film, and sculpture as distinguishable art forms. Any art work that includes elements that are not ordinarily found in one art can be collaborative.

This definition emphasizes the arts rather than the artists. I make no distinction between collaborations completed by one artist and those completed by several artists working together. While the individual contributions of the artists who create a collaborative form are certainly of interest to anyone wishing to interpret such a work, the concept of collaborative form is constructed to direct the viewer to the completed form rather than to its constituent parts. Attention is focused on the interactions of the separable arts (where separable) rather than on the relationships (however fascinating) of the contributing artists. Thus, whether one artist, two, or four work to create the composite form, the definition of the form will not change to reflect its single or multiple composers.

My definition implies a further limitation. I have ruled out those combinations where several artists collaborate in the same art. For example, the surrealist collaborations of André Breton and Phillippe Soupault in *Les Champs Magnétiques* (1919) and of Breton, Paul Eluard, and René Char in *Ralentir Travaux* (1931) must be placed in another category. Where the first goal of collaborative form is that of combining the arts, works that combine elements of the same art must be treated within the conventions of that art. *Ralentir Travaux,* then, poses interesting problems of interpretation, but these problems can be explained within the conventions of literary criticism. They are different and somewhat simpler problems than those I am trying to solve in this essay.

Given the preliminary definition, I want then to propose the following five rules of collaborative form:

I. *Collaborative form results from the interactions of the arts.*

In each of the preceding chapters, my central problem was to show how the various arts in each work were related. More specifically, I wanted to show how the observer could come to understand these relationships. My method was usually to analyze the parts (the elements of each art), then suggest how the parts interacted to create the work (*l'ouvrage*). In doing so, I tried to follow the practice of the artists and to avoid emphasizing one art at the expense of the others. I discovered that if the viewer were to allow the separate arts (the *Klänge,* according to Kandinsky) to manifest their effects, the interactions of these arts would create a composite form.

However, to break down the "barriers" that separate the individual arts, I found that the audience (the viewers, readers, or listeners) has to suspend its normal sets of expectations long enough to experience the work at hand. If the work itself can break down those expectations, as I think *Der gelbe Klang* and *Triad* do, then the elements of the different arts can be perceived. However, some collaborative works do not actively function to bring their constituent arts into relation. For these, an active audience is needed, an audience that can "bracket" its expectations and alter its ways of perceiving art works. Such an audience must always be the exception rather than the rule. More often, the performance of collaborative form is met by tumult (as in the riot incited by *Le Sacre du Printemps*) or withdrawal (as in the incomprehension brought about by the John Cage-Merce Cunningham performances).

Any concept of the relation of the arts must be based on the assumption that, paradoxically, "something happens" between arts that are combined in one work. The rules of collaborative form clarify and limit what "might happen" when different arts are brought together. The first rule implies that there are demonstrable effects that can be derived from such interaction. It also excludes all combinations of the arts that do not create such effects. The mere juxtaposition of several arts in an exhibition or a performance does not guarantee collaboration any more than does writing music for a poem or making a film from a novel. The test of collaborative form is the presence of the effects of interaction. Each composite form is the sum of these effects, an art form that is different from its parts.

In my set of examples of collaborative forms, the first work, *Lettera amorosa*, was shown to depend upon the interactions of the lithographs and the poem as these were combined specifically (page-by-page) and structurally (in the intertwined development of themes by the two arts). In my subsequent examples, the effects of interaction were neither as clear nor as thoroughgoing as in *Lettera amorosa*. Instead, with the examples from *Der Blaue Reiter*, I examined a variety of kinds of interaction that ranged from nonspecific relations between texts and reproductions in the almanac to the precise counterpoints and paradoxes of relation between "Das Verhältnis zum Text" and "Herzgewächse." In both instances, the theoretical statements of Kandinsky and Schoenberg were given full play in the analysis of their works.

The nature of the interactions between the arts in complex forms as examined here followed no set pattern. Thus, even where a larger theory of monumental art (and an essay on *Bühnenkomposition*) provided a key for interpreting the effects of Kandinsky's *Der gelbe Klang*, these effects were multiple and difficult to unravel. The 1982 performance of *Der gelbe Klang* both helped and hindered my understanding of Kandinsky's color opera. In the premiere production, certain sets of interactions between color, light, and sound that I had predicted from the text of the play were, for one reason or another, deleted. While no one could expect any performance of Kandinsky's brief text to conform in all ways to Kandinsky's theories of inner-vibrations, the reduction of the text on the stage was still disappointing. On the other hand, the presence of a musical score where none had heretofore been thought possible added enormously to the effects of the individual scenes. The numerous effects of interaction initiated by the chamber orchestra more than compensated for the absence of other, isolated effects in the other arts.

The major difference between the simple collaborative works and *Der gelbe Klang* cannot be fully defined by my categories of simple and complex collaboration. In the "Pictures" that Kandinsky creates, there is no part that is not created to interact with other elements. If we were to separate the constituent arts in works such as *Lettera amo-rosa, A la santé du serpent,* or *Herzgewächse,* we would still have a set of recognizable forms. That is, we would still have poetic texts and either a set of lithographs or a short musical composition. In *Der gelbe Klang* and *Triad,* no such comfortable separation into constituent arts can occur. If we pull out the colors from the figures, the choreography from the lighting, or the music from the staging, we would discover that each part comprises a set of fragmentary elements that no longer retains a complete sense of disciplinary identity. Each of these elements, abstracted from its traditional artistic home, becomes more dependent on the other elements. In interpreting complex forms, we discover both a greater necessity for and a greater frequency of interaction. We also find that the works seem charged with a greater level of underlying symbolic meaning. This is one reason why I have claimed that the tendency of every *Gesamtkunstwerk* is toward abstraction. This tendency is shown in *Mörder, Hoffnung der Frauen* as well as in *Der gelbe Klang* and *Triad.* In all three, the underlying meaning is symbolically represented in the various fragmented elements of the arts. In each case, the artists can use multiple elements to parallel (or present serially) a consistent symbolism. However, instead of creating an overbearing effect (as often occurs in a single art), the presence of several arts disperses the cumulative effect of symbolism. In this way, the symbols (the yellow giants, the circle of dancers, the triangle) function to state themes (in one art) and counterpoint themes (in the others).

II. *There can be no primary form in collaborative art. Collaboration sub-ordinates each constituent art to the combined effect of the whole.*

In each of the examples I studied, the singular contributions of the individual arts are less important than the part each plays in relation to the others and to the whole. The key to sustaining inter-actions between the arts is the artists' capacity to balance each art against the others. Whether there are two arts involved (as in *Lettera amorosa* and *Herzgewächse*) or a larger number (as in *Der gelbe Klang* or *Triad*), no single art becomes the basis for comparison or contrast. According to this rule, combinations of the arts that are based upon one art are not collaborative because they cannot be centrally depen-dent on the effects of interaction. They are (by definition) incapable of achieving either the harmonic or counterpointal relation of the arts assumed in all effects of interaction. I am not denying that there are combinations of the arts based on one art. Nor do I deny that such combinations can function effectively as works of art. But I am excluding all such works from this category of forms. The rules of collaboration (as we shall see) will make the inclusion of works based on primary forms a logical impossibility.

Certainly one result of this rule will be to narrow the field of com-binations of the arts. (I divide the field of combinations between col-laborative forms and primary forms.) Most combinations of the arts feature a primary form. The prevalent forms of combination in the arts usually are based upon the theory, if not the practice, of pri-mary form. Most examples in opera, drama, television, and film are created and discussed in terms of primary form. Furthermore, nearly all criticism of combinations of the arts operates upon one variation or another of the theory of primary form. Wherever a critic or a scholar employs the critical conventions of one art to in-terpret works of collaboration, we can suspect that he or she is ap-plying the measure of that art to the other arts as well. While this practice is often excused as an extension to other disciplines of a convenient critical language, it should nevertheless be labeled as one of the fallacies of primary form. The application of the conventions of one art (the criticism of that art) to the practices of other arts presupposes the dominant effects of that art. It is a sign of the fail-ure of the critic to transcend the critical categories of his specialty. We should recognize the themes of primary form when we hear op-era discussed only in terms of music, illuminated texts treated merely as poetry, plays as literary texts, and films as occasions for lectures on semiology.

III.   *All collaborations create an original work.*

The effects of interaction, integration, and relation of the arts in collaboration create an original form. Each collaboration is thus a new artwork that does not function exactly like any of its constituent arts. As a result, the traditions, conventions, and effects of each art in a collaboration will not suffice to describe the sum of the effects of combination. Those who divide a collaborative work into its respective parts (i.e., arts) will miss exactly those effects that are the result of combination. To divide opera, for example, into music on the one hand and drama on the other may permit discussion of the two essential parts, but such a division denies implicitly the interaction of the two which defines the new work.

The form created by the effects of the interactions of the arts in a composite work is unique to that particular combination of the arts. This form is distinguished from other forms (musical, literary, painterly, choreographic, etc.) by its composite nature. It cannot be derived outside of a combination of the arts.

IV.   *The subtraction, deletion, or separation of any of the constituent arts in a collaboration destroys the form.*

The issue here is as simple as any equation where the whole is the sum of its parts. Collaborative form is the creation of the sum of the interactions of its parts. Thus the absence of even one of these parts changes the nature of (sum of) the interactions in such a way that the total effect is negated. On the level of "simple" collaborations, the result of taking away one of the arts should be obvious. René Char's poem, *Lettera amorosa,* appears by itself in several collective editions of his poems. Yet, without Braque's lithographs, it is never the same work that it becomes in combination. The absence of the pages of combined text and lithography is, in effect, the absence of *Lettera amorosa,* the collaborative form. Similar examples abound and the differences between the isolated parts (Maeterlinck's poem "Feuillage du coeur" apart from Schoenberg's musical setting, Blake's *Songs of Innocence* without the illuminations, Kandinsky's *Klänge* without the woodcuts) and the composite forms are obvious even though the separated part may suffice in other contexts as a work of art.

In "complex" combinations, this formula has been less frequently emphasized and the original integrity of a number of modern collaborations has been destroyed by those who imagined that minor deletions would not matter. In this way, some of the most original and admired collaborations of this century are regularly performed in part as if the effect of the whole were somehow present. Igor Stravinsky's music for *Le Sacre du printemps* has become something of a standard in the repertoire of contemporary orchestras. Even though Nijinsky's choreography and costumes (not to mention the performance of a troupe of dancers) have consistently been deleted from the original, collaborative form, audiences respond to the music without the other parts of the collaboration. In this case, the deletion of the other parts is treated as an unimportant sacrifice because the part of the original that is performed is a powerful work of art in its own right. It is nonetheless revealing that *Le Sacre du printemps* is recognized primarily as the title of a musical composition rather than an original collaborative form. In the case of such deletions, the interactions between the arts are lost completely and all sense of collaborative form destroyed.

There are many examples of collaborative works that are cut apart for subsequent publication or performance. Often the destruction of the original form is carried out with the best intentions though with apparent ignorance of the fundamental principles of the art forms thus pirated. Perhaps it would require "a harrassing master" to insist that every performance of Erik Satie's *Parade* include the dancers, costumes, and sets of the original work or that each projection of René Clair's *Entr'acte* be inserted between acts of Massine's ballet for Satie's *Relâche*. However, the ease of representation of certain parts of a larger work should not obscure the effects of the original collaboration. The collaborative form is destroyed in each of these cases by deletion and, perhaps because of the success of one of the parts, the destruction is ignored by a culture that persists in refusing to recognize the collaborative nature of some of its most celebrated works of art.

Admittedly, in complex collaborations, it is difficult to reproduce (publish, display, or perform) the total work. But this should not deter us from insisting that the total work cannot be reduced without losing the original. We should not always have to view fragments in place of the work itself. As audiences become aware of how much is lost each time a composite form is divided, they will value complete representations more highly.

V. *The effects of combining the arts are never additive.*

Combining two arts in a collaborative work does not enhance or increase the effect of the resultant combination in any proportionate or additive way. Every completed form is a whole. Thus, just as every painting or every poem is a complete work, so each completed collaboration is a complete work.

From this rule, certain surprising facts are deduced. Often in the writings concerning the relations of the arts (from Lessing to Wagner to Lothar Shreyer), the "obvious" advantages of works that combined the arts were that such *Gesamt* works would be "greater," more "resonant," more "powerful," and more spiritually expressive than any single art. However, according to the rule of nonaddition, collaborative artworks will not necessarily be superior to or even more interesting than works in any single art. In fact, if one were to follow the logic of nonaddition, works of art that combined arts will be no more effective, no more powerful, and no more moving than any other work of art. Music added to drama can thus produce (in some cases) a collaborative form, opera. Yet opera will not, a priori, become twice as rich or twice as effective as either music or drama.

This rule of collaborative form dictates completed forms as wholes. Each art work, whether a single art or a combination, is, in theory, equal to every other art work. The differences that one finds in accessibility, in value, and in memorability between works of art are not caused by the number of arts incorporated in those works. The expectations of any audience should not be unnecessarily elevated merely because the work at hand is collaborative. While an audience might be instructed to expect differences such as those I have discussed here, it should not expect a quantitative change in its experience. The unity of the form of combination, though more difficult to achieve, is still the essential unity analogous to that of any artwork.

It should be clear that these limitations are not merely quantitative. For just as opera is not inherently better art than piano music, so other collaborative forms retain no natural advantage in quality. One consequence of this rule is that we can begin to see why so much was expected of the ideal of the *Gesamtkunstwerk* and how lamentably mistaken those expectations were. At the same time, it is to the health of the arts that such unrealizable and unrealistic goals should be corrected. For surely part of the explanation for the usefulness of this study is that it breaks down the myth of the transcendent work, a myth that held, as a matter of faith, that the difficulties inherent in combining the arts were to be repaid handsomely by the sublimity to be achieved. The paradox, of course, is that occasionally these beliefs are fulfilled. The most far-reaching effect of this rule should be to lower the threshold of interaction and appreciation in combinations of the arts. I would be satisfied, however, if my study shows other artists how simple the effects of interaction can be and how inevitably unique any such combination of the arts becomes.

Notes

INTRODUCTION: *Collaborative Form*

1. *Richard Wagner and the Synthesis of the Arts* (Detroit: Wayne State University Press, 1960), 3.
2. Schelling, "Concerning the Relation of Plastic Arts and Nature," trans. Michael Bullock, in Herbert Read, *The True Voice of Feeling: Studies in English Romantic Poetry* (New York: Pantheon Books, 1953), 332.
3. See Richard Wagner, *Opera and Drama* in *Richard Wagner's Prose Works*, trans. William Ashton Ellis (London: 1895–99) 2:351–76.
4. Compare, for example, *Opera and Drama*, 375–76 to the later essay "Zukunft-musik" (1861) in *Sämtliche Schriften und Dichtungen* 7 (Leipzig: Breitkopf und Härtel, 1912), 87–137.
5. "Über die Bestimmung der Oper" (1871), in *Sämtliche Schriften und Dichtungen*, 9:146.
6. Kandinsky, "Über Bühnenkomposition," in *Der Blaue Reiter*, ed. Wassily Kandinsky and Franz Marc (Munich: Piper Verlag, 1912), 108–9.
7. "Über Bühnenkomposition," 108.
8. "The painter writes himself with difficulty." Braque's phrase is ambiguous since it could as well mean "the painter writes of or to himself with difficulty." Georges Braque, *Cahier 1917–1947* (Paris: Maeght Editeur, 1965), unpaged.

1 THE WORK ADMIRED IN EVERY AGE: *Lettera amorosa*

1. Related to the author in conversations with the poet at L'Isle-sur-Sorgue, May 23–25, 1972.
2. See the explanatory note by François Chapon in Chapon, ed. *Georges Braque-René Char* (Catalogue de l'exposition Georges Braque-René Char à la Bibliothèque littéraire Jacques Doucet) (Université de Paris, May 1963), 55–56.
3. "The Work admired in every age." Trans. Jackson Matthews, *Hypnos Waking* (New York: Random House, 1956), 229. *Lettera amorosa* (1953; new edition, Genève: Edwin Engleberts, 1963), 9. Unless otherwise noted, all citations to *Lettera amorosa* will be from this edition and will be cited parenthetically in my text.

4. *La Conversation souveraine*, Char's phrase, is precise here, for the work imposes an active exchange rather than a passive reading, two voices in rise and fall of conversation remembered only afterward as one.

5. "A time for shoring up, years of affliction. . . . This is natural law! This age, despite itself, will give existence to the Work admired in every age." Trans. Matthews, *Hypnos Waking*, 229.

6. *Lettera amorosa*, 9.

7. The epigraph to Char's poem is from Claudio Monteverdi, the Italian composer (1587–1643), whose *Lettera amorosa* is quoted: "Non è già part'in voi che con forz'invincibile d'amore tutt'a se non mi tragga" ("There is no part of you that does not draw me with the invincible force of love." Trans. author), *Lettera amorosa*, 9.

8. A phrase distilled from Braque's *Cahiers* by Jean Paulhan.

9. "It is not simple to stay balanced upon the wave of courage when one looks at some bird flying at the decline of day." Trans. author, 47.

10. "Sunday Morning," in *The Collected Poems of Wallace Stevens* (New York: Knopf, 1955), 74.

11. "He that watches awake at the summit of pleasure is the equal of both sun and night. He that watches has no wings, he does not pursue." Trans. Matthews, *Hypnos Waking*, 239.

12. "My comic desire, my frozen wish: to seize your head like a bird of prey perched on the abyss. I have many times held you in the rain of cliffs, like a hooded falcon." Trans. Matthews, *Hypnos Waking*, 241.

13. "Moons and night, you are a black velvet mask, village, on the watching window of my love." Trans. author, 16.

14.

Song of Insomnia

Love, calling, the beloved will come,
Gloria of summer, O fruit!
The sun's arrow will pierce her lips,
The naked clover will curl upon her flesh,
Miniature likeness of the Iris, the Orchid,
Oldest gift of the meadow's pleasure instilled
By the waterfall, delivered by the mouth.

(*Lettera amorosa*, 19; trans. author)

2 THE WARMTH OF THE FACE OF THE NEWBORN:
A la santé du serpent

1. At the Bibliothèque nationale, Paris, from 16 January to 30 March 1980.

2. Most of Char's early books published between 1928 and 1934 contained illustrations (for example: *Arsenal* [1929]; *Arsenal* [1930]; *Le Tombeau des secrets* [1930]; and *Artine* [1930]).

3. Paris: GLM, 1936.

4. *Le Marteau sans maître suivi de Moulin premier: 1927–35* (Paris, Librairie José Corti, 1945). The first twenty-five exemplaires contain an eau-forte in black by Pablo Picasso. *L'Escalier de Flore* (Alès: PAB, 1958) has two engravings in color by Picasso and *Pourquoi la journée vole* (Alès: PAB, 1960) includes one engraving by Picasso.

5. Here I refer to specific works that each artist has completed with the poet: Jean Hélion in *Dix poèmes de la sieste blanche, manuscrit enluminé* (1950–51); Jean Hugo in

Chanson des étages (Alès: PAB, 1955) and *La Fauvette des roseaux* (Alès: PAB, 1955); Pierre André Benoit in *Visage de semence* (Alès: PAB, 1963) and *Songer à ses dettes* (Alès: PAB, 1964); Victor Brauner in *Le Viatique ou non, manuscrit enluminé* (1950); Luis Fernandez in *Le Deuil des Névons* (Brussels: Le Cormier, 1954); Greta Knutson in *Le Visage nuptial* (Paris: n.p., 1938); and Denise Esteban in *Le Nu perdu et autres poèmes plus distants, manuscrit enluminé* (1974). All references to *manuscrits enluminés* are to those single copies exhibited at the *Bibliothèque nationale*, 1980, which were lent by the poet from his collection.

6. *Le Soleil des eaux* (Paris: H. Matarasso, 1949) with four eaux-fortes by Georges Braque; *La Bibliothèque est en feu* (Paris, Louis Broder, 1956) with frontispiece (eau-forte and aquatinte en couleurs) by Georges Braque; and *Lettera amorosa* (Geneva, Edwin Engelberts, 1963) with twenty-seven color lithographs by Georges Braque; *Poèmes des deux années*, 1953–54 (Paris: GLM, 1955) with an eau-forte by Alberto Giacometti as frontispiece; *Retour Amont* (Paris: GLM, 1965) containing four eaux-fortes by Alberto Giacometti; *Guirlande terrestre, manuscrit enluminé* (1952), in which sixteen of the thirty-six pages are illustrated by *papiers découpés et collés*, some of which are painted with water colors, by Jean Arp; *A la santé du serpent* (Paris: GLM, 1954) with twenty-seven *vignettes* and one color lithograph by Joan Miró; *De moment en moment* (Alès: PAB, 1957) including two *gravures* by Joan Miró; and *Nous avons* (Paris: Louis Broder, 1959) illustrated by five eaux-fortes in color by Joan Miró.

7. "The poet and the painter came to know each other, came across one another during the period of surrealism, meetings of such warmth and brevity that they each would remember the other. But a storm was in the sky and each so absorbed by the necessity of strengthening his language in order to resist the monstrous rise of danger that they would have to wait until after the war for a more serene space in which their friendship could produce its first fruits" (Dupin in catalogue for the exposition *René Char* [St.-Paul-de-Vence and Paris: Foundation Maeght, Musée d'art moderne de la Ville de Paris, 1971]).

8. "Miró who proved often and with explosiveness an almost infallible feeling for the book and a remarkable graphic intelligence for the poem, treated here as Wifredo Lam would do four years later, each double page as a whole, alternating brilliantly colored surfaces with darker spaces, playing the entire keyboard of possibilities offered him. Indian Ink, *gouaches*, water colors, crayons, charcoal, wax, mixed or used separately, thus determine the zones creating a rhythm in the collection with a graphic accompaniment which matches the poems in a way so fitting to the economy of means and the paradox of signs . . . that we are confounded by so much freedom and fantasy in his response, his graphic punctuation" (Coron, in catalogue *René Char: Manuscrits enluminés par les peintres du XXᵉ siècle* [Paris: Bibliothèque nationale, 1980], 1).

9. "Things come slowly. My vocabulary of forms, for example, I did not discover all at once. It formed itself almost in spite of me." *Je travaille comme un jardinier* (Paris: XXᵉ siècle, 1963), 46. Miró also collects his various writings from the period in question in *Carnets catalans*, a two-volume set of illustrated *cahiers* published by Skira in the series *Les Sentiers de la création* (Geneva: Editions Albert Skira, 1976).

10. "I wanted to consider this series of canvases as poignant schematic signs, of pure poetry, a cry of the spirit as eaux-fortes of the future." *Carnets catalans* 2:43.

11. "These schematic signs have an enormous suggestive power, otherwise they would have been abstract and, as a consequence, dead." *Carnets catalans* 2:43.

12. These books are: *Fête des arbres et du chasseur* (Paris: GLM, 1948); *Homo poeticus* (Alès: PAB, 1953); *L'Alouette* (Paris: GLM, 1954); *Nous avons* (Alès: PAB, 1958) and *Le Chien de coeur* (Paris: GLM, 1969).

13. As is the case in *Fête des arbres et du chasseur* and *Le Chien de coeur*.

14. *Six patiences pour Joan Miró*, n.p., n.d., is an illuminated two-page manuscript containing six poems written for and illustrated by Miró. This manuscript was subsequently printed privately and then reproduced in the catalogue of the exposition *René Char* (1971).

15. *Fontaine 56* (November 1946), 520–33. *Le Poème pulvérisé* (Paris: Fontaine, 1947).

16. Lam, in the *manuscrit enluminé* of *A la santé du serpent*, Braque in his illustrations for *Le Soleil des eaux*, and Fernandez in his vignettes drawn to accompany *A une sérénité crispée* had each demonstrated effective uses of the spaces between Char's fragments.

17. "Miró who does not declare, Miró who points, Miró who imagines marriages." René Char, *Flux de l'aimant* (Paris: Maeght editeur, 1964), unpaged.

18. René Char, *A la santé du serpent* (Paris: GLM, 1954), 18–19, Hereafter references to this book will occur parenthetically in the text.

19. In a parallel structure, the opposite order of events may occur as well. In this case, following the order of presentation, the effect of the *signe* may precede and thus modify, a priori, the reading of the text. The order of these effects is reversible, depending on the reader's disposition to attend to either *signe* or text first.

20. "You are in your essence constantly a poet, constantly at the high point of your love, constantly avid for truth and justice. No doubt it is a necessary evil that you cannot be assiduously in your conscience." Trans. author, 20.

21. "It is unworthy of the poet to mystify the lamb, to invest himself in its fleece." Original, 26; translation, Matthews, *Hypnos Waking*, 205.

22. "Tears despise their sympathizer." Original, 22; translation, Matthews, *Hypnos Waking*, 203.

23. "If we live in a lightning flash, it is the heart of the eternal." Original, 27; translation, Matthews, *Hypnos Waking*, 205.

24. René Char, *La Bibliothèque est un feu* in *Oeuvres complètes* (Paris: Editions Gallimard, 1983), 378.

25. *Héraclite d'Éphèse*, traduction nouvelle et intégrale avec introduction et notes par Yves Battistini, avant-propos de René Char (Paris: Editions Cahiers d'Art, 1948), 44.

26. I have numbered the *signes* in the order of their first appearance in the book, reading from left to right on every full page (6, 7, 10). The unique group on p. 15 is not given a number even though it would represent the twenty-eighth *signe* in the series.

27. "In the loop of the swallow a storm is informed, a garden is built." Original, 17. Trans. author.

28. "A rose that it may rain. At the end of innumerable years, that is your wish." Original, 28; translation, Matthews, *Hypnos Waking*, 207.

3 ON THE SPIRITUAL IN ART: *Der Blaue Reiter*

1. *Der Blaue Reiter*, herausgegeben von Wassily Kandinsky und Franz Marc (München: R. Piper and Co. Verlag, 1912). This edition and the second edition,

which appeared in 1914, were published in relatively small runs and are, consequently, extremely rare. A new documentary edition of *Der Blaue Reiter* was published in 1965 by Klaus Lankheit (Munich: R. Piper Verlag) with accompanying documents, facsimiles, and notes. In citing *Der Blaue Reiter*, I shall refer to the Lankheit edition as *DBR*. Subsequently, Lankheit's edition was translated into English as *The Blaue Reiter Almanac* by Henning Falkenstein with the assistance of Manug Terzian and Gertrude Hinderlie in the Documents of 20th-Century Art (New York: Viking, 1974); hereafter referred to in the text as *TBRA*.

2. Will Grohmann, *Wassily Kandinsky: Life and Work* (New York: Abrams, 1958), 44–60. A more suggestive account of Kandinsky's activities in Munich has been presented in Peg Weiss's *Kandinsky in Munich: The Formative Jugendstil Years* (Princeton: Princeton University Press, 1978). The exhibition, *Kandinsky in Munich*, organized by Weiss at the Solomon R. Guggenheim Museum in New York (1982), further documented the various influences on Kandinsky's development between 1896 and 1914.

3. Will Grohmann, *Wassily Kandinsky* (New York: Abrams Library of Great Painters, 1971), 4. Paul Overy states that it would be more accurate to say that Kandinsky began to experiment with abstraction in 1910; Overy recognizes, at the same time, that the claim of "the first abstract painting" is still disputed among art historians. The date of Kandinsky's first "abstract" painting may be less important than the fact that much of what he accomplished between 1909 and 1914 was directly related to his desire to experiment with nonobjective, symbolic, and "pure" paintings. See Overy, *Kandinsky: The Language of the Eye* (London: Elek, 1969), 13, 35.

4. Rose Carol Washton Long, in her book *Kandinsky: The Development of an Abstract Style* (Oxford: Clarenden Press, 1980), argues persuasively that Kandinsky built a set of symbolic motifs and figures into otherwise nonfigurative paintings during the period that preceded the war. Her argument must modify previous positions on Kandinsky's development as an abstract painter even though no one would have claimed that he painted pure abstraction during the period 1910–14.

5. At the conclusion of his book, *Über das Geistige in der Kunst* (Munich: Piper Verlag, 1912), 124, Kandinsky outlines the distinctions that he began to make in titling his works (c. 1910). This passage appears in English in *Concerning the Spiritual in Art* (New York: Wittenborn, 1947), 77:

> As examples of the new symphonic composition, in which the melodic element plays an infrequent and subordinate part, I have added reproductions of four of my own pictures. They represent three different sources of inspiration:
>
> 1) A direct impression of nature, expressed in purely pictorial form. This I call an "Impression."
>
> 2) A largely unconscious, spontaneous expression of inner character, nonmaterial nature. This I call an "Improvisation."
>
> 3) An expression of a slowly formed inner feeling, tested and worked over repeatedly and almost pedantically. This I call a "Composition." Reason, consciousness, purpose, play an overwhelming part. But of calculation nothing appears: only feeling.

6. *Über das Geistige in der Kunst*, 110–13. Of the several translations in English, the most accurate is that published as *Concerning the Spiritual in Art* (New York: Wittenborn, 1947). This edition is a revision and retranslation (by Francis Golffing, Michael Harrison, and Ferdinand Ostertag) of the early English translation, *The Art of Spiritual Harmony*, by Michael Sadleir (London: Constable, 1914). Hereafter I shall refer to

the Wittenborn translation as CSA in my text. "Über die Formfrage" was composed especially for *Der Blaue Reiter* in 1911 and appears in *DBR*, 74–100.

7. "A work of art consists of two elements, the inner and the outer. The inner is the emotion in the soul of the artist; this emotion has the capacity to evoke a similar emotion in the observer. As long as the soul is connected with the body, it is affected through the medium of the senses—the felt. Emotions are aroused and stirred by what is sensed. Thus, the sensed is the bridge, i.e., the physical relation between the immaterial which is the artist's emotion and the material, which results in the production of a work of art. And again, what is sensed is the bridge from the material (the artist and his work) to the immaterial to (the emotion of the soul of the observer).

"Emotion—Feeling—Work—Feeling—Emotion" (Kandinsky, "Malerei als reine Kunst," *Der Sturm* 178/179 [September 1913]: 98–99; trans. author).

8. "Malerei als reine Kunst," 98.

9. "Here we see that in principle it makes *no difference whether the artist uses real or abstract forms. Both forms are internally equal. . . .* To express it abstractly: *in principle, there is no question of form.*" "Über die Formfrage," *DBR*, 162; translation from *TBRA*, 168 (Kandinsky's emphasis).

10. "I had then the idea of a 'synthetic' book which was to have eradicated the superstitions, destroyed the walls between the arts divided from each other, between official art and 'unacceptable' art, and finally to have proven that the question of art was not that of form, but of content. The separation of the arts, their isolated existence in little huts made of high, hard, and opaque walls, was to my eyes one of the false and dangerous consequences of the analytic method which suppressed the synthetic method in science and was beginning to do the same in art. The results followed: inflexibility, narrow points of view and feelings, loss of the freedom of emotion, perhaps even the definitive death of art" ("Franz Marc," *Cahiers d'Art* 11 [1936]: 274; emphasis Kandinsky's, trans. author).

11. "My idea then was to show by example that the difference between official art and 'ethnographic' art had no basis; that the pernicious custom of not seeing, beneath the different, exterior forms, the interior, organic roots of art in general would end by a total loss of reciprocal interaction between art and human society. Even the differences between children's art, art of the dilettante and academic art—these gradual differences between forms that are said to be 'successful' and 'unsuccessful' covered over the force of the expression and the communal roots [of all art]" ("Franz Marc," 274, trans. author).

12. Kandinsky to Marc, 19 June 1911, in "Die Geschicht des Almanachs," ed. Klaus Lankheit; *Der Blaue Reiter: Dokumentarische Neuausgabe* (Munich: Piper Verlag, 1965), 259. In the letter Kandinsky observes:

> I have a new idea. Piper must be the publisher and the two of us editors. A kind of almanach (yearbook) with reproductions and articles . . . and a chronicle!! that is, reports on exhibitions reviewed by artists, and artists alone. In the book the entire year must be reflected; and a link to the past as well as a ray to the future must give this mirror its full life. The authors will probably not be remunerated. Maybe they will have to pay for their own plates, etc. We will put an Egyptian work beside a small Zeh, a chinese work beside a Rousseau, a folk print beside a Picasso, and the like. Eventually we will attract poets and musicians. The book should be called "The Chain" or some other title. . . . Don't

talk about it. Or only if it could be directly useful to us. In cases like this discretion is most important. (Translation from *TBRA*, 16)

13. Lankheit reproduces facsimile versions of the projected contents of *Der Blaue Reiter* from letters. The first version is from a letter from Franz Marc to Reinhard Piper dated 10 September 1911. The second version, considerably shorter, is taken from the draft of a press release written by Kandinsky in early October 1911. The third prospectus (from the estate of Auguste Macke) is dated October 1911. See *DBR*, 307–12; *TBRA*, 244–49. While Lankheit traces the history of the compilation, changes, and production of the almanac, he does not explain why the format for the book changed nor how the final copy assumed the order (reproductions and articles) we now have.

14. Kandinsky, *Catalogue for the First Blaue Reiter exhibition*, 18 December 1911 at the Thannhauser Gallery in Munich, quoted in Grohmann, 67.

15. Grohmann, 67. From the advance announcement of *Der Blaue Reiter Almanach* inserted in the catalogue of the First Blaue Reiter exhibition and attributed to Kandinsky by Grohmann and Lankheit.

16. Reproduced in facsimile in Lankheit, *DBR*, 311–12. Also in *TBRA*, 248–49.

17. Reproduced in facsimile in Lankheit, *DBR*, 309. Also in *TBRA*, 247–48.

18. "As for the production of the book, you and Mr. Kandinsky acted entirely independently of us. You never asked for our advice about accepting articles, the number of articles, or the size of the plates. You just ordered us to print or make plates. You also fixed the retail price at ten marks without considering the cost of production. It was correct of you to assume that a promotional pamphlet should not be too expensive . . . but now you must not be surprised when despite rather active sales, the cost of the book is out of proportion to the money received. . . . You did not respect our calculation whatsoever, *and we on our part could not influence your editorial work*" (Reinhard Piper to Franz Marc, 9 December 1912, reproduced in *DBR*, 273; translation from *TBRA*, 26–27, emphasis author's).

19. A number of artists declined to participate: Matisse contributed photographs but refused to write an article and Picasso and Braque did not answer Kandinsky's letters (though Kahnweiler sent several reproductions of Picasso's paintings). Pechstein did not complete his article on *die Brücke* and the *Sturmkreis*. Certain painters in the *Neue Künstlervereinigung München* were dropped because of their opposition to Kandinsky. Thomas de Hartmann's music for *Der gelbe Klang* was not composed in time for publication.

20. "It is terribly difficult to present one's contemporaries with spiritual gifts." Original in *DBR*, 22; translation, *TBRA*, 213. Subsequent page references will appear in parentheses in the text.

21. Piper published only fifty copies of the *luxus Ausgabe* in the 1912 edition of *Der Blaue Reiter* and of these, very few have survived.

22. This account occurs in spite of the fact that he and Kandinsky had recently had to walk out on the NKVM because of the group's refusal to allow Kandinsky to hang "Composition V" in the third (Fall 1911) exhibit. The jury claimed the canvas was "too large" to fit in the show, a spurious claim as Will Grohmann remarks in *Wassily Kandinsky*, 65–66.

23. That August Macke had not shown with the NKVM did not prevent Marc from substituting him for the movement.

24. Kandinsky and Marc could have illustrated the three groups with representative examples, had they so desired, using only those artists who otherwise appear in

Der Blaue Reiter. The point of their choice is not necessity or availability, but the interesting possibilities of the internal *"vibrationen"* thus created.

25. *TBRA,* 67; *DBR,* 37. Marc does not explain how he can account for the particulars of the history of feeling for 1832. Rather, he appeals to the reader's nostalgia for a more Romantic age.

26. Grohmann, 91.

27. *DBR,* 154–55; *TBRA,* note on pp. 162–63.

28. *TBRA,* 168. In *DBR,* this reads, " . . . dass es auch im Prinzip gar keine Bedeutung hat, ob eine reale oder abstrakte Form vom Künstler gebraucht wird. Da beide Formen innerlich gleich sind" (162).

29. "Abstractly said, there is, in principle, no question of form." Original in *DBR,* 162; translation from *TBRA,* 168.

30. "If the reader is able to rid himself of his own desires, his own ideas, his own feelings for a while and leafs through this book, going from a votive painting to a Delauney, from Cézanne to a work of Russian folk art, from a mask to Picasso, from a glass painting to Kubin, etc. etc., then his soul will experience many vibrations and he will enter the sphere of art. Here he will not find shocking defects and annoying faults, and instead of a minus he will attain a spiritual plus. And these vibrations and the plus arising from them will enrich his soul as no other means can do.

"Later the reader can go on with the artist to objective reflection and scholarly analysis. Then he will find here that all the examples respond to the same inner call— composition, that they will restore *the same inner basis—construction"* (Original in *DBR,* 180–81; translation from *TBRA,* 186).

31. *DBR,* 33-38; *TBRA,* 65–69.

32. "As with everything genuine, its inner life guarantees its truth." *DBR,* 36; translation from *TBRA,* 67.

33. A third painting of Delauney, *Le Tour Eiffel* (1911) is reproduced at the end of Arnold Schoenberg's essay, "Das Verhältnis zum Text," *DBR,* 68; *TBRA,* 98.

34. *Der Sumpf* (c. 1909–10) is, by way of analogy, more similar to the formal experiments in Cézanne's *Mont Sainte Victoire* series (1890–1905) or Braque's *Maison à l'Estaque* (1908), each of which represents an early stage of a process that led to analytic cubism as developed by Braque and Picasso during 1909–11. However, Le Fauconnier's *Le Marais* is (like early paintings by Cézanne or Braque) not yet cubist either in conception or in manner. A number of Le Fauconnier's paintings in 1911 and 1912 were in the cubist manner: see especially *L'Abondance* (1911) as reproduced on page 127 of *DBR.*

35. Except, of course, for the fact that Allard refuses to recognize Picasso's importance, an attitude of chauvinism and ignorance that characterized much of the Parisian art public during the years 1910–12, during which Braque and Picasso were painting together and holding back their work. This might explain Allard's emphasis on "those who followed" the first attempts of Braque, Picasso, and then Derain toward a formal cubism. Apparently Metzinger, Le Fauconnier, Albert Gleizes, Fernand Leger, and Robert Delauney are the "new painters" from whom all the "signs of a renewal" are to come.

36. *DBR,* 107–24; *TBRA,* 127–40.

37. Mircea Eliade, *The Sacred and the Profane: The Nature of Religion* (New York: Harcourt, Brace and World, 1959), 69–70.

38. *DBR,* 125–31; translated as "Free Music," in *TBRA,* 141–46.

4 THE RELATION OF THE TEXT: *Herzgewächse*

1. *DBR*, 60–75; *TBRA*, 90–102, translated as "The Relationship to the Text."

2. *DBR*, 62; *TBRA*, 92.

3. Thus during the most turbulent and productive years of Schoenberg's life, more than half of his works were composed to texts, beginning with *Das Buch der Hängenden Gärten*, Op. 15 (1909), composed to a cycle of poems by Stefan George, and including *Gurrelieder*, which, though composed in 1900, was first orchestrated in 1911 and performed in 1913; *Erwartung*, Op. 17 (1909), a monodrama composed to a text by Marie Pappenheim; *Die Glückliche Hand*, Op. 18, a drama written by Schoenberg and set to music between 1910 and 1913; *Herzgewächse*, Op. 20 (1911), a song set to a poem by Maurice Maeterlinck; *Pierrot Lunaire*, Op. 21 (1912), a cycle of twenty-seven songs to poems by Albert Giraud; and finally the *Four Orchestral Songs*, Op. 22 (1913–16), orchestral settings of a text by Ernest Dowson (translated by Stefan George) and three poems by Rainer Maria Rilke.

4. "These are the symptoms of a gradually spreading recognition of the true essence of art. And with great joy I read Kandinsky's book, *Concerning the Spiritual in Art*, in which a way is shown for painting that arouses hope that those who demand a text will soon stop demanding" (*DBR*, 74–75; translation from *TBRA*, 102).

5. "He [the critic] helplessly faces the pure musical effect and he prefers, therefore, to write about the kind of music that is somehow related to a text, [hence] about program music, lieder, operas, etc." *DBR*, 63–64; translation from *TBRA*, 93.

6. "Such judgements actually originate in a very trite idea. In a traditional scheme a certain incident in the poetry must be absolutely parallel with a certain loudness or speed in music. This parallel may also occur, may even be much *more profound* when externally the opposite is true—when a delicate idea is rendered by a fast and vigorous theme. A subsequent vigor can develop from it more organically; but aside from that, such a scheme is surely contemptible because it is traditional. Moreover it makes us think of music as a language that is "creating and thinking" for everybody" (*DBR*, 64–65; translation from *TBRA*, 94).

7. Kandinsky received the scores rather late in the composition of the almanac and, for reasons that are not clear, had them reproduced and placed at the very end of the book. While the placement of the scores may merely be a result of the tardiness of Schoenberg's contributions, it is more likely that it is due to the difficulty of reproducing scores within the format of the book. Other works, including those of the editors, were inserted more belatedly than these musical materials. See Franz Marc, *Briefe Aufzeichnungen und Aquarelle* (Munich: Piper Verlag, 1920); August Macke and Franz Marc, *Briefwechsel* (Cologne: Dumont, 1964), 108 ff.; and W. Kandinsky, *Der Blaue Reiter* (Rückblick) in *Das Kunstblatt*, 14 (1930): 59.

8. See Jelena Hahl-Koch, ed., *Arnold Schoenberg—Wassily Kandinsky: Briefe, Bilder, und Dokumente einer aussergewohnlichen Begegnung* (Salzburg and Vienna: Residenz Verlag, 1980), 32, 35, 55, 58–59.

9. While the possibility of placing the scores next to the text may have occurred to Kandinsky, such a direct juxtaposition of "illustration" and musical example to Schoenberg's text was probably deemed inappropriate since the composer's text emphasized the rarity of such relations and gave no explicit indication that *Herzgewächse* (much less the settings of Webern and Berg) was in any way related to the general comments he made.

10. To conclude the subject of placement of the musical scores, I find that on Kandinsky's part at least, the "appended" scores need not be thought to break apart the various relations of illustration with text that are suggested throughout *Der Blaue Reiter*. In each case, the music is reproduced already in relation to its own text. Schoenberg, Webern, and Berg are thus juxtaposed mainly to each other and each score stands only in an indirect relation to any other text or illustration. In other contexts such as collections of scores, songs, or settings, this particular presentation of the scores would seem normal. However, in a book that is an example of collaboration, such an isolation draws attention to itself.

11. Maeterlinck, "Feuillage du coeur," *Serres Chaudes* (Paris: Vanier, 1889), 19. Also in *Poesies Complètes,* J. Hanse, ed. (Brussels: La Renaissance du Livre, 1965), 109–10.

12. I do not mean to imply that Maeterlinck is dealing with poetic clichés but rather that his poetic vocabulary was as conventional as the musical vocabulary that Schoenberg was trying to escape.

13. Translation from original French to English by author; from French to German unknown (not credited on score); and from German to English by author.

14. This melancholy is an emotion particularly favored by late symbolist poets as the passport to exploration of the "inconnu" whether understated as in Mallarmé's "La chair est triste, hélàs, et j'ai lu tous les livres" ("Brise Marine," *Oeuvres Complètes* [Paris: Gallimard, 1945], 161), or overstated as in Valéry's "Dans la sérénité d'un rêve sans limite . . . / Je méprise les sens, les vices, et la femme, / Moi qui puis évoquer dans le fond de mon âme / La lumière . . . le son, la multiple beauté!" ("Solitude," *Le Figaro littéraire* [11 September 1954], written in 1887).

15. Thomas Clifton, "On Listening to *Herzgewächse*," *Perspectives in New Music* 11, No. 2 (Spring-Summer 1973): 89.

16. The first publication (in autograph facsimile) of *Herzgewächse* was in *Der Blaue Reiter*. Subsequent publication in 1922 by Universal (Vienna) included several corrections and minor changes. I shall use the standard Universal Edition score except where there is an important difference between the original published version and the Universal edition.

17. Schoenberg, "Analysis of the Four Orchestral Songs, Opus 22," trans. Claudio Spies, *Perspectives on Schoenberg and Stravinsky,* ed. Benjamin Boretz and Edward T. Cone (Princeton: Princeton University Press, 1968), 26–27. Schoenberg was to have delivered the essay by radio on the occasion of the premiere of the *Four Orchestral Songs,* Op. 22 on 21 February 1932.

18. A step analogous to a poet's throwing out syntax, something achieved neither as easily nor as often as modern critics would have us believe.

19. "Analysis of the Four Orchestral Songs, Opus 22," 27.

20. Ibid., 27–28.

21. Ibid., 26–27.

22. Two of Arnold Schoenberg's paintings are reproduced in *Der Blaue Reiter* although neither is directly juxtaposed with either the text or the music of the composer. See *Vision* (1910), *DBR,* 144; *TBRA,* 156; and *Selbstporträt* (1911), *DBR,* 158; *TBRA,* 166.

5 THE STAGE COMPOSITION: *Der gelbe Klang*

1. Sponsored by the Solomon R. Guggenheim Foundation and the Guggenheim Museum, Kandinsky's stage composition was given its first full "historically accurate"

performance at the Marymount-Manhattan Theater on 9–14 February 1982 under the title "The Yellow Sound." The "color opera" was produced and directed by Ian Strasfogel with the original score by Thomas de Hartmann reconstructed, arranged, and orchestrated by Gunther Schuller, choreographed by Helmut Fricke-Gottschild and danced by the Zero Moving Dance Company with scenery, costumes, and lighting by Robert Israel and Richard Riddell. Instrumental music was performed by Speculum Musicae and conducted by Gunther Schuller. Vocal parts were sung by the Y Chorale and directed by Amy Kaiser.

2. Kandinsky's term *Bühnenkomposition* (stage composition) carries special significance as I shall demonstrate.

3. *Über das Geistige in der Kunst*, 36.

4. As when he refers to both painters in *UGK* and *DBR* as examples of the recent thrust toward the nonrepresentational in painting. See *UGK*, 34–35; *CSA*, 36–39; *DBR*, 178–82; *TBRA*, 182, 186.

5. Grohmann, *Kandinsky: Life and Work* (New York: Abrams, 1958), 99, dates both of the Russian plays from 1909 and implies that *Der gelbe Klang* was first written the same year. In the *Vorwort zur Zweiten Auflage* to *UGK*, Kandinsky notes that *UGK* "was im jahre 1910 geschrieben."

6. See *UGK*, 36–37; *CSA*, 39–40.

7. See Grohmann, 99, 413.

8. Peg Weiss in her book *Kandinsky in Munich: The Formative Jugendstil Years* (Princeton: Princeton University Press, 1979), 196–97, calls attention to these transcriptions in the notebooks. However, Susan Stein claims that B-I is neither *DGK* nor its earlier version *Die Riesen*, and that Weiss is simply wrong in comparing the two. See Stein, "The Ultimate Synthesis: An Interpretation of the Meaning and Significance of Wassily Kandinsky's 'The Yellow Sound.' " M.A. thesis, SUNY–Binghamton, 1980, 78, 97, n. 2.

9. In a comment on the section of *Violett* that he published in the Bauhaus quarterly (*bauhaus* 3 [July 1927]: 6), Kandinsky noted that he had written the play during the summer of 1914.

10. Both essays and the stage composition appeared in *Der Blaue Reiter* (Munich: Piper Verlag, 1912). Their placement (in series and at the end) emphasizes their importance to the larger statement that Kandinsky intended in the almanac.

11. See my discussion of "Über die Formfrage" in chapter 3.

12. "There are numerous combinations between these two poles: collaboration and contrast." *DBR*, 208; translation from *TBRA*, 206.

13. One cannot extend this analogy very far, of course, since the aims of the artist, Kandinsky, are radically different from those of the physicists. Thus, where Heisenberg or Paul Dirac constructed "ideal experiments" as preliminary examinations of the ramifications of a new concept to discover how established principles would be affected, these experiments were always understood to be theoretical test situations, the necessary groundwork for future experiments. For Kandinsky, the experimental composition permits the same freedoms from the constraints of actual production, but there is an advantage the scientist does not usually have. The artist's ideal experiment is also composed for its own sake and allowed to stand as an artwork as well as an evidence of conceptual development.

14. Weiss argues that the physical features of the relatively new Munich Künstlertheater, opened in 1908, with its shallow stage and variable drop backstage, were controlling factors in Kandinsky's scenario for *Der gelbe Klang*. She also implies that the

lighting designs and sets at the Jacques Dalcroze Dance School in Hellerau (near Dresden) were the source for Kandinsky's ideas about lighting and color. See *Kandinsky in Munich*, 92–98.

15. In defense of those who created the 1982 New York production, their stated goal of a historically accurate production imposed strict limits on the lighting techniques and color values. Kandinsky's scenario is relatively free of just those historical restrictions.

16. The standard works on Kandinsky give short shrift and almost no interpretation to *Der gelbe Klang*. The composition merits two paragraphs of description in Grohmann, 56, 99; a few notes in Paul Overy, *Kandinsky: The Language of the Eye*, 19, 64; a chapter about influences on Kandinsky's theatrical works in Weiss 92–103; and a few pages on sources and themes in Washton Long, *Kandinsky: Development of an Abstract Style*, 52–64. Others, such as Max Bill in *Kandinsky: Essays Über Kunst und Künstler* (Bern: Bentali Verlag, 1963) and H. K. Roethel in *Kandinsky: Das graphische Werk* (Köln: Dumont Schauberg, 1970), mention the title with no further comment. Several recent critics have, however, offered detailed and interesting commentaries, including R. W. Sheppard, "Kandinsky's Abstract Drama *Der Gelbe Klang*: An Interpretation," *Forum for Modern Language Studies* 11 (April 1975); 165–76; and Stein, "The Ultimate Synthesis: An Interpretation of the Meaning and Significance of Wassily Kandinsky's 'The Yellow Sound.'" Both take into account the themes and theories of Kandinsky's paintings in their interpretations. Apparently neither interpreter had access to de Hartmann's music (or to Schuller's completed versions) and thus each is limited to the visual and verbal elements.

17. *UGK*, 107; *CSA*, 71.

18. Rolf Liebermann produced the most advanced "color-opera" of the 1970s with his presentation of *Klydex I*, a collaborative performance of light and sound and color which enjoyed a successful run in Hamburg, Germany during 1972–73. The wide variety of multimedia performances is a reflection of a renewed interest in the idea of the total work of art since the end of the Second World War. I shall discuss this phenomenon further in the next chapter.

19. See Weiss, where she lists the innovative features of Münchner Künstlertheater. In addition to the shallow stage, there was "an advanced lighting system, a broad inner proscenium, adjustable in height and width by a system of moveable screens and an upstage area that could be raised or lowered." Weiss even calls the Müncher Künstlertheater "a *Jugendstil Gesamtkunstwerk*" in emphasizing the harmonious total design of the theater itself (94).

20. Hans Poelzig created the Grand Theater of Berlin *(Das Grosses Schauspielhaus)* as an example of Expressionist architecture. This grotto-like structure (also called the Max Reinhardt Theater) opened on 20 November 1919, and though it featured "mountainous looking reliefs" and molded interiors that looked like stalactites, all designed to improve the acoustics of the hall, the physical properties of the stage were no different from the opera halls of the preceding century. See Dennis Sharp, *Modern Architecture and Expressionism* (London: Braziller, 1967), 52–54.

21. "The stage must be as deep as possible. At the rear, a broad green hill. Behind the hill, a flat, mat blue, rather deep colored curtain." *DBR*, 215–16; translation from *TBRA*, 213.

22. In *UGK*, Kandinsky writes: "Gerade in diesem Falle von ausschliesslich grosser Wichtigkeit soll man nicht vergessen, das es auch andere Mittel gibt, die materielle Fläche zu behalten, eine ideelle Fläche zu bilden und die letztere nicht nur als eine

flache Fläche zu fixieren, sondern sie als dreidimensionalen Raum auszunützen. Schon die Dünne oder die Dicke einer Linie, weiter das Stellen der Form auf der Fläche, das Überschneiden einer Form durch die andere sind als Beispiele für die zeichnerische Ausdehnung des Raumes genügend. Ähnliche Möglichkeiten bietet die Farbe, die, richtig angewendet, vor-oder zurücktreten und vor-oder zurückstreben kann und das Bild zu einem in der Luft schwebenden Wesen machen kann, was der malerischen Ausdehnung des Raumes gleichbedeutend ist.

"Das Vereinen der beiden Ausdehnungen im Mit-oder Widerklang ist eines der reichsten und gewaltigsten Elemente der zeichnerisch-malerischen Komposition" (*UGK*, 94–95; see also *CSA*, 67).

23. For example, the deep and medium blue backgrounds, the mountains, and the indistinct, large figures in the middle ground dominate an entire series of paintings from the Murnau period beginning with *Improvisation 4* (1909) and including the following paintings over a period of several years during which the painter explored new directions in organization as he moved toward abstraction in his canvases: *Paradise* (1909); *Improvisation 7* (1910); *Composition II* (1910); *Improvisation 11* (1910); *Improvisation 12* (1910); *Improvisation 13* (1910); *Improvisation 14* (1910); *Improvisation 16* (1910); *Das jüngste Gericht* (1910); *Impression III* (1911); *Composition IV* (1911); and *Improvisation 19* (1911). The larger drama of movement and contrast of colors gradually replaces (and becomes symbolic of) the specific figures of the spiritual (St. George, the riders of the Apocalypse, the Biblical saints, and other religious figures).

24. Paul Overy remarks that during the Bauhaus period, Kandinsky used "dynamic methods of composition to create a lyrical energy from contradictory tensions which are set up between colour and forms. . . . For calmer, more meditative works he made use of a second, more traditional method of composition, exploiting the rectangular picture plane to the full as in *At Rest* (1928). In the second method, the elements are so freely arranged that the rectangular shape of the picture plane is disregarded and does not contribute to the 'sound' of the composition, merely existing as a convenient format. The result, Kandinsky says, is 'that the picture plane disappears so to speak and the elements hover in space, which, however knows no precise limit (especially in depth)'!" (Overy, 122, is citing Kandinsky at the end of this comment from *Concerning the Spiritual in Art*.)

25. Many of these effects were subsequently achieved by motion pictures. The window illusion, the fast cut from a long shot to a close up (simulating rapid expansion of subject), the zoom shot, optical printing, and a number of the special effects suggested by the scenario for *Der gelbe Klang* were duplicated in the films of the following decade. Kandinsky was certainly aware of motion pictures though he preferred the effects of live performance on a stage. Standish Lawder claims that "Kandinsky's original plan was to film *Der gelbe Klang*." However, as Lawder explains in a footnote, it is he who has inferred Kandinsky's intention (from Eichner's comment in his *Kandinsky und Gabriele Münter* [Munich: Bruckmann Verlag, 1957], 91) to film his stage composition. While not impossible, such a plan to film this "stage composition" remains difficult to verify. Kandinsky does not mention this possibility in his notebooks from this period. See Lawder, *The Cubist Cinema* (New York: New York University Press, 1975), 31–33, and esp. 246 n. 12.

26. Overy, 101–2.

27. Overy, 101. See also L. D. Ettlinger, *Kandinsky's "At Rest"* (Oxford: Oxford University Press, 1961), 11.

28. *UGK*, 87; *CSA*, 64.

29. Overy, 103 and Christina Ladd-Franklin, *Colour and Colour Theories* (London: Kegan Paul, 1929), 36 ff.

30. For physicists, the "colors" black and white are not an issue since they do not exhibit the wavelengths or frequencies of the spectrum. However, Ladd-Franklin's color theory, based on psychological effects rather than on wavelengths, includes both.

31. Dreams hard as stones . . . talking rocks
    Clouds with justifying questions . . .
    Heaven shakes . . . Stones melt. . . .
    (DBR, 212; translated from TBRA, 210)

32. Tears and Laughter . . . Prayers and Curses . . .
    Happiness and Blackest slaughter together . . .
    (DBR, 213; translation from TBRA, 210-11)

33. Although the language is idiosyncratic, the mood evoked in these passages is similar to that created in the apocalyptic poems by Georg Heym, Jakob von Hoddis, Alfred Lichtenstein, and Georg Trakl written during this same period (1910-13). The accretion of paradoxes was a technique that became an identifying mark of Expressionism just before and during the war.

34. Dark night on the . . . sunniest . . . day . . .
    (vanishing fast and suddenly)
    . . . Blindingly bright shadow in darkest night!!
    (DBR, 213; translation from TBRA, 211)

35. *DBR*, 216; *TBRA*, 214.

36. The flowers cover everything. Cover everything. Cover Everything.
    Shut your eyes! Shut your eyes!
    We are looking. We are looking.
    Cover conception with innocence
    Open your eyes! Open your eyes!
    Gone. Gone.
    (DBR, 219; translation from TBRA, 217)

37. Hellmut Fricke-Gottschild's choreography for this section of *Der gelbe Klang* as danced by his Zero Moving Dance Company in the premiere performance (1982) appeared to be an attempt to recapture a style that might have been appropriate for an earlier production. However, Fricke-Gottschild's choreography succeeded in adopting a curious appearance that resembled neither the dance of the pre–World War I period (in which case he might have emulated the dance of Jacques Dalcroze, the inventions of Isadora Duncan or even the choreographies of Mary Wigman) nor that of contemporary dance. The Zero Moving Dance Company seemed determined to create an anachronism composed of static poses and dramatic, emotive postures (but stiff and arhythmic) like the early dances of Ruth St. Denis, Ted Shawn, and Martha Graham. The choreographer succeeded in the sense that the dance does not dominate the collaborative performance.

38. "From all sides come dazzlingly colored rays (blue, red, purple, green alternating rapidly several times). Then all these rays become focused in the center and blend." *DBR*, 222; translation from *TBRA*, 219.

39. Each color projection creates an instantaneous effect that might best be illustrated by one of Kandinsky's paintings from this period (1910-12). Thus, the suffusing green light over the yellow and blue of giant and background might well be imagined by viewing the same effect represented in *Composition V* (1911). The sweep-

ing red effect is seen in the *Study for Composition VII* (c. 1911) and the dominance of blue in *Improvisation 19* (1911). For those who cannot reproduce the actual effect of a stage composition, a review of Kandinsky's paintings from the period in question suggests not the source of the pictures in the composition, but rather the common vision from which both the paintings and the scenario came.

40. Several paintings from this same period dramatize the invasion and conquest of a scene by yellow: the earliest is from 1910, *Improvisation 10*. In this painting, several large figures in the background reflect the yellow that commands the foreground and center of the canvas. The force of the yellow is reflected all around the canvas. In *Impression III (Konzert)* (1911), the canvas is divided diagonally by the intrusion of a bright yellow mass and the large figures on the left side of the canvas seem to be tilted against this intrusion. As in this section of *Bild 3* of *Der gelbe Klang*, the combat between the outgoing yellow and the surrounding darker lines seems to be drawn in favor of the former.

41. Professor Washton Long credits Klaus Brisch's pioneering dissertation with originating the argument that Kandinsky retained imagery in his paintings through 1914 and that this imagery "contained apocalyptic motifs. He [Brisch] stressed that Kandinsky's seven large compositions originated from eschatalogical themes and that such imagery persisted in a number of his paintings until 1912 and in a few of 1913" (vii). For other views of the dark tone and pessimistic atmosphere of these paintings, see Weiss, 97–98 and Sheppard, 165–76.

42. Washton Long, 108–22.

43. Other versions of this view have emphasized either the mysticism of *Der gelbe Klang* from a gnostic perspective, as in, for example, Lothar Schreyer's commentary in *Expressionistisches Theater* (Hamburg: J. P. Toth Verlag, 1948), 64–68, 80–88; or from the perspective of the rather rich tradition of Christian mysticism, from the writings of St. Augustine and St. Thomas Aquinas to compilations of medieval and renaissance mysticism, as in Susan Stein's thesis, "The Ultimate Synthesis: An Interpretation of the Meaning and Significance of Wassily Kandinsky's 'The Yellow Sound,'" 103–43.

44. See "Für Kandinsky," *Der Sturm* 3, Nos. 150–151 (March 1913): 277–79.

45. Grohmann, 66.

46. Ian Strasfogel, *Opera News* (30 January 1982), 8–11. See also Klaus Lankheit, "The History of the Almanac," *TBRA*, 43 for an account of de Hartmann's lecture and how it was that *Der gelbe Klang* was not understood in Russia.

47. Stein, 78–79.

48. This offprint of the scenario of *Der gelbe Klang* was contained in the papers de Hartmann bequeathed to the Music Library at Yale University and was displayed in the exhibition of paintings and documents in *Kandinsky in Munich* at the Solomon R. Guggenheim Museum in New York (22 January–21 March 1982). The notations in this offprint are in the handwriting of both artists and support the argument that their collaboration was not completed (if it was ever completed) until after the final version of *Der gelbe Klang* was set in print as part of *Der Blaue Reiter* between December 1911 and March 1912; these are the earliest possible dates for the appearance of an offprint from the publisher. This clue established with much greater certainty the enduring nature of de Hartmann's collaboration with Kandinsky, which was reported to have begun during 1908–9.

49. All the materials (the annotated scenario, the parts of de Hartmann's score, and other documentation) are held in the Yale Music Library and were the basis upon

which Gunther Schuller completed and orchestrated a full performing score for the 1982 New York production of *The Yellow Sound.*

50. "You know, twice a performance was offered to me. The first time right before the war; the production was to have taken place in Munich in the late fall [of 1914]; the second time in Berlin *(Volksbühne)* 1922. And this second time the war didn't stand in the way, rather my composer, Th. v. Hartmann, who was out of touch. So I had to refuse. I suddenly remember a third time. Schlemmer wanted to produce the piece [at the Bauhaus theater], but once again, it didn't work out. . . . Such things have their own destinies." (Kandinsky in a letter to Hans Hildebrandt in 1937. See Hildebrandt, "Drei Briefe von Kandinsky," in *Werk: schweizerische Zeitschrift für Baukunst, Gewerbe, Malerei, und Plastik* 42, No. 10 [October 1955]: 330.)

51. Grohmann, 56.

52. Peg Weiss reports that *Der gelbe Klang* was first produced in the United States by Zone, Theater of the Visual (associated with the Massachusetts School of Art, Boston) in May 1972 at the Guggenheim Museum in New York. Weiss adds that unfortunately the production was not historically accurate and demonstrated a very weak understanding of Kandinsky's ideas. Nor, she comments, did those who attempted the performance show any familiarity with the theatrical or musical possibilities available to Kandinsky at the time of composition. (See *Kandinsky in Munich,* 197 n.6.)

6. DER STURM: *Mörder, Hoffnung der Frauen*

1. The play was first published under the title *Hoffnung der Frauen,* in a limited edition by Herwarth Walden (Berlin: Der Sturm Verlag, 1909), with five line engravings by the artist and a musical score composed by the publisher. The collaborators privately sold most of the copies to collectors, and the edition was never reprinted. This text and the line engravings were reprinted for the public on the front page of *Der Sturm,* which, given the readership of *Sturm* in Munich, Vienna, Dresden, and Berlin, assured the play of a notoriety that one small performance could never give it.

2. Oskar Kokoschka, *Oskar Kokoschka: Mein Leben* (Munich: Verlag F. Brukmann, 1971), 28–30. The first performance of the play took place on the evening of 4 July 1909, and in his autobiography Kokoschka gives a full account of events surrounding the premiere.

3. See, for example, the review of the play, "Theater und Kunstnachrichten: Kokoschka-Abend in der Kunstschau," *Neue Freie Presse* (Vienna), 5 July 1909, 8.

4. For two succinct accounts of the play, see Peter Vergo, *Art in Vienna: 1898–1918* (London: Phaidon Press, 1975), 248, and Carl E. Schorske, *Fin de Siècle Vienna: Politics and Culture* (New York: Alfred A. Knopf, 1980), 335–38. For a more complete interpretation, see Henry Schvey's *Oskar Kokoschka: The Painter as Playwright* (Detroit: Wayne State University Press, 1982), 31–45.

5. *The Sacred and the Profane,* trans. Willard Trask (New York: Harcourt Brace, 1959), 44.

6. We were the flaming wheel around him,
   We were the flaming wheel around you,
   Destroyer of locked fortresses!
         (*Der Sturm,* 156)
All translations are based on the first important published edition of the play in *Der Sturm* (Wochenschrift für Kultur und die Künste), 20 (14 July 1910): 156–57. This text was reprinted with the engravings in *Dramen und Bilder* (Leipzig: K. Wolff, 1913)

under the original title, *Hoffnung der Frauen* and then once again as *Mörder, Hoffnung der Frauen* (Berlin: Der Sturm Verlag, [1916]), with neither engravings nor music. Subsequent editions of the play incorporate the textual revisions and deletions that Kokoschka made in 1916 and 1917. Some of Kokoschka's fervor may very well have been dampened by his experiences in the war and by the serious head wound he received while serving on the Eastern Front. At any rate, his revisions of this play tend to take away the mystery from the rite. These revisions were published in *Schriften, 1907–1955*, ed. Hans Maria Wingler (Munich: A. Langen and G. Müller, 1956).

7. "Who was the stranger who looked at me?"

8. "Am I a real one? What did the shadows say?"

9. "Did you see me, did I see you?"

10. "We saw him stride upon the fire, his feet unharmed."

   "He tortured animals to death, killed neighing mares with the pressure of his thighs."

   "Birds, that ran before us, he made blind; and red fish we had to stifle in the sand."

11. "Why do you bind me, man, with your look? Strange light confounds my flame,

   Devouring life overcomes me, endflame.

   O take away my terrible hope . . .

   And may anguished agony overcome you. . . ."

12. "(The Man, in convulsions, singing with a bleeding, visible wound)

   'Senseless craving from horror to horror,

   Unappeasable rotation in the void.

   Birth pangs without birth,

   Crashing of the sun, quaking of space.

   The end of those who praised me.

   O your unmerciful word. . . .' "

13. "(She slinks in circles around the cage like a panther. She crawls up to the cage inquisitively, handles the bars lasciviously, then inscribes a large, white cross on the tower and cries out:) 'Open the cage; I must be with him.' (She shakes the bars in despair, in desperation.)"

14. "Lascivious malevolent panting, like a snake."

15. "(The Man, breathing heavily, lifts his head with difficulty; later, he moves one hand, then slowly rises up, singing higher and higher, soaring:)

   'Wind that wanders

   Time repeating Time

   Solitude, Repose, Hunger confuse me

   Worlds that circle past

   No air

   World drawn out like evening.' "

16. "(The Woman, beginning to be afraid): 'So much life flows from the gap, so much power runs through the gate, so pale is he, like a corpse.' "

17. "Am I the real One, you the entrapped dead? And why do you turn pale?"

18. Stars and Moon! Bright shining lights! Woman!

   In disfiguring Life, in waking or dreaming

   I saw a singing essence shining out.

Breathing brings dark visions to me.
Who gives me suck?
19. *Der Teufel! Bändigt ihn, rettet Euch, rette, wer kann . . . verloren!* ("The Devil! Tame him, save yourselves . . . save who you can . . . lost!"), 157.

7 THE SACRED AND THE PROFANE: *Triad*

1. Just such a total work of art was also in the minds of those who collaborated in such famous avant-garde performances as Stravinsky's *Sacre du Printemps* (1913) and *Parade* (1917). I distinguish here between "multimedia" performances such as those carried out by the Futurists and Dadaists, where different arts were performed, and the more coherent "collaborations" of the artists and the arts which, like *Parade*, were created before their first performance. In the arts, there is a difference between occasions where several arts are presented or performed in juxtaposition (not as part of a larger experience, but as disparate parts calculated to shock an audience) and those other occasions where an attempt is made to create a single performance by combining several arts. For, where the order and the content of the performance are dependent on the audience's reaction, it is difficult to discuss the relation of the arts (even though the Futurists worked toward breaking down the barriers between the arts as well as breaking down the arts themselves).

2. Alwin Nikolais in an interview with the author, 8 December 1976.

3. For example, one need only imagine a failure in spotlighting (in cues or the electrical system) which would result in an unilluminated dancer on a dark stage beside (in, on, or under) a scarcely visible prop. Even a failure in the timing of the change of lighting, projectors, film, or scrim will wreck certain dances despite the fact that the dancers' timing and performance are perfect. The more elements combined, the greater the risk of mistakes in performance. This rule explains Nikolais's habitual involvement with every element of the Dance Theater.

4. These issues have been debated from the inception of The Alwin Nikolais Dance Theater, though mainly by critics and reviewers who claimed to feel sympathy for the company dancers and the way in which they were apparently rendered inhuman by the choreographies.

5. In many cases, the dancers themselves report that they do not know what a dance looks like from the perspective of the audience. Seeing a performance of a dance such as *Tribe* or *Styx* or *Triad* on video tape or film can occasionally be a surprising experience for them. Their sense of the dance is radically different from that of the spectator since their understanding of the form and structure is reached through a series of creations, rehearsals, and performances within the piece.

6. Marcia B. Siegel, ed. "Nik: A Documentary" in *Dance Perspectives* 48 (Winter 1971), 17. Special number devoted to Alwin Nikolais.

7. Nikolais began his career in dance as a student, then an assistant and dance partner of Trudy Kaschmann, who had studied with Mary Wigman in Kassel and with Rudolph von Laban in Hamburg.

8. In the history of the critical reception of the Alwin Nikolais Dance Theater some of the best and the worst critics of dance have found themselves in the same dilemma in resorting to labels like the "Wizard of Henry St." or New York's resident "magician" instead of offering sensible commentary on the performances.

9. The standard technical baggage with which they perform includes three portable dimmer boards, twelve projection machines, twenty slide carriages, twenty-eight leko spotlights, a main switch box and control panel, eight speakers and amplifiers, and tape decks as well as electrical cable and connections for the varying electrical systems. Stages with additional lights can be patched into Nikolais's system.

10. *Nik: A Documentary,* 16.

11. Ibid.

12. To say, for example, that most dance takes place without language is, of course, to announce a convention that even Nikolais has not always obeyed. The language of dance (in the semiological sense) is the codified structure of movement that is symbolized in the various notations (the shorthand symbol systems) of dance. In performance, the absence of language takes the viewer back, imaginatively, to a prehistoric, prelinguistic period. The choreographer's play between prelinguistic expression and the linguistic meaning defines, in one broad area, the limits dance imposes upon itself. This tension can also be invoked to describe one of the areas of shared experience with the viewer.

13. Here, I want to signal a motif in Nikolais's works, the structural break that is repeated with variations throughout most of his more recent choreographies. At times, the whole performance begins (as in *Triad*) with the presentation of the mystery. A visually fascinating prop is revealed and, in the course of the dance, the dancers and the audience must habituate themselves to it. If this "revelation" occurs in the middle of the performance, then its demystification follows (i.e., its apprehension, its approach, the dancers' experiments with it). In more complex works, there are several props, sets, or costumes to deconstruct. In none of these cases does the motif suffice to explain the performance.

14. The choreography of mythic experience is not new to modern dance since the origins of modern dance incorporated in one way or another the performance of imagined mythic or sacred experience. In the dances of Isadora Duncan (who subsequently became a myth), Mary Wigman and others, the choreographies were embodiments of primitive expression. More recently, Martha Graham incorporated elements of Greek myth, Indian rituals and contemporary sacrality. Dance finds its origins in tribalism. As a natural, prelinguistic expression of the body and thus as one of the preconscious forms that might have preceded painting and writing, dance maintains an extraordinary, prior position among the sister arts.

BIBLIOGRAPHY

Ashmore, Jerome. "Sound in Kandinsky's Painting." *Journal of Aesthetics and Art Criticism* 35, No. 3 (Spring 1977): 329–36.

Birringer, Johannes H. "Constructions of the Spirit: The Struggle for Transfiguration in Modern Art." *Journal of Aesthetics and Art Criticism* 42, No. 2 (Winter 1983): 137–50.

Blake, William. *Vala or The Four Zoas: A Facsimile of the Manuscript, A Transcription of the Poem, and a Study of Its Growth and Significance.* Ed. G. E. Bentley, Jr. Oxford: Clarendon, 1963.

Bowlt, John, and Rose Carol Washton Long. *The Life of Vasili Kandinsky in Russian Art: A Study of* Über das Geistige in der Kunst. Newtonville: Oriental Research Partners, 1980.

Braque, Georges. *Cahier de Georges Braque: 1917–1947.* Paris: Maeght Editeur, n.d.

Breitenbach, Edgar. "Arnold Schoenberg and the Blaue Reiter." *Quarterly Journal of the Library of Congress* 31, No. 1 (1977): 32–38.

Brinkman, Heribert. *Wassily Kandinsky als Dichter.* Köln: Universität Köln, 1980.

Char, René. *Commune Présence.* Paris: NRF Gallimard, 1964.

———. *Hypnos Waking: Poems and Prose by René Char.* Selected and trans. Jackson Mathews. New York: Random, 1956.

———. *Lettera amorosa.* Paris: NRF Gallimard, 1953.

———. *Les Matinaux.* Paris: NRF Gallimard, 1950.

———. *La Parole en Archipel.* Paris: NRF Gallimard, 1962.

———. *Oeuvres complètes.* Paris: Bibliothèque de la Pléiade. NRF Gallimard, 1983.

———. *Poèmes et Prose Choisi.* Paris: NRF Gallimard, 1957.

———. *Recherche de la base et du sommet.* Paris: NRF Gallimard, 1955.

———. *Le Soleil des Eaux.* Paris: Librairie H. Matarasso, 1949.

Char, René, and Georges Braque. *Lettera amorosa.* Geneva: Edwin Engelberts, 1963.

Clifton, Thomas. "On Listening to Herzgewächse." *Perspectives of New Music* 11, No. 2 (Spring–Summer 1973): 87–103.

Comini, Alessandra. "Through a Viennese Looking-Glass Darkly: Images of Arnold Schoenberg and his Circle." *Arts Magazine* 58, No. 9 (May 1984): 107–19.

Eichner, Johannes. *Kandinsky and Gabriele Münter: von Ursprungen moderner Kunst.* Munich: Bruckmann, 1957.

Eliade, Mircea. *The Sacred and the Profane: The Nature of Religion.* Trans. Willard R. Trask. New York: Harcourt, Brace and World, 1959.

Ettlinger, L. D. *Kandinsky's "At Rest."* Oxford: Oxford University Press, 1961.

Giedion-Welcker, Carola. "L'élan vers le monumental." In *Hommage à Wassily Kandinsky: XXe Siècle* (numero spécial) Paris, 1974, 50–58.

Grohmann, Will. *Wassily Kandinsky: Life and Work.* New York: Abrams, 1958.

———. *Wassily Kandinsky.* New York: Abrams Library of Great Painters, 1971.

Hahl-Koch, Jelene, ed. *Arnold Schoenberg-Wassily Kandinsky Briefe, Bilder, und Dokumente einer aussergewöhnlichen Begegnung.* Salzburg and Vienna: Residenz Verlag, 1980.

Hildebrandt, Hans. "Drei Briefe von Kandinsky." *Werk: Schweizerische Zeitschrift für Baukunst, Gewerke und Plastik* 2, No. 10 (October 1955): 327–31.

Kandinsky, Wassily. *Concerning the Spiritual in Art.* Trans. Michael Sadleir with Francis Golffing, Michael Harrison, and Ferdinand Ostertag. New York: Wittenborn, 1947.

———. "Der Blaue Reiter (Rückblick)." *Das Kunstblatt* 14 (1930): 59.

———. *Die gesammelten Schriften.* Band I. hrsg. Hans K. Roethel and Jelena Hahl-Koch. Bern: Benteli, 1980.

———. *Essays über Kunst und Künstler.* Ed. with notes by Max Bill. Stuttgart: Hatje, 1955.

———. "Franz Marc." *Cahiers d'Art* 2 (1936): 274.

———. *Kandinsky 1901–1913.* Berlin: Der Sturm, 1913.

———. *Klänge.* Munich: Piper Verlag, 1913.

———. "Malerei als reine Kunst." *Der Sturm* 178/179 (September 1913): 98–99.

———. *Point and Line to Plane.* Trans. Howard Dearstyne and Hilla Rebay. New York: Dover Books, 1979.

———. *Punkt und Linie zu Fläche: Beitrag zur Analyse der malerischen Elemente.* Munich: Albert Lange, 1926.

———. "Réponse à une enquête...." *Cahiers d'Art* 10, Nos. 1–4 (1935): 53–55.

———. *Über das Geistige in der Kunst.* Munich: Piper Verlag, 1912.

———. "Über Kunstverstehen." *Der Sturm* 3, No. 129 (October 1912): 157–58.

———. *Violett. bauhaus* 3 (July 1927): 6.

———. *The Yellow Sound (Der gelbe Klang).* World Premiere. Music by Thomas de Hartmann. Reconstructed, arranged, and orchestrated by

Gunther Schuller. Marymount Manhattan Theater. New York. 9 February 1982.

Kandinsky, Wassily, and Franz Marc, eds. *Der Blaue Reiter.* Munich: Piper Verlag, 1912.

———. *Der Blaue Reiter: Dokumentarische Neuausgable von Klaus Lankheit.* Munich: Piper Verlag, 1965.

———. *The Blaue Reiter Almanac:* The Documents of Twentieth-Century Art. New Documentary Edition, edited and with an introduction by Klaus Lankheit. Trans. by Henning Falkenstein. New York: Viking, 1974.

Kokoschka, Oskar. *Briefe I: 1905–1919.* Ed. Olda Kokoschka and Heinz Spielman. Düsseldorf: Claasen, 1984.

———. *Dramen und Bilder.* Leipzig: K. Wolff, 1913.

———. *Hoffnung der Frauen.* Berlin: Der Sturm Verlag, 1909.

———. *Mörder, Hoffnung der Frauen. Der Sturm* 20 (Berlin, 14 July 1910): 156–57.

———. *My Life.* Trans. David Britt. New York: Macmillan, 1974.

———. *Oskar Kokoschka: Mein Leben.* Munich: Verlag F. Bruckmann, 1971.

———. *Schriften.* Ed. Hans Maria Wingler. Munich: A. Langen and G. Müller, 1956.

Ladd-Franklin, Christina. *Colour and Colour Theories.* London: Kegan Paul, 1929.

Lawder, Standish. *The Cubist Cinema.* New York: New York University Press, 1975.

Lessem, Alan Phillip. *Music and Text in the Works of Arnold Schoenberg: The Critical Years 1908–1922.* UMI Research Press, 1979.

Lindsay, Kenneth, and Peter Vergo, eds. *Kandinsky: Complete Writings on Art.* Boston: G. K. Hall, 1983.

Long, Rose Carol Washton. *Kandinsky: The Development of an Abstract Style.* Oxford: Clarendon Press, 1980.

McCabe, Cynthia Jaffee. *Artistic Collaboration in the Twentieth Century.* With essays by Robert C. Hobbs and David Shapiro. Washington, D.C.: Smithsonian Institution Press, 1984.

Macke, Wolfgang, ed. *August Macke: Franz Marc Briefwechsel.* Cologne: M. DuMont Schauberg, 1964.

Mackie, Alwynne. "Wassily Kandinsky and Problems of Abstraction." *Artforum* 17, No. 3 (November 1978): 58–63.

Maegaard, Jan. *Studien zur Entwicklung des dodekaphonen Satzes bei Arnold Schoenberg.* Copenhagen: Wilhelm Hansen, 1972.

Maeterlinck, Maurice. *Serres chaudes.* Paris, Vanier, 1889.

———. *Poésies Complètes.* Ed. J. Hanse. Brussels: La Renaissance du Livre, 1965.

Mallarmé, Stéphane. *Oeuvres Complètes.* Paris: Gallimard, 1945.

Marc, Franz. *Briefe, Aufzeichnungen und Aphorismen.* 2 vols. Berlin: P. Saffirer, 1920.

Miró, Joan. *Catalan Notebooks.* Trans. Dinah Harrison. New York: Skira-Rizzoli, 1977.

———. *Joan Miró Lithographs.* Vol. 2 (1950–70). New York: Leon Amiel, 1974.

———. *Obra gráfica.* Barcelona: Museo Español de Arte Contemporáneo, 1979.

———. *Obra pintura.* Barcelona: Museo Español de Arte Contemporáneo, 1979.

Nikolais, Alwin, choreographer. *Triad.* Nikolais Dance Theater. The Beacon Theater. New York, 25 February 1977.

Nogacki, Edmund. "Peinture et poésie de René Char." In *Des Mots et des Couleurs: Études sur le rapport de la littérature et de la peinture* (19ème et 20ème siècles), ed. Phillippe Bonnefis and Pierre Reboul. Lille: Publications de l'université de Lille, 1979. 165–71.

Osborne, Harold. *Abstraction and Artifice in Twentieth-Century Art.* Oxford: Clarendon Press, 1979.

Overy, Paul. *Kandinsky: The Language of the Eye.* London: Elek, 1969.

Pehnt, Wolfgang. *Expressionist Architecture.* Trans. J. A. Underwood and Edith Kustner. New York: Praeger, 1973.

Reich, Willi. "Der 'Blaue Reiter' und die Musik." *Schweizerische Musikzeitung* 85 (1945): 341–45.

Roethel, Hans K. *Kandinsky: Das graphische Werk.* Cologne: DuMont Schauberg, 1970.

Roethel, Hans K., and Jean K. Benjamin, eds. *Kandinsky: Catalogue raisonné of the Oil Paintings: 1900–1915.* Ithaca: Cornell University Press, 1984.

———. *Kandinsky: Catalogue raisonné of the Oil Paintings: 1915–1944.* Ithaca: Cornell University Press, 1984.

Rufer, Josef. *The Works of Arnold Schoenberg: A Catalogue of His Compositions, Writings, and Paintings.* Trans. Dika Newlin. London: Faber and Faber, 1962.

Schelling, Friedrich W. J. "Concerning the Relation of the Plastic Arts and Nature." In *The True Voice of Feeling: Studies in English Romantic Poetry,* ed. Herbert Read. New York: Pantheon Books, 1953.

Schoenberg, Arnold. "Analysis of Four Orchestral Songs, Opus 22." Trans. Claudio Spies. *Perspectives of New Music* 3 (1965): 1–21.

———. *Harmonielehre.* Leipzig and Vienna: Verlagseiguntem der Universal-Edition, 1911.

———. *Herzgewächse,* Op. 20. Vienna: Universal Editions, 1920.

———. *Theory of Harmony.* New York: Philosophical Library, 1947.

Schorske, Carl B. *Fin de Siècle Vienna: Politics and Culture.* New York: Alfred A. Knopf, 1980; paperback edition, New York: Vintage Books, 1981.

Schreyer, Lothar. *Expressionistisches Theater.* Hamburg: J. D. Toth Verlag, 1948.

Schuller, Gunther. "The Case of Thomas de Hartmann." In program notes, *The Yellow Sound.* New York: Solomon R. Guggenheim Foundation, 1982. n.p.

Schvey, Henry. *Oskar Kokoschka: The Painter as Playwright.* Detroit: Wayne State University Press, 1982.

Sharp, Dennis. *Modern Architecture and Expressionism.* New York: Braziller, 1967.

Sheppard, R. W. "Kandinsky's Abstract Drama *Der gelbe Klang:* An Interpretation." *Forum for Modern Language Studies* 2, No. 2 (April 1974): 165–76.

Siegel, Marcia B. "Nik: A Documentary." *Dance Perspectives* 48 (Winter 1971): 1–56.

Stein, Erwin, ed. *Arnold Schoenberg Letters.* Trans. Eithen Wilkins and Ernst Kaiser. New York: St. Martin's Press, 1965.

Stein, Jack M. *Richard Wagner and the Synthesis of the Arts.* Detroit: Wayne State University Press, 1960.

Stein, Susan A. "Kandinsky and Abstract Stage Composition: Practice and Theory." *Art Journal* 43, No. 1 (Spring 1983): 61–66.

———. "The Ultimate Synthesis: An Interpretation of the Meaning and Significance of Wassily Kandinsky's 'The Yellow Sound.' " M.A. Thesis. SUNY, Binghamton, 1980.

Stevens, Wallace. *The Collected Poems of Wallace Stevens.* New York: Alfred Knopf, 1955.

Stich, Sidra. *Joan Miró: The Development of a Sign Language.* St. Louis: Washington University Gallery of Art, 1980.

Strasfogel, Ian. "A Radical Vision." *Opera News* (30 January 1982): 8–11.

Stuckenschmidt, H. H. *Arnold Schoenberg: His Life, World and Work.* Trans. Humphrey Searle. London: John Calder, 1977.

———. "Kandinsky et la musique." *Hommage à Wassily Kandinsky: XXe Siècle*, numero spécial (Paris, 1974), 27–30.

———. "Was ist musikalischer Expressionismus." *Melos* 1 (1969), 1–5.

"Theater und Kunstnachtrichten: Kokoschka—Abend in der Kunstschau." *Neue Freie Presse* (Vienna), 5 July 1909, 8.

Tobias, Tobi. "Nickolais and Louis: A New Space." *Dance Magazine* 45, No. 2 (February 1971): 46–54.

Valéry, Paul. *Oeuvres.* (Bibliothèque de la Pléiade). 2 vols. Paris: NRF Gallimard, 1957.

———. "Solitude." *Le Figaro littéraire* (11 September 1954): 12.

Vergo, Peter. *Art in Vienna: 1898–1918.* London: Phaidon Press, 1975.

Wagner, Richard. *Gesammelte Shriften und Dichtungen von Richard Wagner.* Vols. 3 and 4. Leipzig: CFW Siegels Musikalienhandlung 1903.

———. *Richard Wagner's Prose Works.* Vol. 2. Trans. William Ashton Ellis. London: Paul, Trench, Trubner, 1893–99.

———. *Sämtliche Schriften und Dichtungen.* 12 vols. Leipzig: Breitkopf und Hartel, 1911.

Walden, Nell, and Lothar Schreyer. *Der Sturm: Ein Erinnerungsbuch an Herwarth Walden und die Künstler aus dem Sturmkreis.* Baden-Baden: Woldemar Klein, 1954.

Watts, Harriett. "The Poetry of Kandinsky and Arp: Transposed Landscapes." In *Turn of the Century: German Literature and Art 1890–1915.* Ed. G. Chapple and Hans Schulte. Bonn: Bouvier, 1981.

Weiss, Peg. "Kandinsky in Munich: Encounters and Transformations." In the catalogue, *Kandinsky in Munich: 1896–1914.* New York: The Solomon R. Guggenheim Museum, 1982. 28–82.

———. *Kandinsky in Munich: The Formative Jugendstil Years.* Princeton: Princeton University Press, 1978.

COLLABORATIVE FORM

was composed in 10-point Baskerville leaded two points
on a Xyvision system with Linotron 202 output
by BookMasters, Inc.;
printed by sheet-fed offset on 55-pound, acid free,
Glatfelter Natural paper stock,
Smyth sewn and bound over .088" binders boards
in Holliston Roxite B cloth,
and wrapped with dust jackets printed in two colors
on 80-pound enamel stock and film laminated
by BookCrafters, Inc.;
designed by Diana Gordy;
and published by

THE KENT STATE UNIVERSITY PRESS
KENT, OHIO 44242

INDEX